I0795017

IMAGES
of America

CLARENDON COUNTY

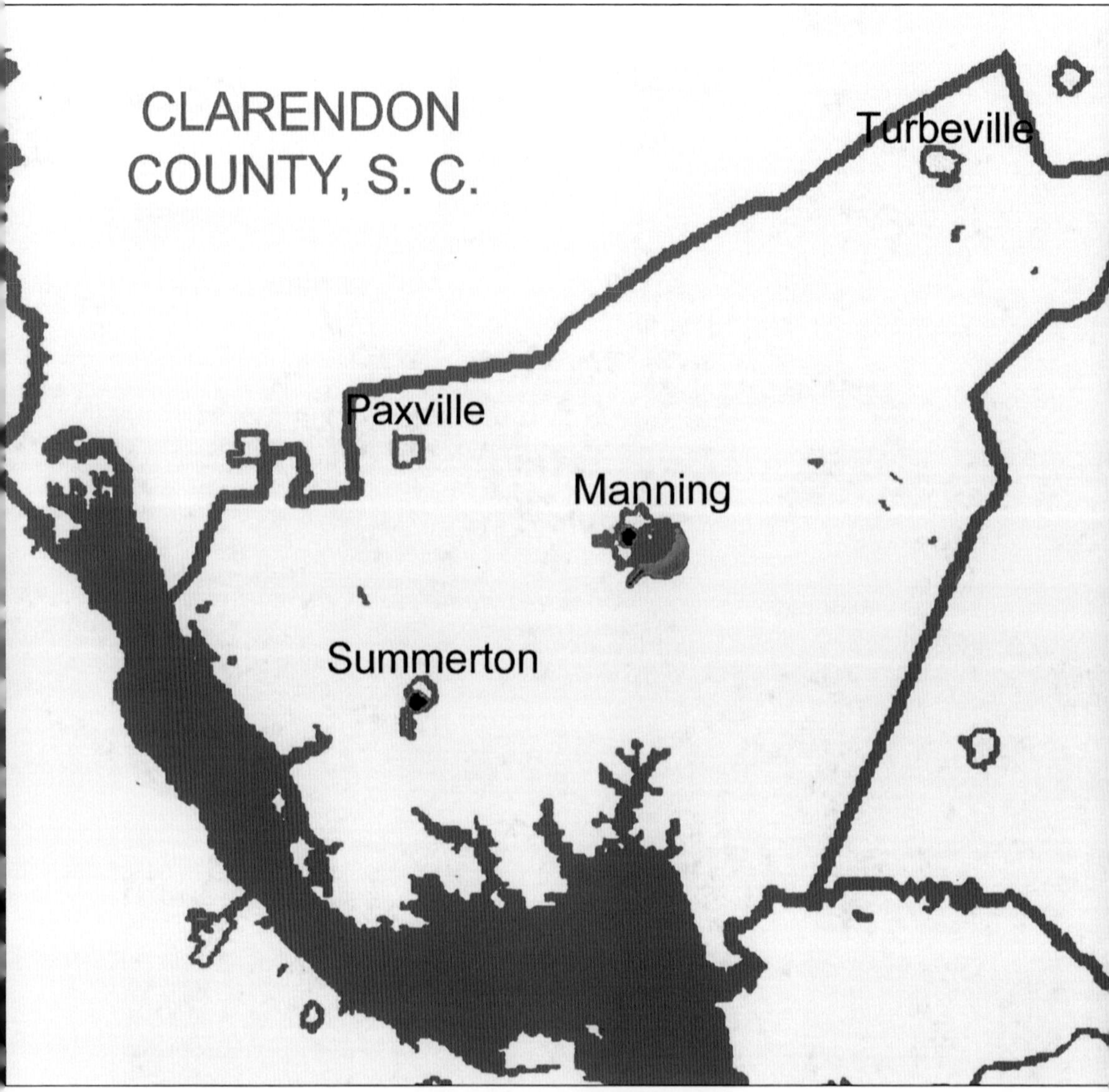

Clarendon County is situated in the east central portion of South Carolina. It has a population of approximately 33,000 people and covers a 590-square-mile land area. In addition, there is another 95 square miles of Lake Marion that is part of the county. The major towns within the county are Manning (county seat), Turbeville, and Summerton. About one-third of the land area is used for the cultivation of agricultural crops, and about ninety-five percent is woodland.

IMAGES
of America

CLARENDON COUNTY

Marguirite De Laine, F.S. Corbett, and Cecil J. Williams

ARCADIA
PUBLISHING

ISBN 978-0-7385-1435-2

Published by Arcadia Publishing
Charleston, South Carolina

Printed in the United States of America

Library of Congress Catalog Card Number: 2002103219

For all general information contact Arcadia Publishing at:
Telephone 843-853-2070
Fax 843-853-0044
E-Mail sales@arcadiapublishing.com
For customer service and orders:
Toll-Free 1-888-313-2665

Visit us on the Internet at www.arcadiapublishing.com

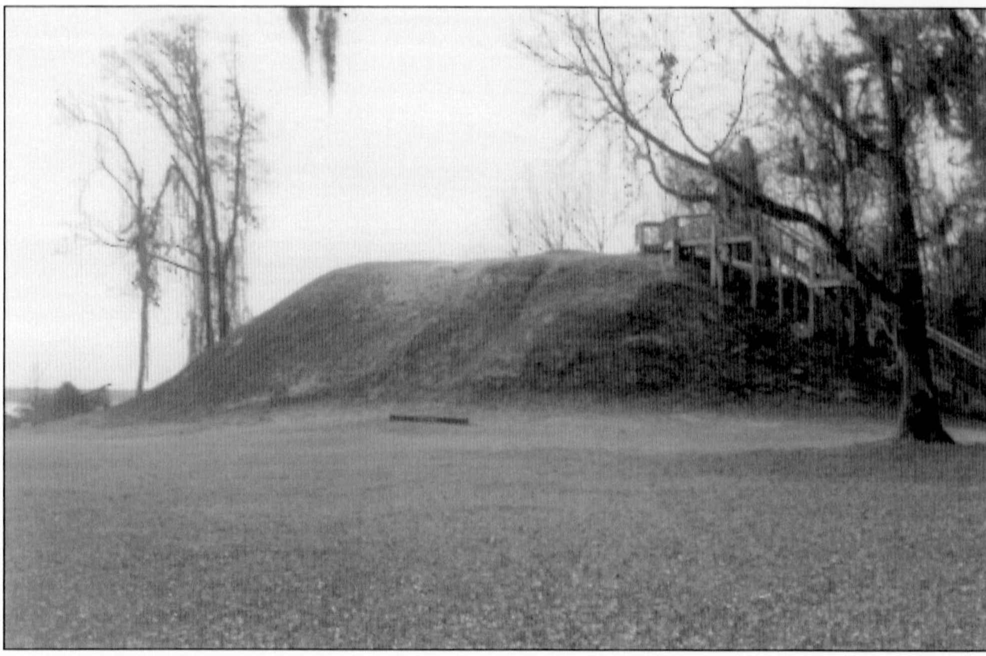

Native Americans constructed this ceremonial mound, probably between 1200 and 1400 A.D. It was built by plastering mud over upright posts and wooden sticks. Located near the Santee River, the mound forms part of the largest prehistoric ceremonial center ever discovered in the coastal plains. It was used for burials and as a focal point for other major community activities. Fort Watson, a small British outpost, was built on top of the mound because of its strategic location connecting the coast with the interior. By taking control of the fort on April 15, 1781, Gen. Francis Marion, the famous "Swamp Fox," and Col. "Light Horse" Harry Lee disrupted the British supply line. The fall of Fort Watson played a significant role in causing the British to abandon the backcountry of South Carolina.

Contents

Acknowledgments		6
Introduction		7
1.	People and Places of Note	9
2.	Military Participation	21
3.	Institutions and Institutional Activities	29
4.	Personalities and Scenes of Bygone Years	57
5.	Civil Rights Movement of the 1950s	125

ACKNOWLEDGMENTS

The Clarendon County Archives serves as a repository for the collection of artifacts and other records depicting the history of the county. Its collection of images of its citizens, their lives, and culture continues to expand as individuals become increasingly aware of the importance of the preservation of their rich history.

The Briggs Reunion Committee viewed this endeavor as an opportunity to assist in the expansion of photographic images on file at this institution. Under the auspices of this group, the South Carolina Humanities Council provided funds for the collection and reproduction of privately-owned photographs to expand this collection.

The authors, working through the Briggs Reunion Committee, defined the criteria for the selection of these images as those depicting individuals, life, scenes, and culture within the county of more than 50 years ago (with few exceptions).

The Clarendon County Archives shared some of the images included in this publication. A special thanks is extended to Larry Hewett for his interest and the donation of images from his collection. The *Manning Times*, the local weekly newspaper, was extremely cooperative through the publication of our efforts to solicit donations from private individuals.

The tireless efforts of Mary Cooper, Dr. Barbara Jenkins, and Beatrice Rivers, who used their personal contacts to generate individual responses, are sincerely appreciated. An expression of appreciation is also extended to all of the individuals who shared their personal photographs to help make this project a reality. In addition, acknowledgement is given to Brumit B. De Laine for his untiring role in assisting with photographic reproductions.

Sites for the collection and reproduction of these images were provided at no cost. These sites were the Clarendon County Archives (Manning), the Walker Gamble School (New Zion), the American Legion Post (Manning), and the Summerton Town Hall.

Thanks to all who have contributed to this window of life depicting days gone by in Clarendon County.

INTRODUCTION

Edward Hyde, the Earl of Clarendon, was the namesake of this county. The Earl of Clarendon was one of the Eight Lord Proprietors of Carolina.

The first settlers to this area are believed to have arrived around 1698. About 70 families of French-Huguenot origin settled along the Santee River. Another group of Scotch-Irish settlers are believed to have crossed over the Black River from the Williamsburg Township around that same time.

Before the American Revolution, the area now known as Clarendon was part of St. Mark's Parish, which included one-third of the Province of Carolina. The name Clarendon was first proposed in 1783 when the state was divided into seven court districts. The district was ultimately named the Camden District and was later divided to form Clarendon and six other counties. A legislative act passed in 1785 to create the county of Clarendon. In 1798, Clarendon, Claremont, and Salem Counties were combined to form the Sumter District. A legislative act passed in 1855 established the Clarendon District with the same boundaries defined in the Act of 1785. The State Constitution of 1868 changed the name Clarendon District to Clarendon County.

In 1855, Capt. Joseph C. Burgess was commissioned to determine the geographical center of the Clarendon District so that a district seat (the town of Manning) could be established. Captain Burgess deeded to the state six acres, which provided sites for the courthouse and jail. The Clarendon District began its separate existence in October 1856. In January 1857, it was established as a separate judicial district. The town of Manning received its charter in January 1861, and was chartered again in March 1904. The earliest settled village in the county was probably Paxville, known originally as Packsland.

Because of the need for transportation and the convenience of the waterways, the early settlers established their homes and business operations in the Wright's Bluff area. Seeking a resort that was more healthful and was away from the daily business operations, these families located an area 10 miles north of Wright's Bluff and began to build homes there. "The Summer Town," as it was first called, soon developed into a year-round settlement, and the name was shortened to Summerton. Michael Turbeville settled in an area just north of the present town of Turbeville in 1840.

Several Revolutionary War confrontations took place in the area now identified as Clarendon County. Most notable were the battles that took place along the Santee River at Fort Watson.

Counted among the most distinguished native sons of Clarendon County are five men from the Richardson and Manning families who served as governors of the State of South Carolina. These are James Burchell Richardson (1802–1804); Richard Irvine Manning (1824–1826); John Peter Richardson (1840–1842); John Laurence Manning (1852–1854), for whom the town of Manning is named; and John Peter Richardson (1886–1890).

The Santee River has played and continues to play an important role in the history of Clarendon County. Some believe that it was the first North American River seen by white men. It is also believed that Spanish explorers traveled up the Santee in the sixth century, and it has been and continues to be a dominant force in the development of this area. The commerce on this river created a thriving community at Wright's Bluff that no longer exists.

South Carolina passed an act to establish a ferry on the lower Santee in 1734, but it did not start operating until 1756. This ferry was first known as Beard's Ferry. In 1762, it was permanently named Nelson's Ferry. The ferry provided the only efficient means of transporting people and goods to and from Charleston.

The Santee Canal, a 22-mile aqueduct, was opened in July 1800, to improve the efficiency of transportation inland from Charleston. This was one of the first canals of its length in the United States. The completion of the railroad from Columbia to Charleston in 1840 rendered the canal almost useless, and in 1850, the waterway was closed.

Almost 90 years later, in 1938, the state turned to the Santee River as a natural resource. The planning and construction of huge hydroelectric plants, dikes, and dams were constructed. This venture provided employment in an area recovering from the depression. The completion of this venture also created economic opportunities through recreational activities, such as fishing, hunting, and water sports for tourism, which we still enjoy today.

Three groups of men from Clarendon County joined with fellow southerners to fight in the War Between the States. These were the Manning Guards, The Sprott Guards, and Keel's Company.

Clarendon County played an important role in the Civil Rights movement of the 20th century. African-American parents began to seek redress for the improvement of educational facilities as they were interpreted under the Separate but Equal doctrine. The first was a lawsuit requesting bus transportation for African-American children within the county. The second effort was centralized in the Summerton area, requesting equal funding of schools for black children. *Briggs v. Elliott* was then filed in federal court, challenging the separate but equal laws requiring the separation of races in public schools as unconstitutional based on the 14th Amendment. In November 1952, it was joined by four other cases and became known as *Brown v. Board, et al.*

The publication of this book is the result of efforts originating among descendants of those individuals responsible for the *Briggs* case.

One

People and Places of Note

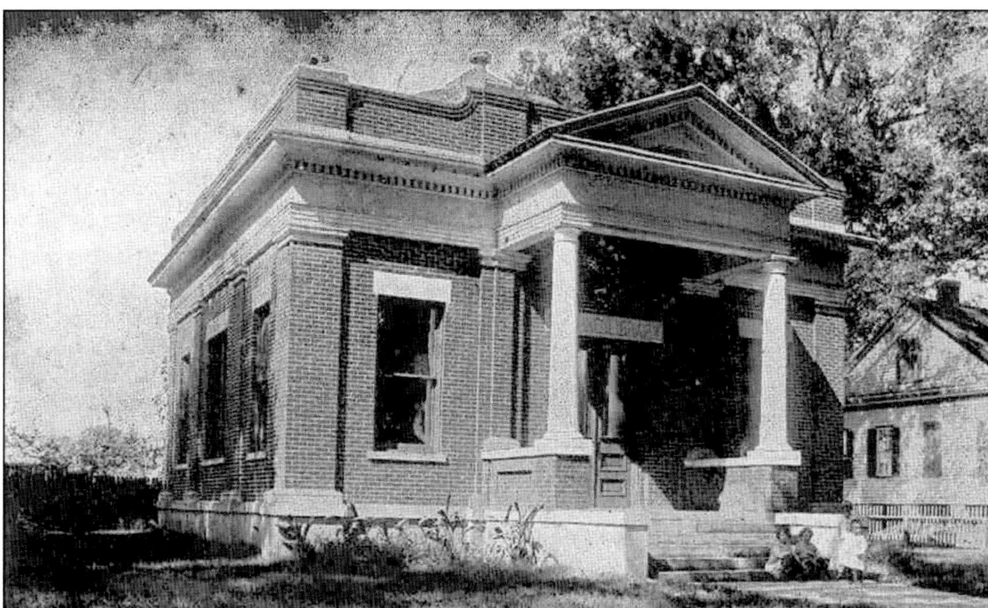

It is believed that the same architects who designed the present Clarendon County Courthouse also designed the old Manning Library in 1909. The children of Moses and Hanna Levi provided over $1000 in memory of their mother Hannah and the rest of the money was raised by the Civic League through bazaars and other fund raisers. The building has housed the Clarendon County Archives and History Center since 1996.

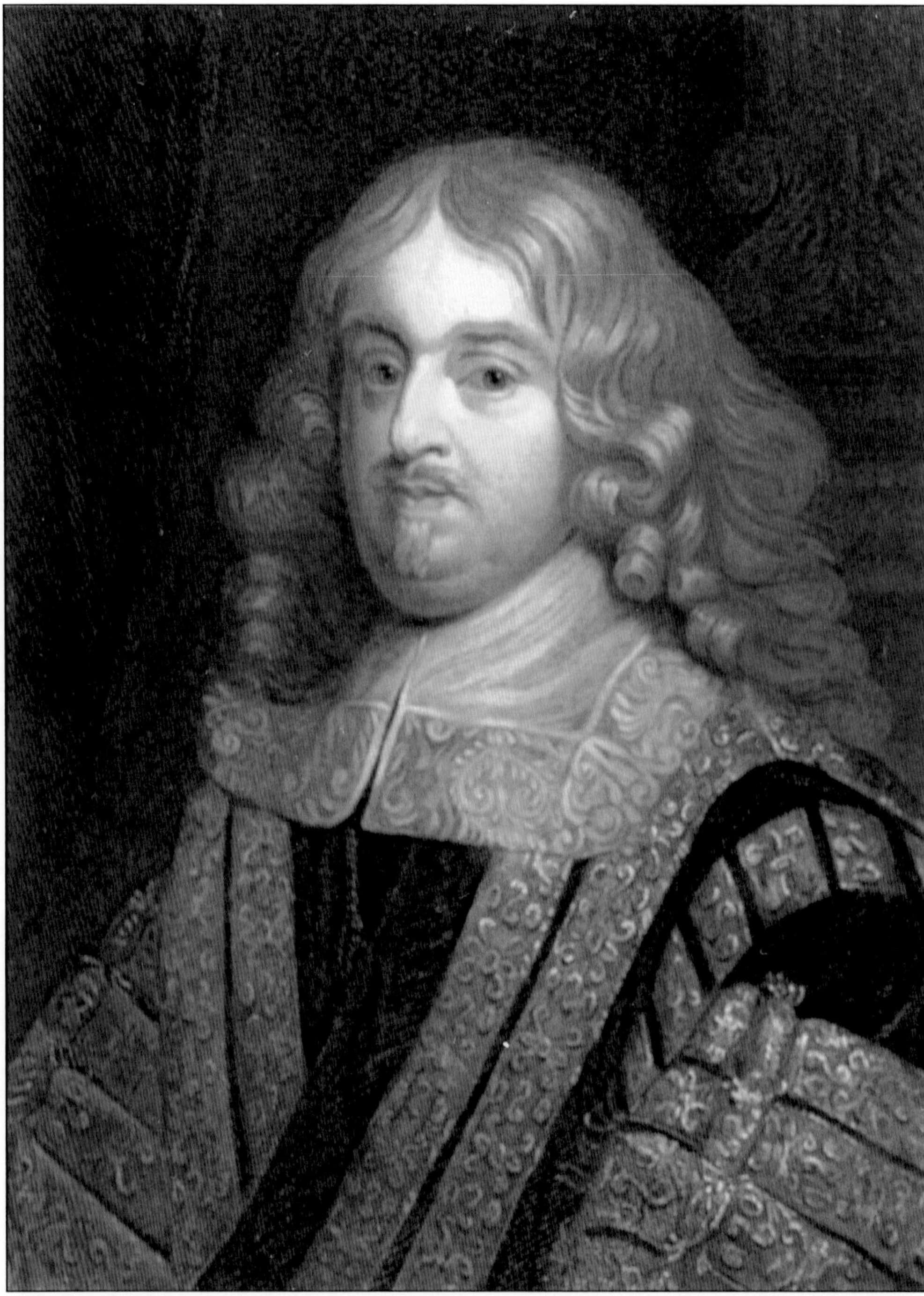

Lord Clarendon (1619–1674), the namesake of Clarendon County, was born in Dinton, England as Earl Hide. The Earl of Clarendon was one of the eight Lord Proprietors of Carolina. He also served as a companion to King Charles II and as Lord High Chancellor of England.

John P. Richardson Sr. was governor of South Carolina from 1840 to 1842. He was a member of the Richardson family, who were plantation owners in the Summerton-Rimini area.

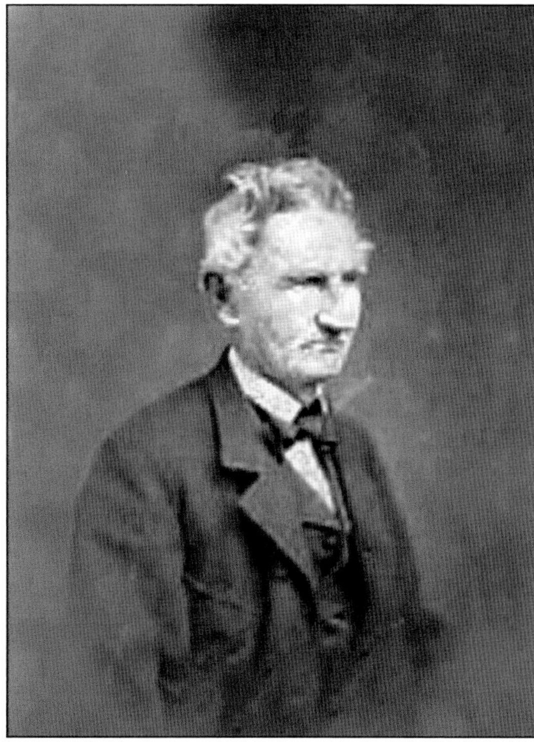

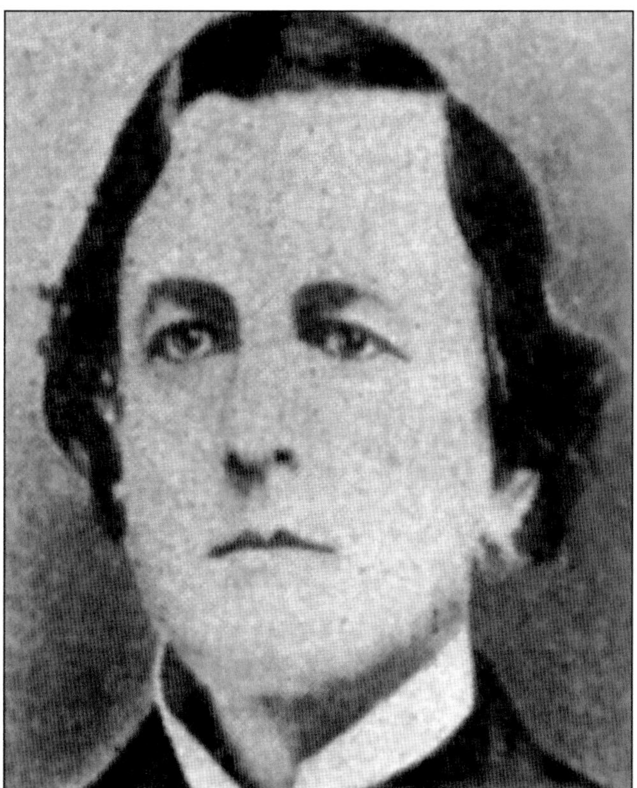

John Laurence Manning (1816–1889) was governor of South Carolina from 1852 to 1854. During his term as governor there was much improvement in public education. Contributions to scholarships at South Carolina College were made out of his own pocket. He was a delegate to the Democratic National Convention in 1856. He opposed secession but voted for the ordinance of secession at the South Carolina Conference in 1860.

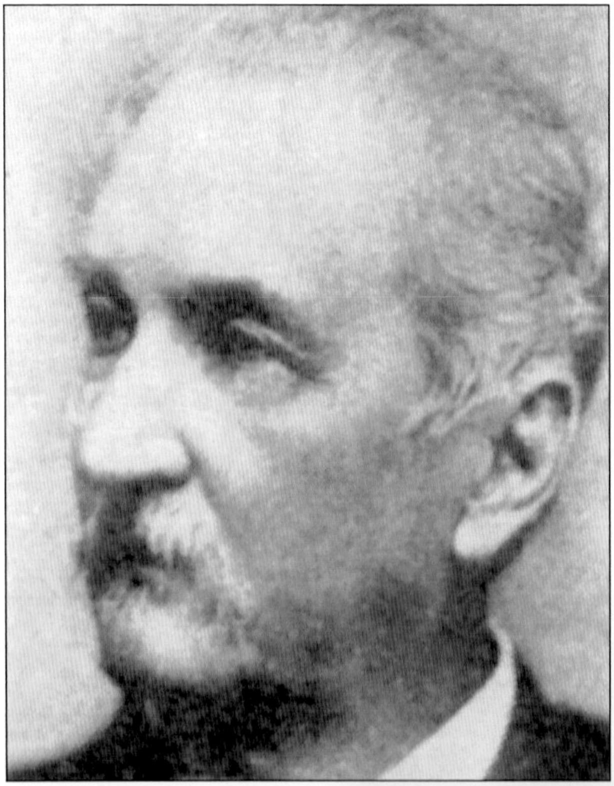

John P. Richardson III (1831–1899) served as governor of South Carolina from 1886 to 1890. He was a descendant of Revolutionary Gen. Richard Richardson and served in the Confederate Army on the staff of General Cantey.

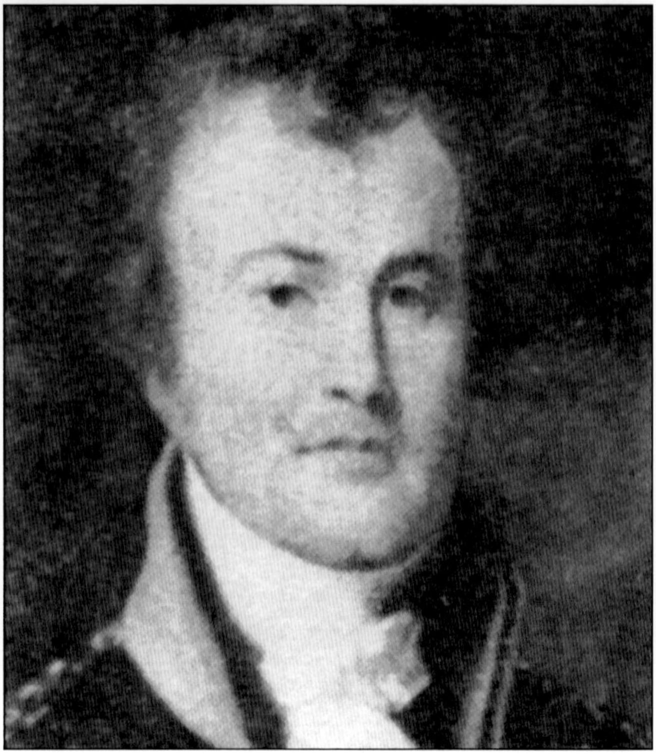

James B. Richardson (1770–1836) was born in the Camden District, now a part of Clarendon County, and served as governor from 1802 to 1804. His father was the direct ancestor of six governors of South Carolina.

Richard Irvine Manning I (1789–1836) served as governor of South Carolina from 1824 to 1826. His mother was the sister of Gov. James Burchill Richardson. He served as a captain in the War of 1812.

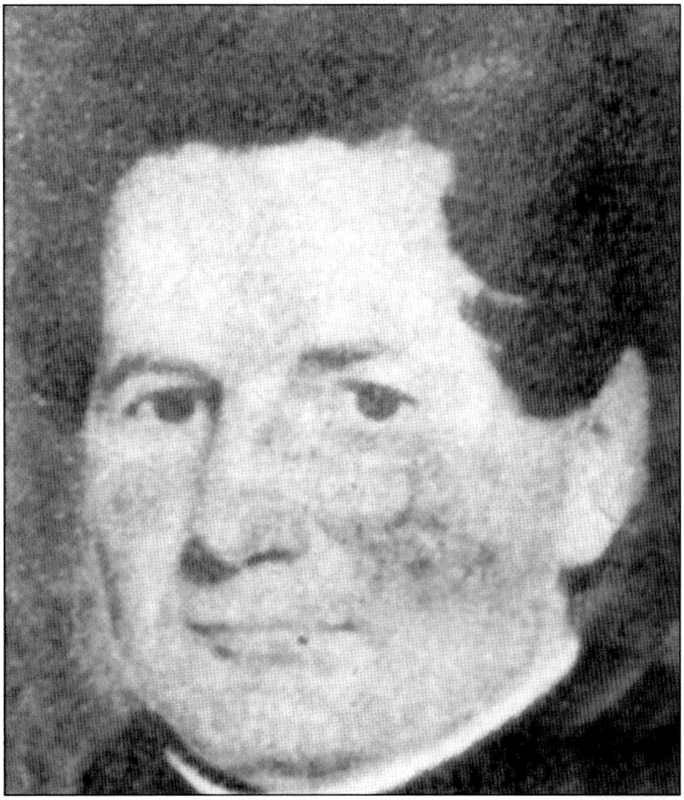

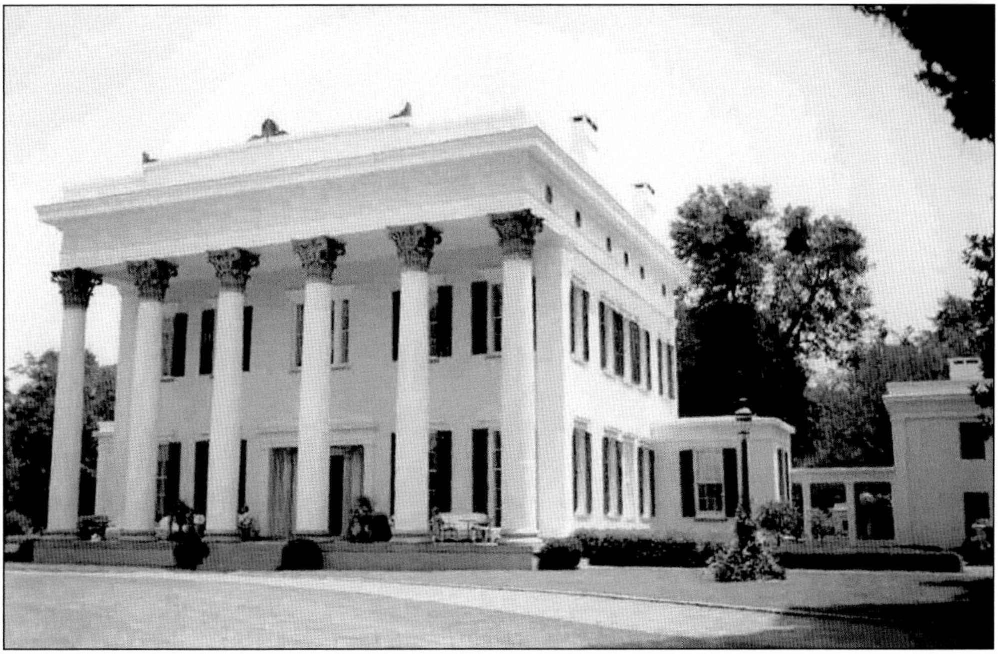

The Milford Plantation is located in what is now Sumter County. John Laurence Manning, the state's 37th governor, built the mansion in 1839 as his family residence. The mansion is situated in what had been known as Claremont, which at one time was a section of Clarendon.

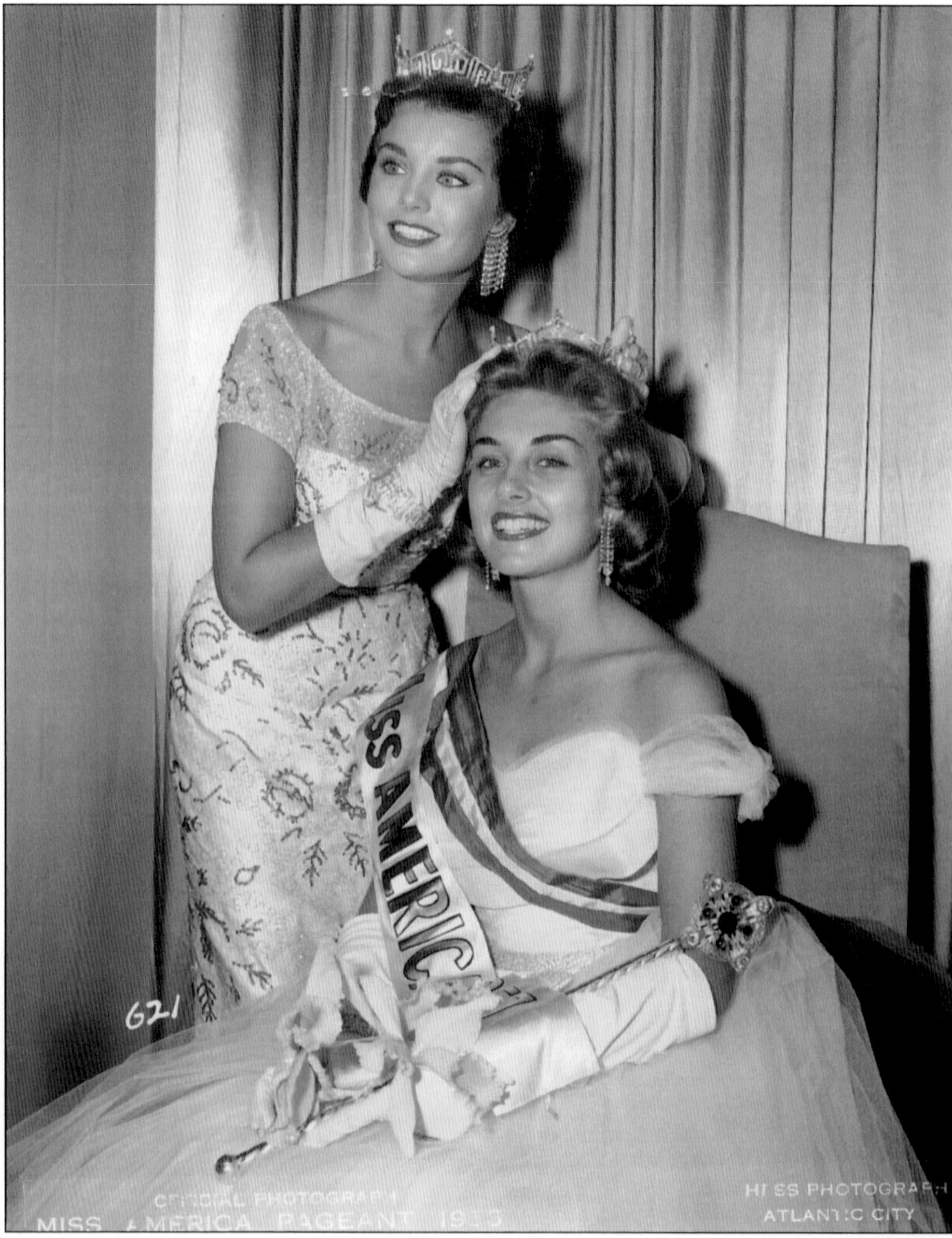

In October 1956 the first South Carolinian crowned as Miss America was Marian McKnight, a native of Clarendon County.

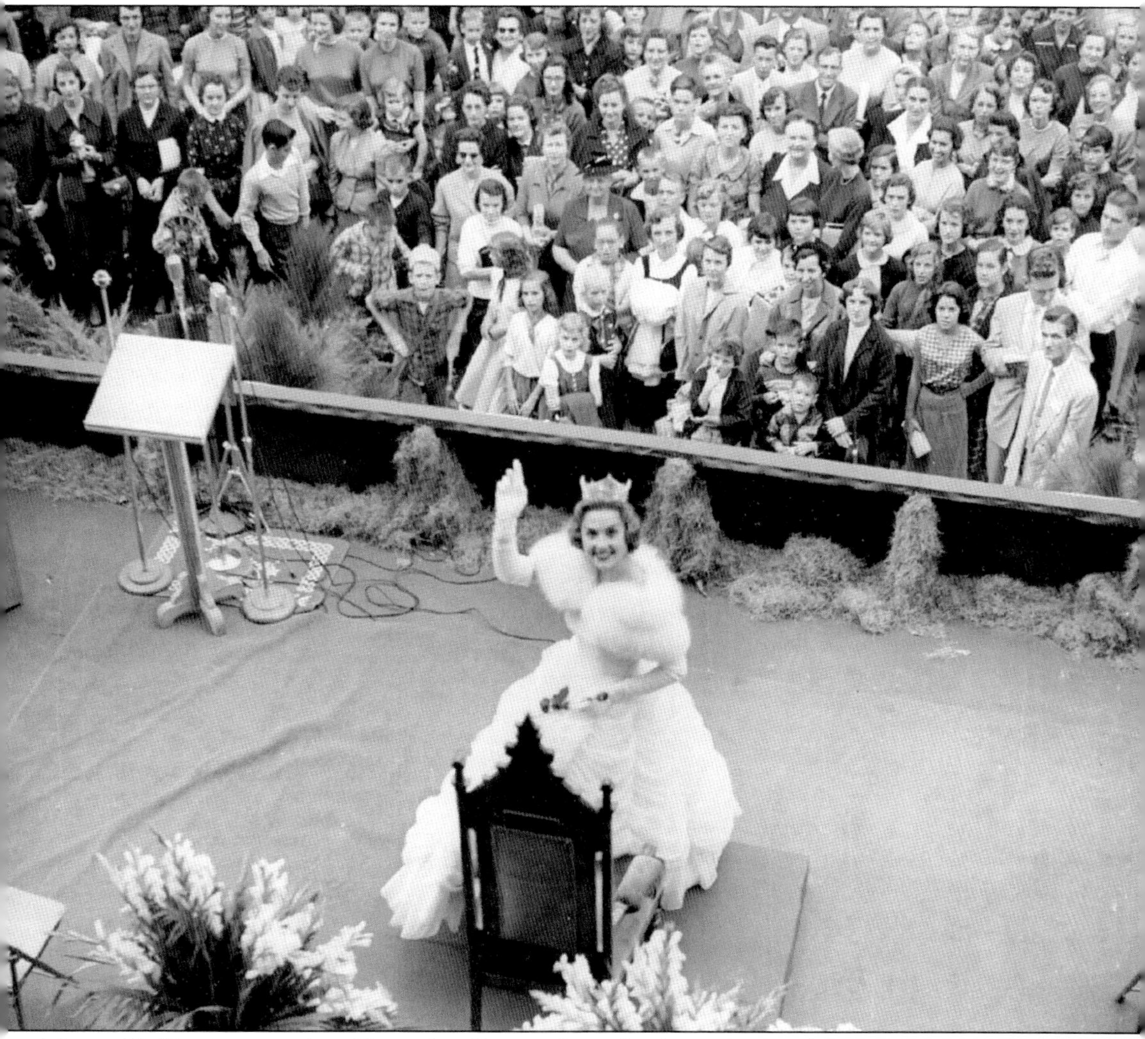

Marian McKnight greets her Clarendon County fans after being crowned Miss America 1957. This photograph was taken during her first visit home after receiving the title. It was indeed a proud moment for many of the citizens of this county.

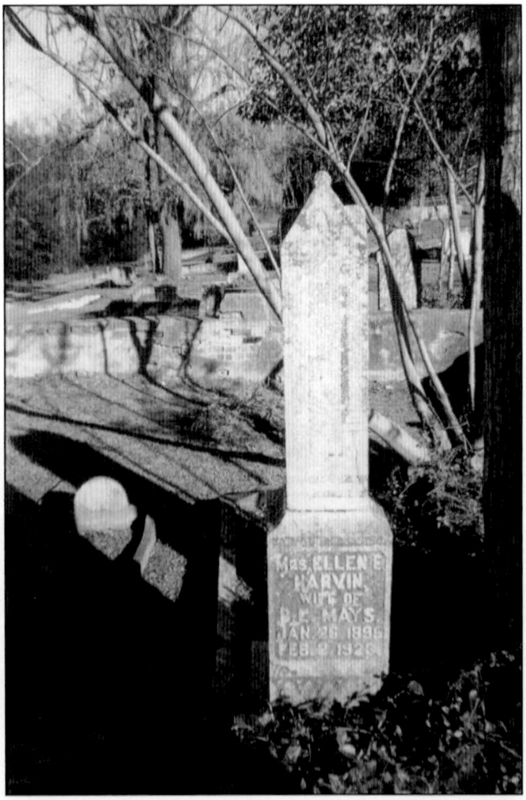

Ellen E. Harvin (1895–1923), the first wife of noted African-American educator Benjamin E. Mays, is buried in her hometown at the Manning Cemetery. Her grave is situated in an enclosed plot, presumably with other family members. The graves of Corp. Rufus Richardson (1899–1919) and Theodosia Richardson (1867–1928) are positioned on either side of Ellen.

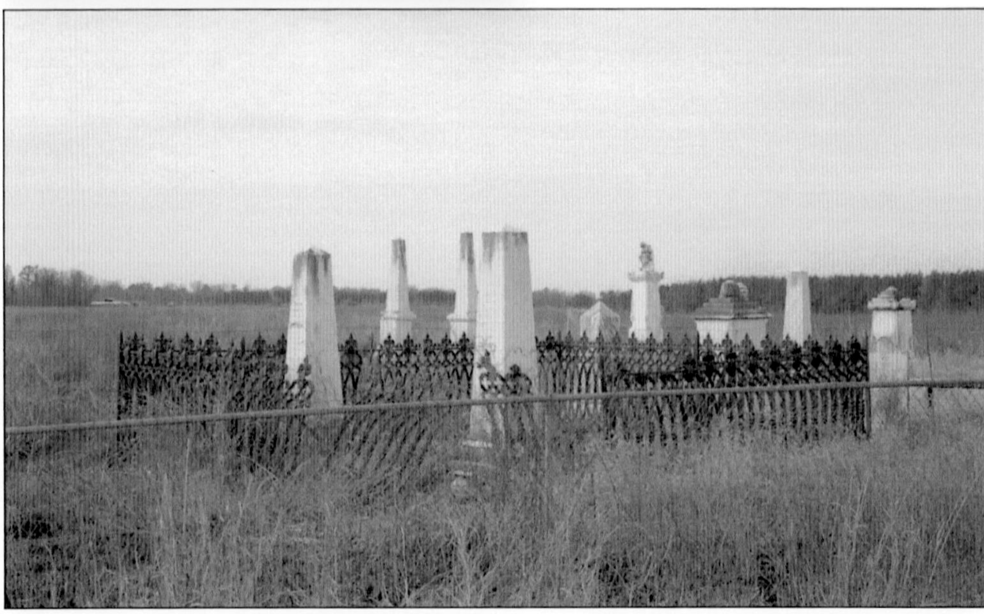

This is a photo of one of the earliest cemetery of the colonial Carolinas, which is located in the St. Mark Parrish. Such notables as Richard Richardson, brigadier in the American Revolution; James Burchell Richardson, South Carolina governor from 1802 to 1804; and John Peter Richardson, South Carolina governor from 1840 to 1842 and the founder of the Citadel, are buried here.

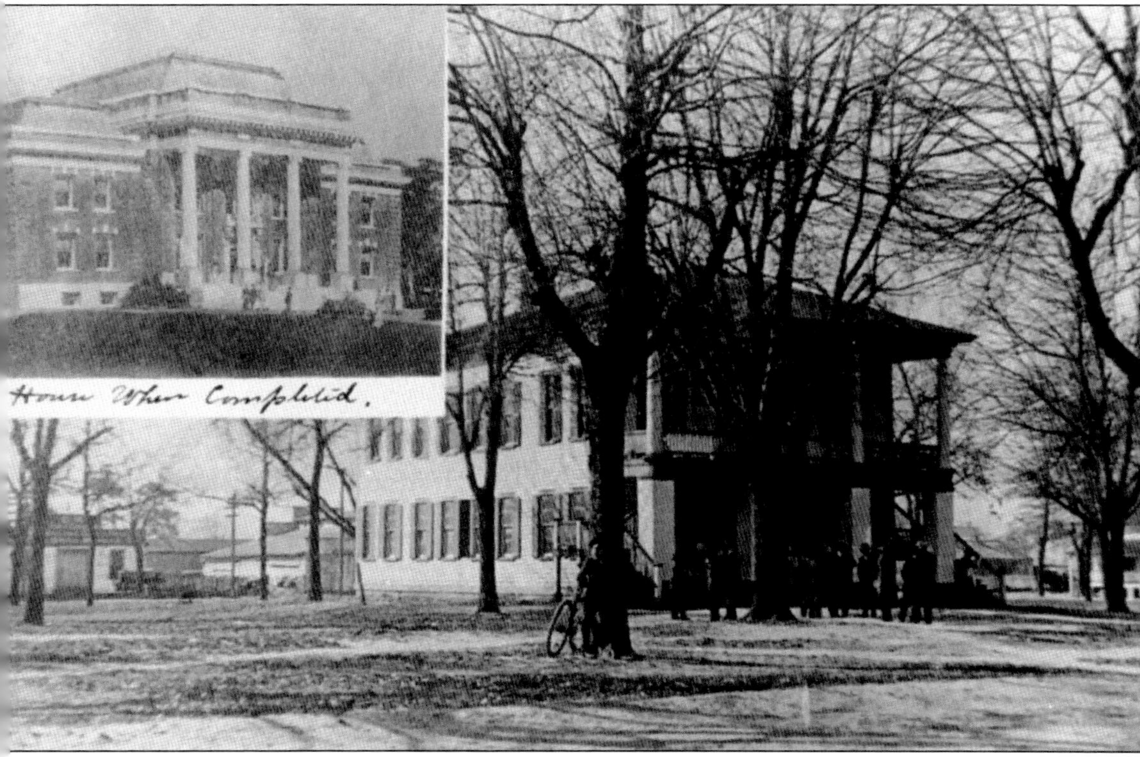

The first courthouse was completed on this site in 1858. That building was destroyed by General Potter's troops during the Civil War. The second courthouse building (above) was constructed in 1878. The structure was deemed inadequate for services required for the governmental center. However, it continued to function as the county's seat of government until 1908 when the building was moved south across Keitt Street to make room for the new courthouse. The present courthouse (inset) was dedicated in January 1910 and continues to the present to serve as the center for governmental services within the county.

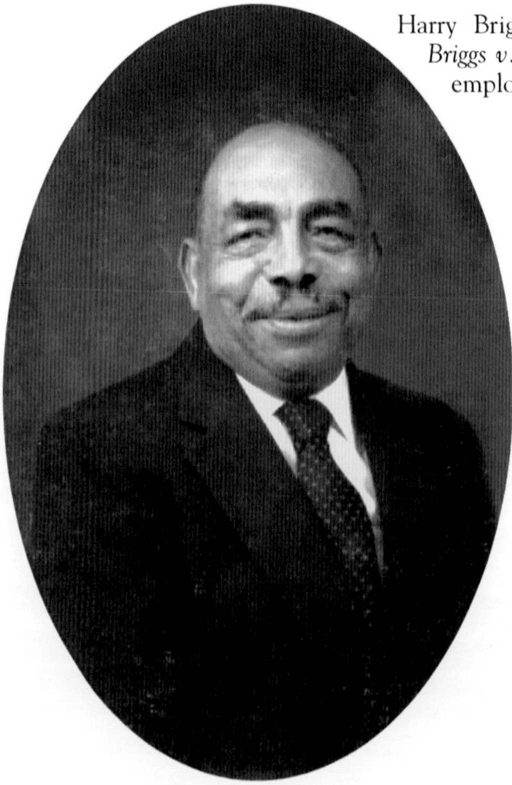

Harry Briggs Sr., one of the 20 petitioners in the *Briggs v. Elliott* case, had to leave South Carolina for employment shortly after signing the petition.

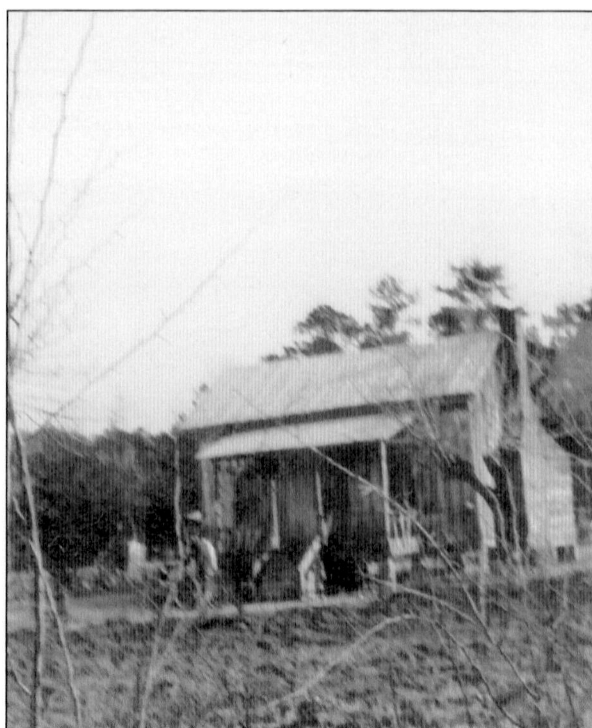

This photograph is of the birthplace of Harry Briggs Sr., a litigant in the South Carolina Court action for the desegregation of public schools.

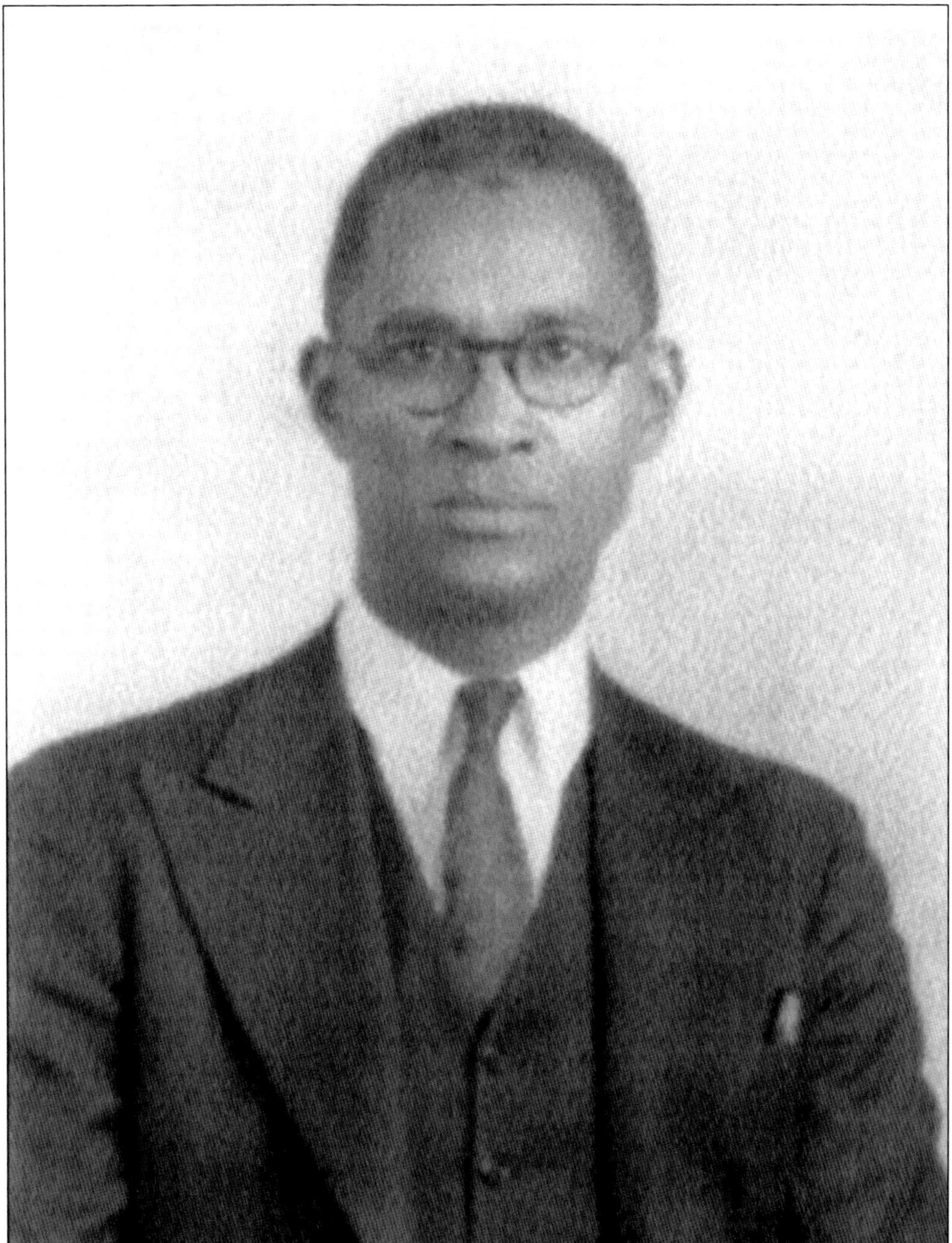

Joseph A. De Laine (1898–1974) was 20 years old when he posed for this picture in 1918. De Laine, who later became a minister, is credited with the primary leadership role in local Civil Rights initiatives within the county during the 1940s and 1950s. Most notable was his involvement in the genesis of *Briggs v. Elliott*, the first case of the 20th century challenging state law requiring the separation of races in public schools. The *Charlotte Observer* named him as one of the 100 most influential Carolinians during the 20th century.

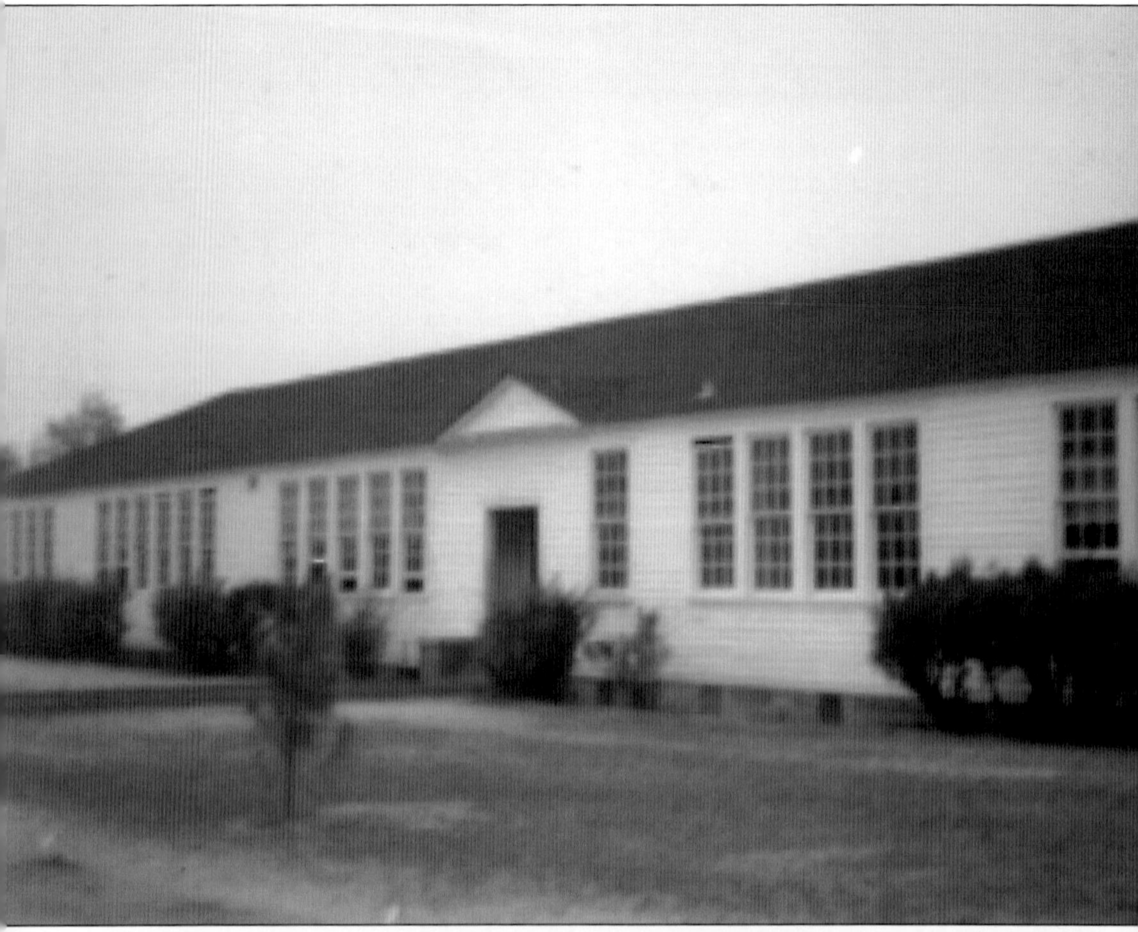

Scott's Branch School, pictured here *c*. 1950, and its school district received national notoriety as the school and district of primary focus in the *Briggs v. Elliott* litigation regarding the desegregation of public schools. This building was replaced with a new structure, a high school, around 1952. The new building houses the middle school for the district.

Two

Military Participation

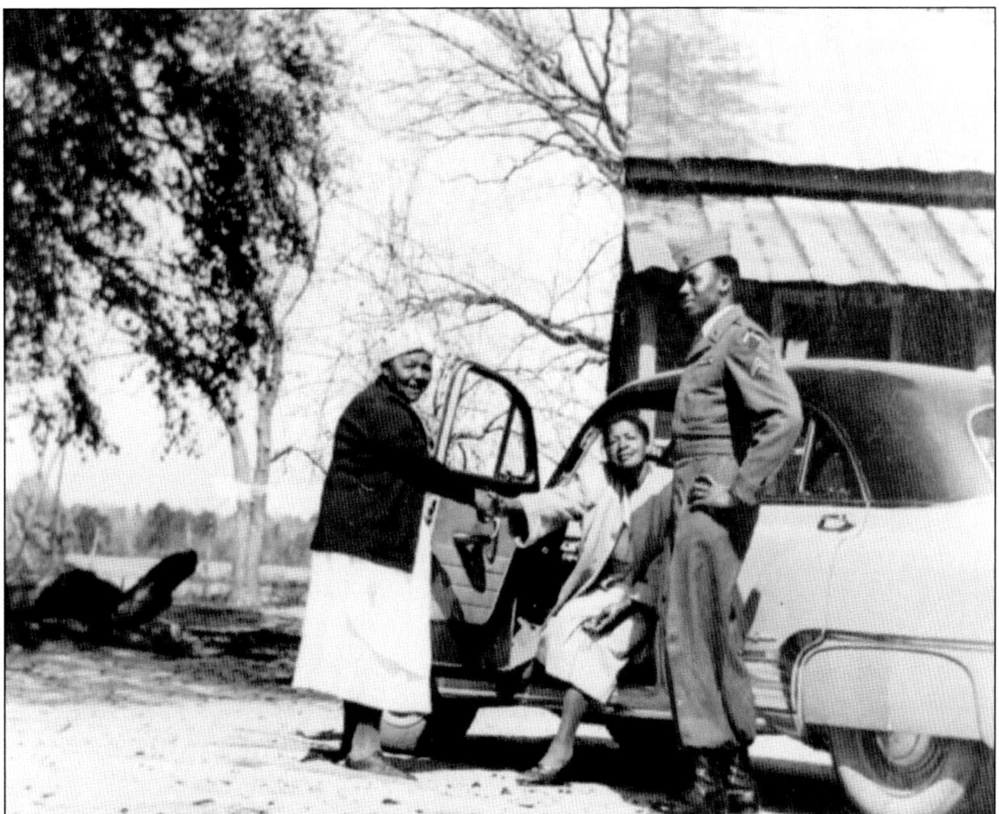

Corporal James Lee Scott is welcomed home by his mother Sallie James Scott and his aunt Mary Lou James Boatwright (standing) in 1955. Families looked forward to having their sons return; soldiers were always a source of pride for the community and were shown great respect. Families usually gathered for a great feast with all of the soldier's favorite foods.

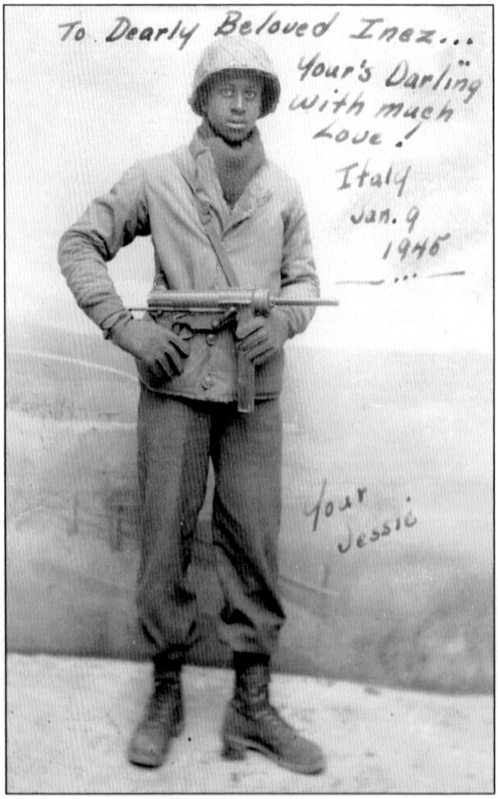

Jessie Pearson is pictured here in full combat gear. During his career in the U.S. Army, he fought in three major battles in central and northern Italy. In this 1943 picture sent from Italy, he expresses his love to his future wife Inez. Pearson is a native of the Davis Station area.

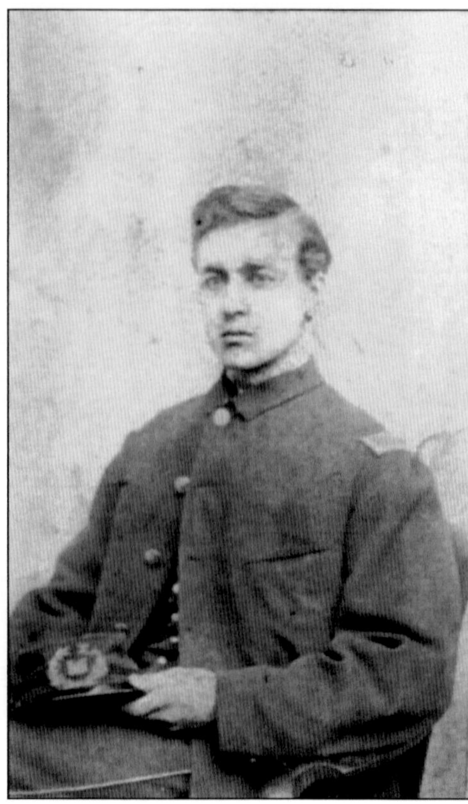

Lt. Harrison Waterman is shown here in uniform, *c.* 1864. He was a Union soldier, and it is reputed that he interceded to spare the lives of several Manning residents when Union soldiers occupied the town.

This is a photograph of Walter McFadden in his navy uniform. Note the tight leggings and long white spats. McFadden is from the New Zion area.

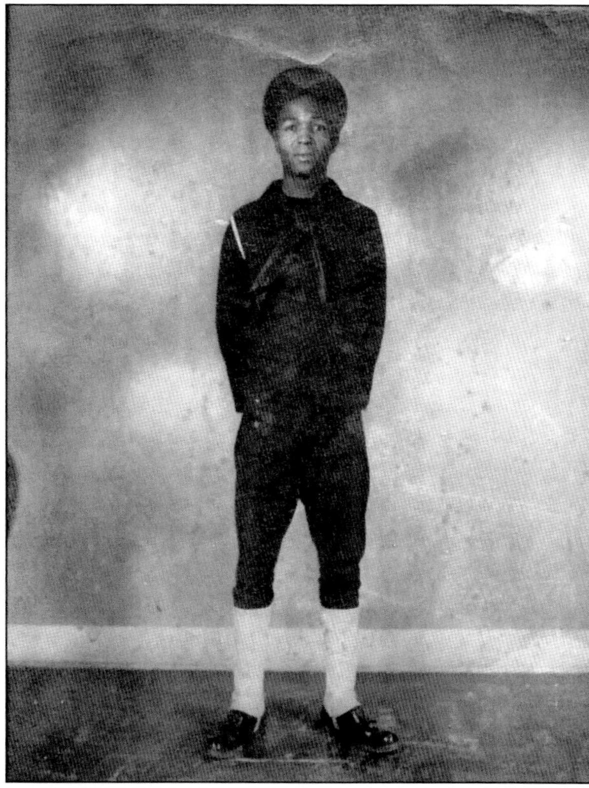

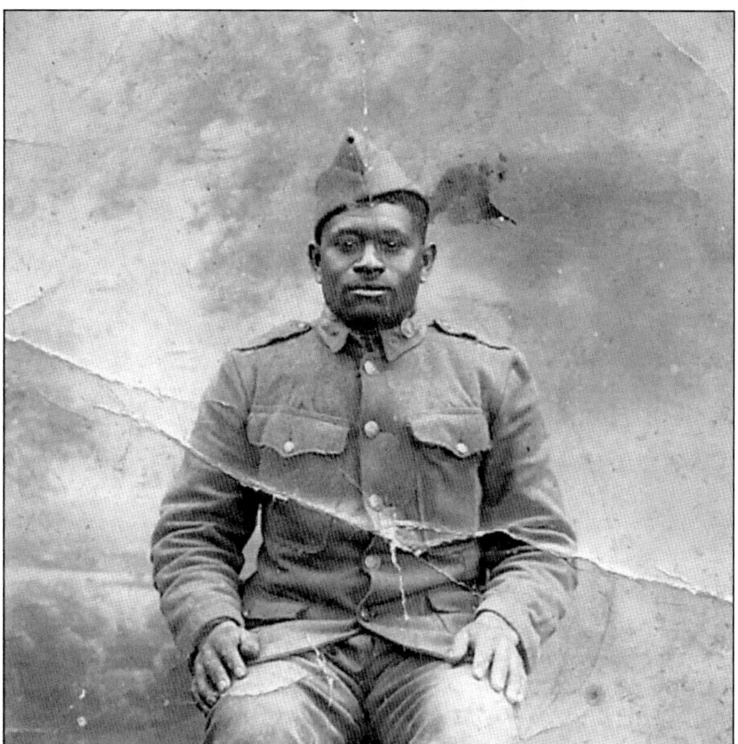

Ben Riley, a native of New Zion, proudly served in the U.S. Army during World War I. Although military units were maintained on a segregated basis until President Truman ended the practice, black men valiantly served and died for their country so that all Americans could enjoy the preservation of our democratic ideals.

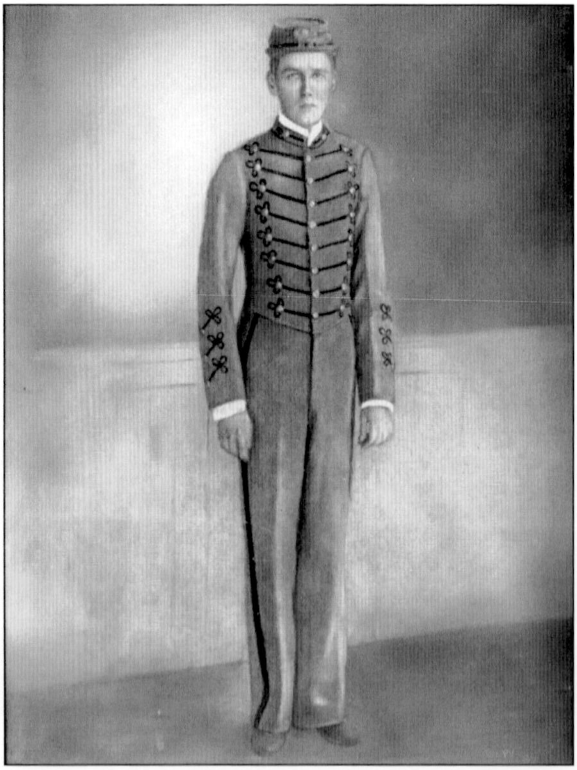

T.Y. Eadon served as mayor of Summerton for several years during the 1930s. He is pictured here, as a young man, in what seems to be the uniform of a cadet.

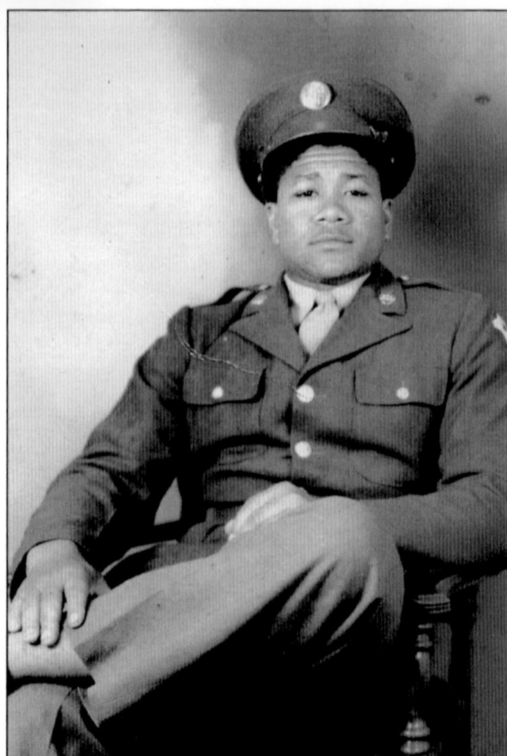

Jonathan Riley proudly shows off his army dress in this 1944 picture. He is believed to have experienced combat in the European Theater during World War II.

James Sumter, a Manning native and a veteran of World War II, poses in this 1942 portrait, which was given to his family.

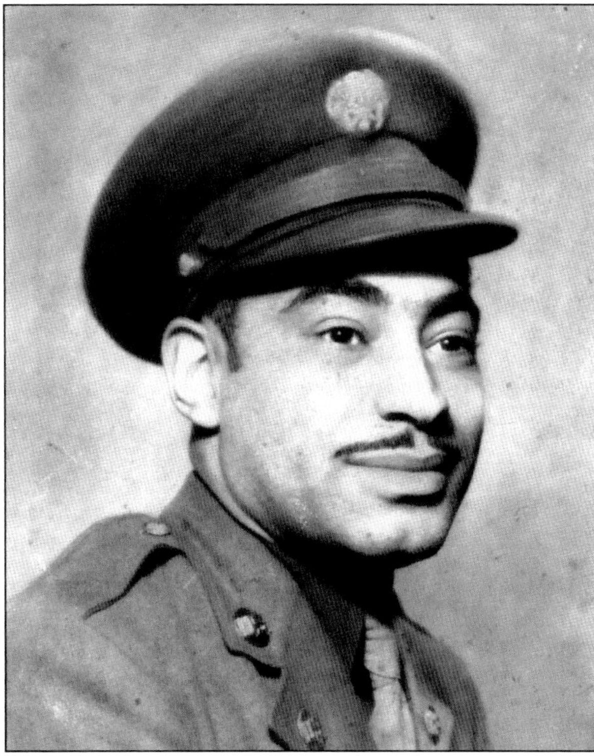

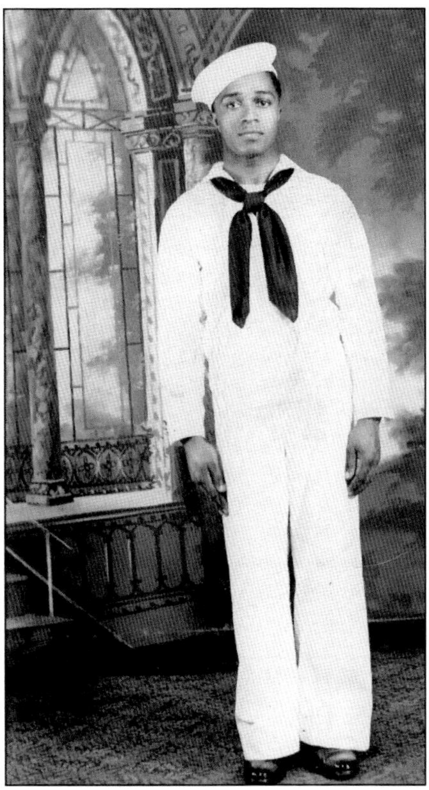

Van Richburg, pictured here *c.* 1940, served in the United States Navy in the late 1930s and early 1940s. His home was Manning.

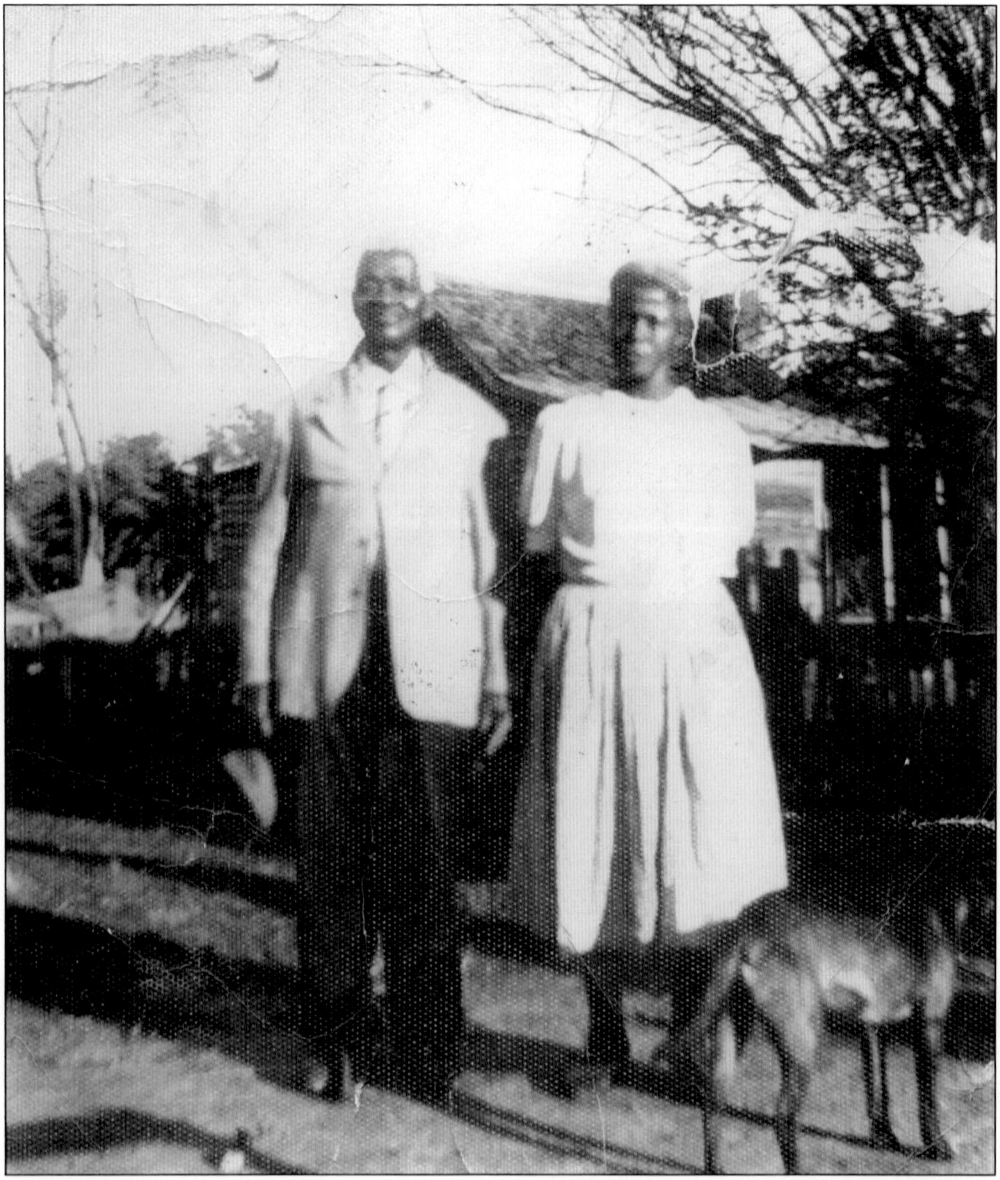

Lucious Cooper, a veteran of the Spanish American War, is shown with his wife, Mariah Rhodes Cooper, as they pose in front of their home *c.* 1931. Mariah, now a centenarian, still resides in the Summerton community.

Three proud World War I soldiers from the Summerton area display the American flag under which they served. They are believed to be the descendants of Dinah Beshet Bowman.

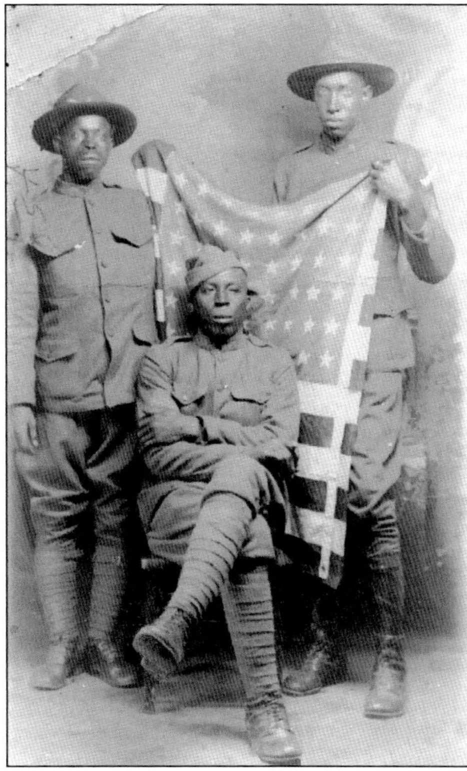

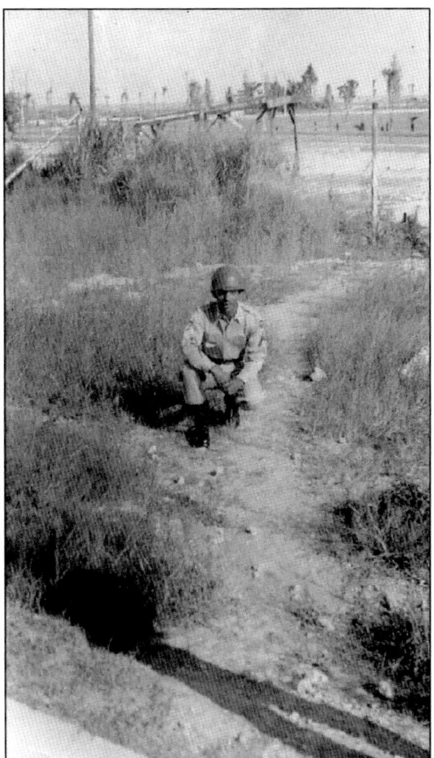

Summerton's Howard Brown is shown in Okinawa while serving in the United States Army.

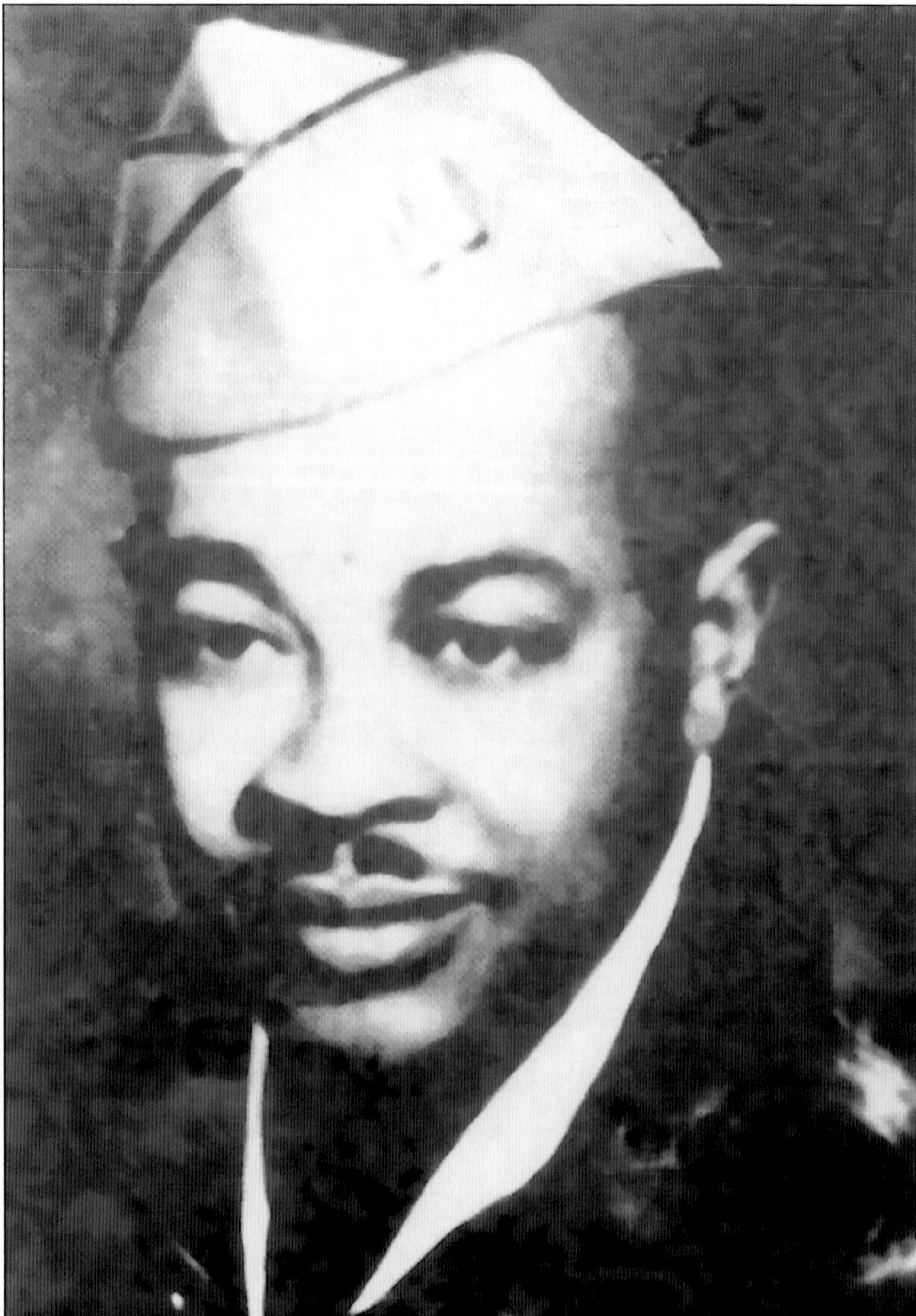

Capt. James Alonza Walker, a native of Manning and a member of the famed Tuskeegee Airmen, completed his aviation training in 1943. He is credited with 107 combat missions during World War II.

Three

INSTITUTIONS AND INSTITUTIONAL ACTIVITIES

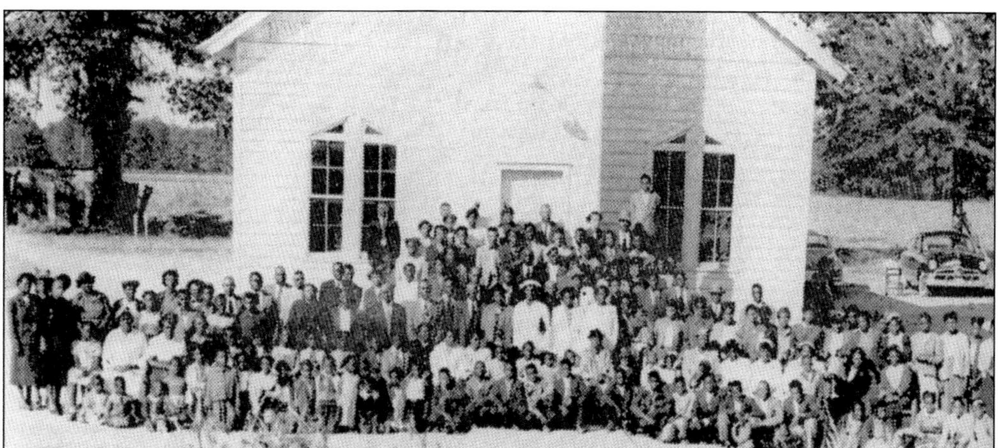

The 1949 Pine Grove AME Church congregation gather for a group picture. The church is located in the Bloomville area of the county. Most families in this community were involved in the growth of seasonal crops such as corn, tobacco, and cotton for their livelihoods.

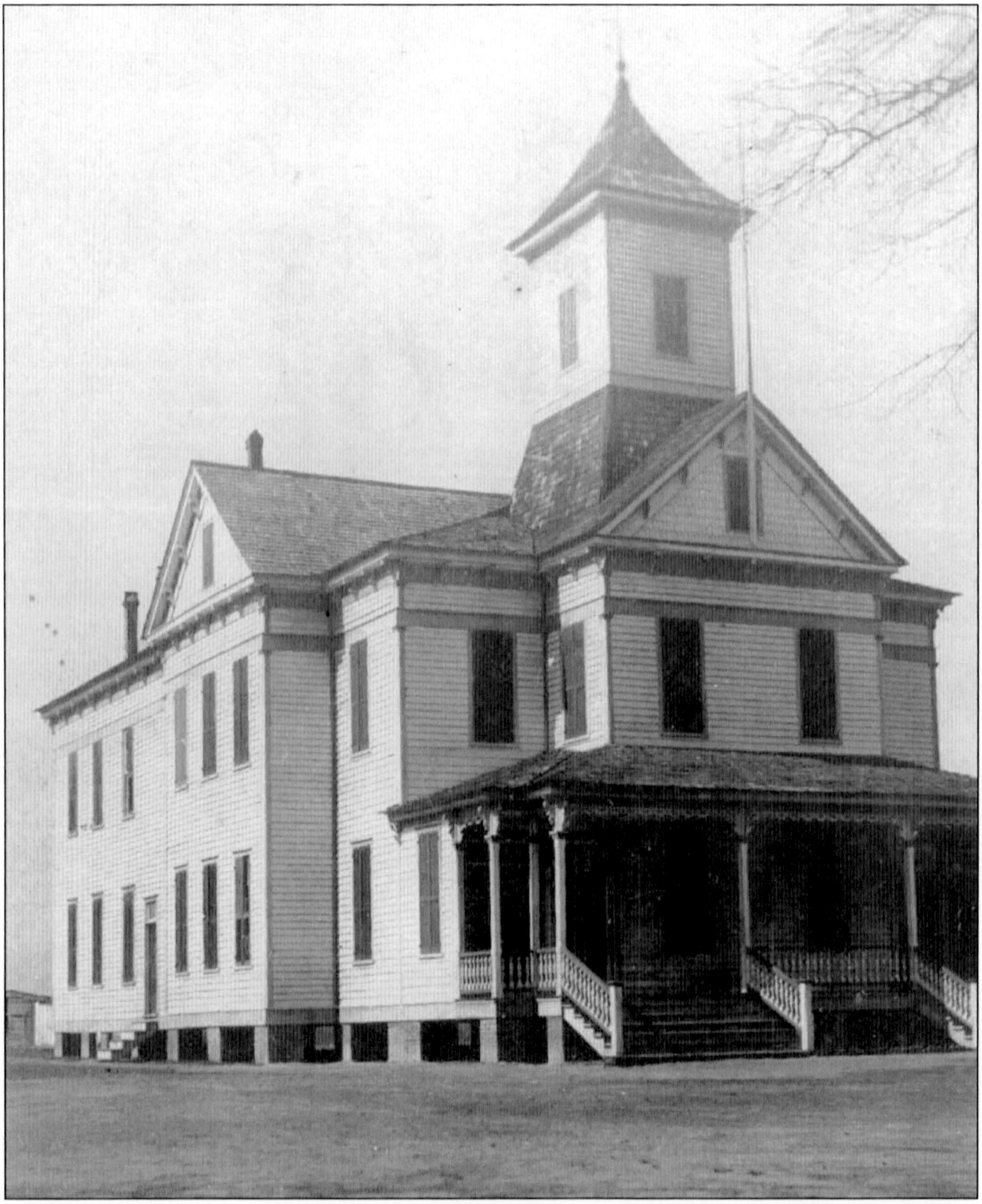

The Moses Levi Institute, originally known as Manning Collegiate Institute, was organized in 1889 and operated until 1910 when it was replaced by the Manning Graded School. It stood on North Brooks Street near the corner of Old Georgetown Road and was later the high school.

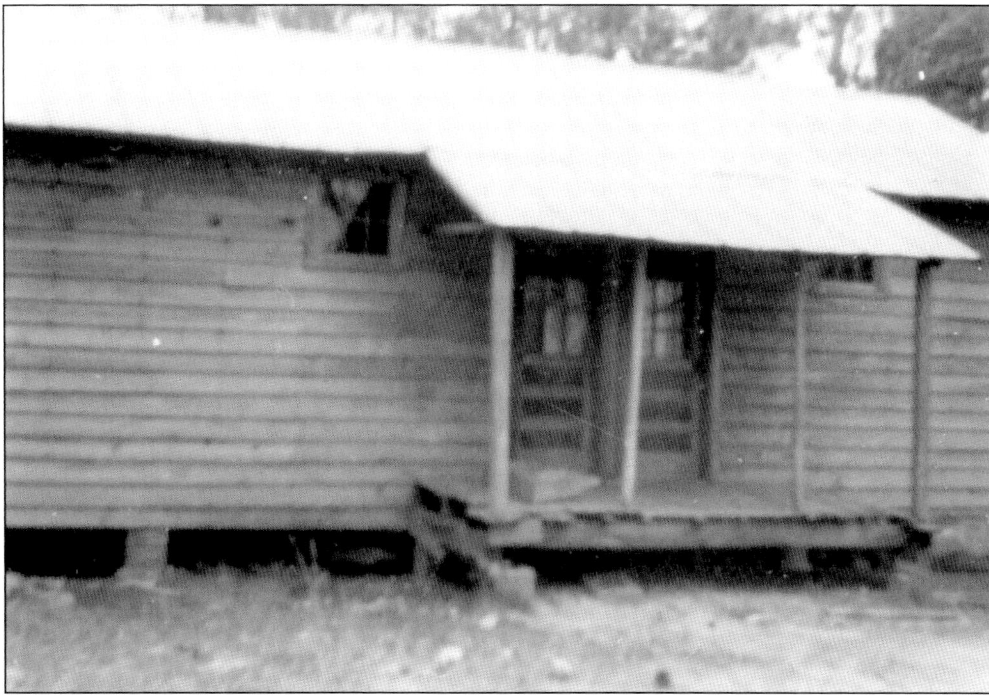

This building was erected by Willie Pearson and once served as the Halleytown School located near the Elizabeth Baptist Church. The principal for the duration of the school's existence was Esther Pearson. The structure no longer exists.

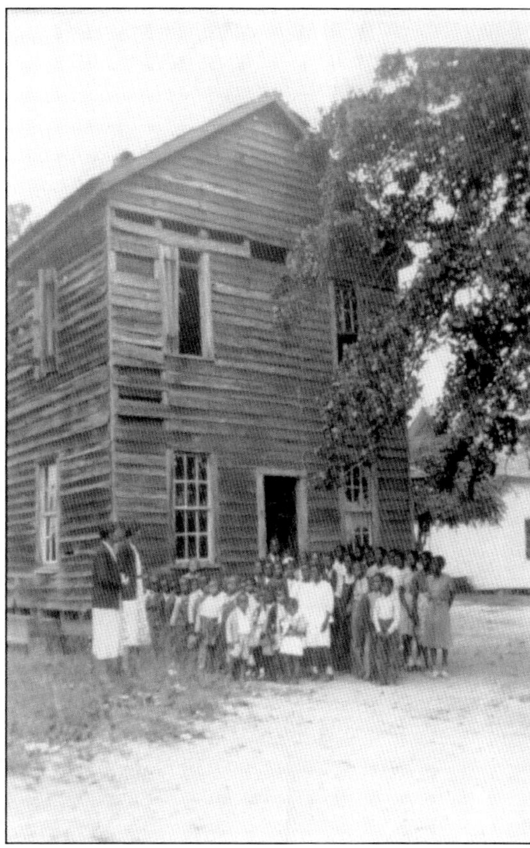

Students pose for a school picture at Spring Hill School. This 1937 photograph includes teachers Mattie B. De Laine and Helen B. Richburg. The school was housed on the first floor of this old Masonic building.

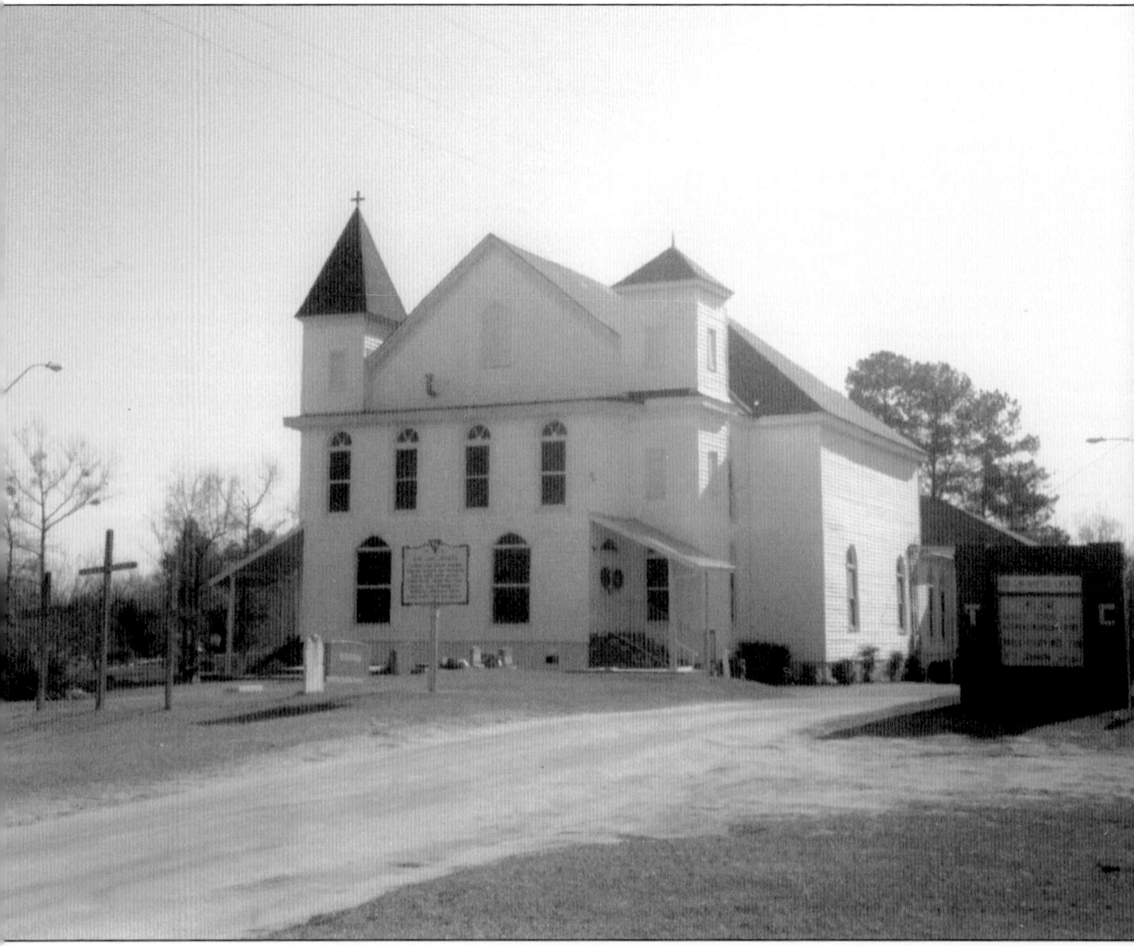

Taw Caw Baptist Church was originally built *c.* 1860 and was used by a white Baptist congregation until 1885. At that time, the church was purchased by a black group to be used as a Baptist church. The church is located on U.S. Route 301, near Summerton.

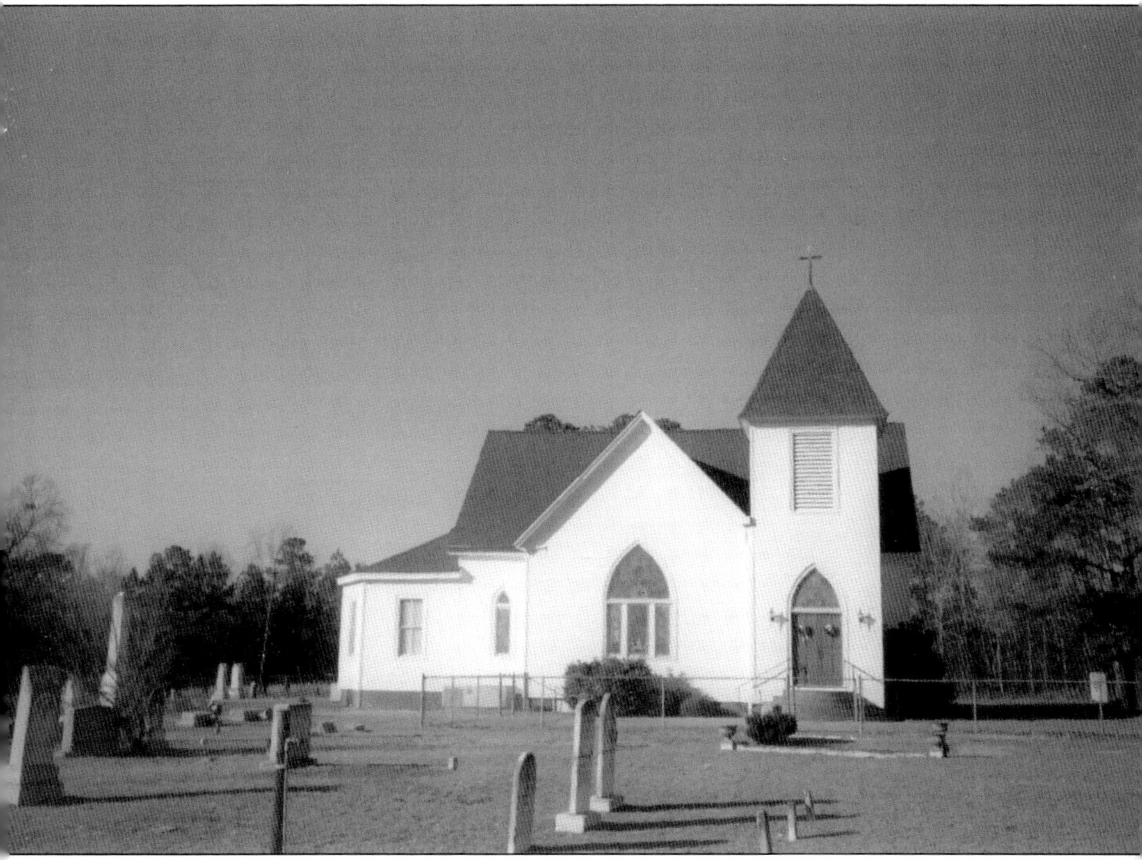

According to local legend, Andrews Chapel Church was first organized as early as 1786. Today, the church stands on land that was donated by Ellis R. Richburg and Mary A. Richburg in 1880.

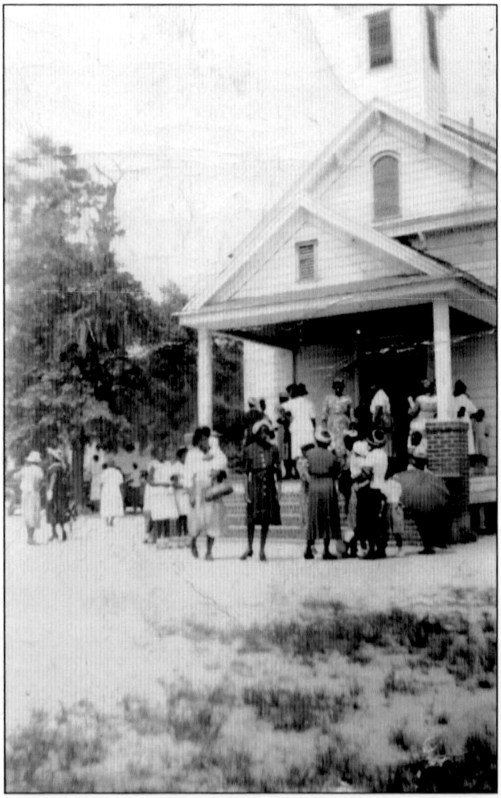

This *c.* 1949 photograph of Melina Presbyterian Church in the New Zion community depicts a typical after-service gathering. Parishioners often gathered briefly after services to socialize.

This photograph of Liberty Hill AME Church was taken shortly after the building's completion in 1904. The pastor at the time, Rev. Henry C. De Laine, was instrumental in the construction of this edifice. Peter De Laine, brother of the pastor, designed and supervised the construction of the building.

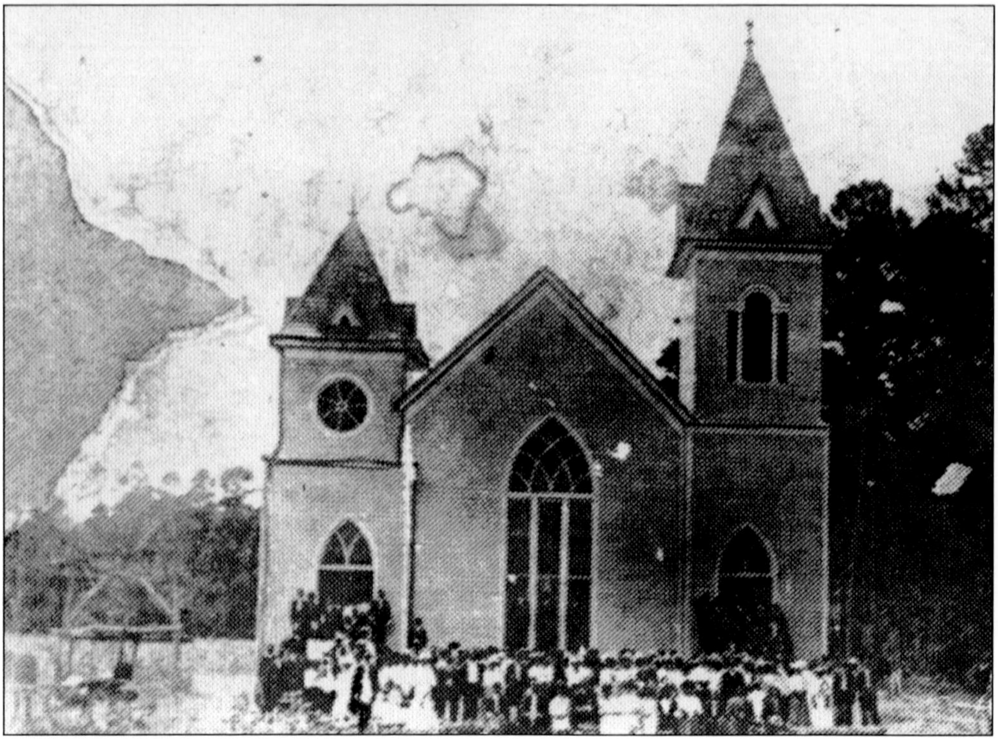

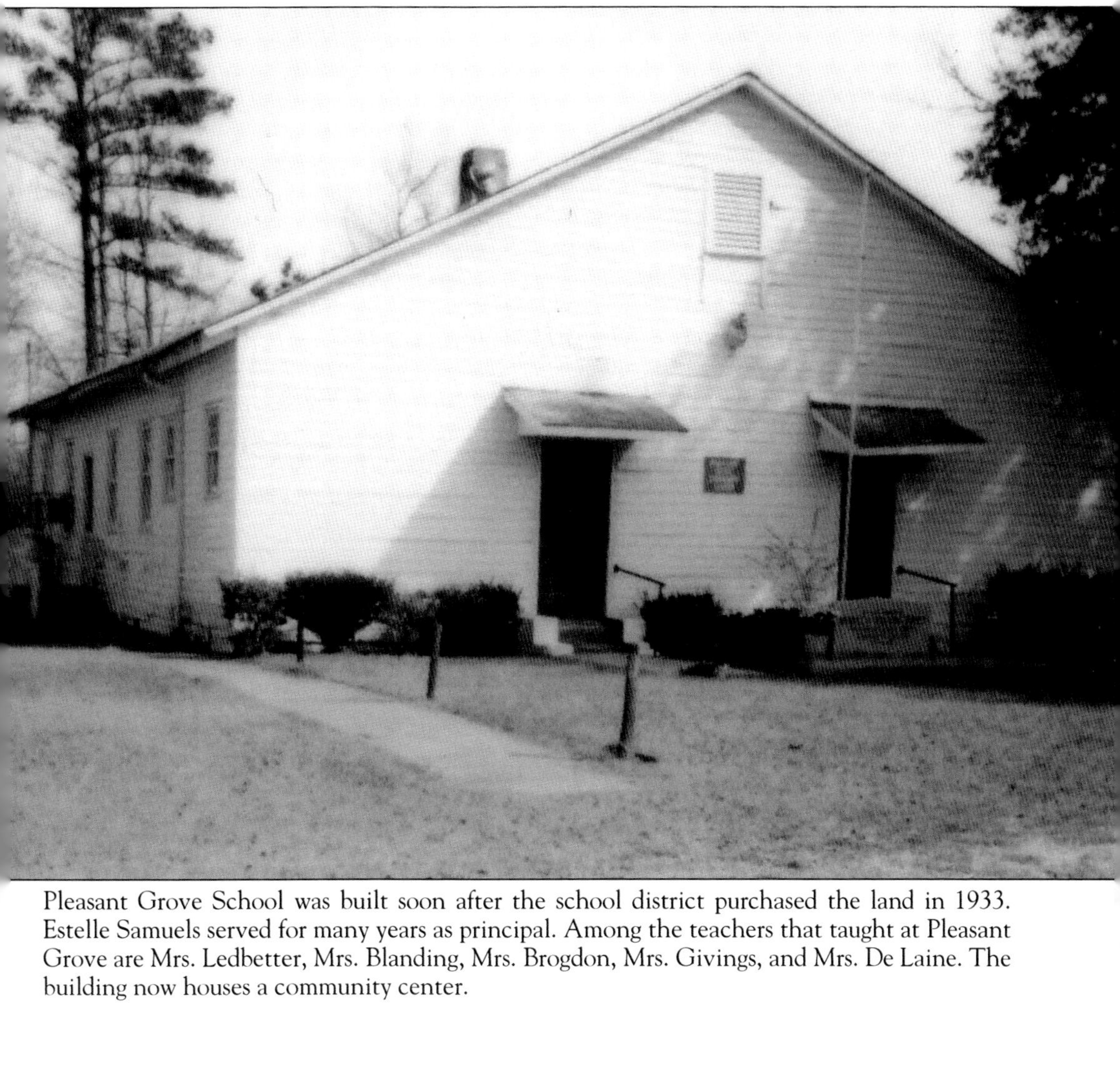

Pleasant Grove School was built soon after the school district purchased the land in 1933. Estelle Samuels served for many years as principal. Among the teachers that taught at Pleasant Grove are Mrs. Ledbetter, Mrs. Blanding, Mrs. Brogdon, Mrs. Givings, and Mrs. De Laine. The building now houses a community center.

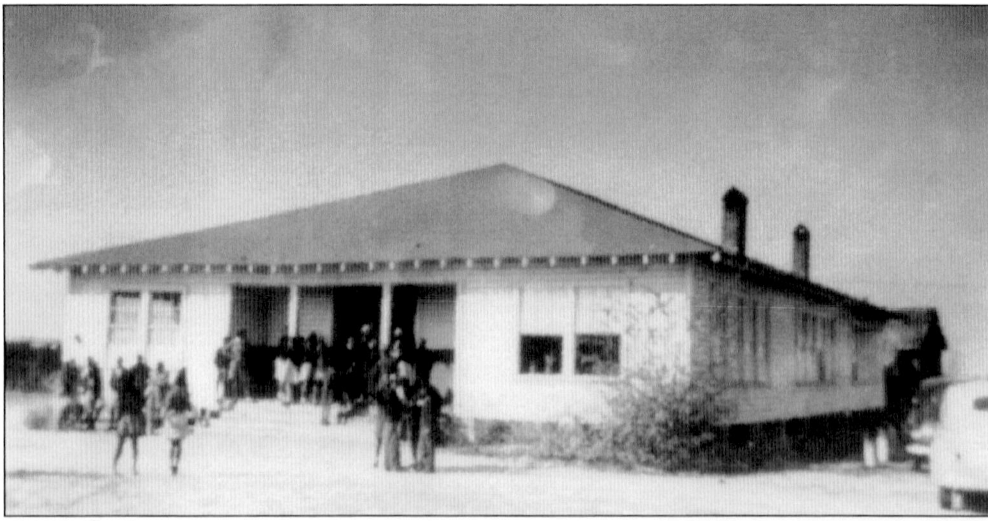

The St. Paul School, pictured here, was located on Nelson's Ferry Road and taught grades one through eleven. The students standing at the front of the building are enjoying a brief recess from their classes.

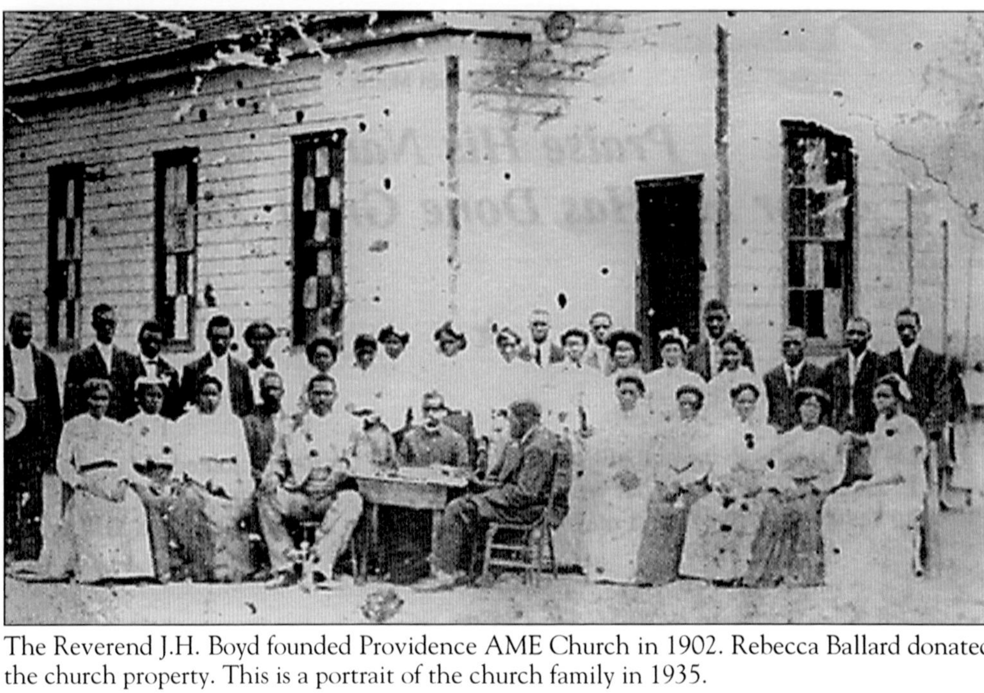

The Reverend J.H. Boyd founded Providence AME Church in 1902. Rebecca Ballard donated the church property. This is a portrait of the church family in 1935.

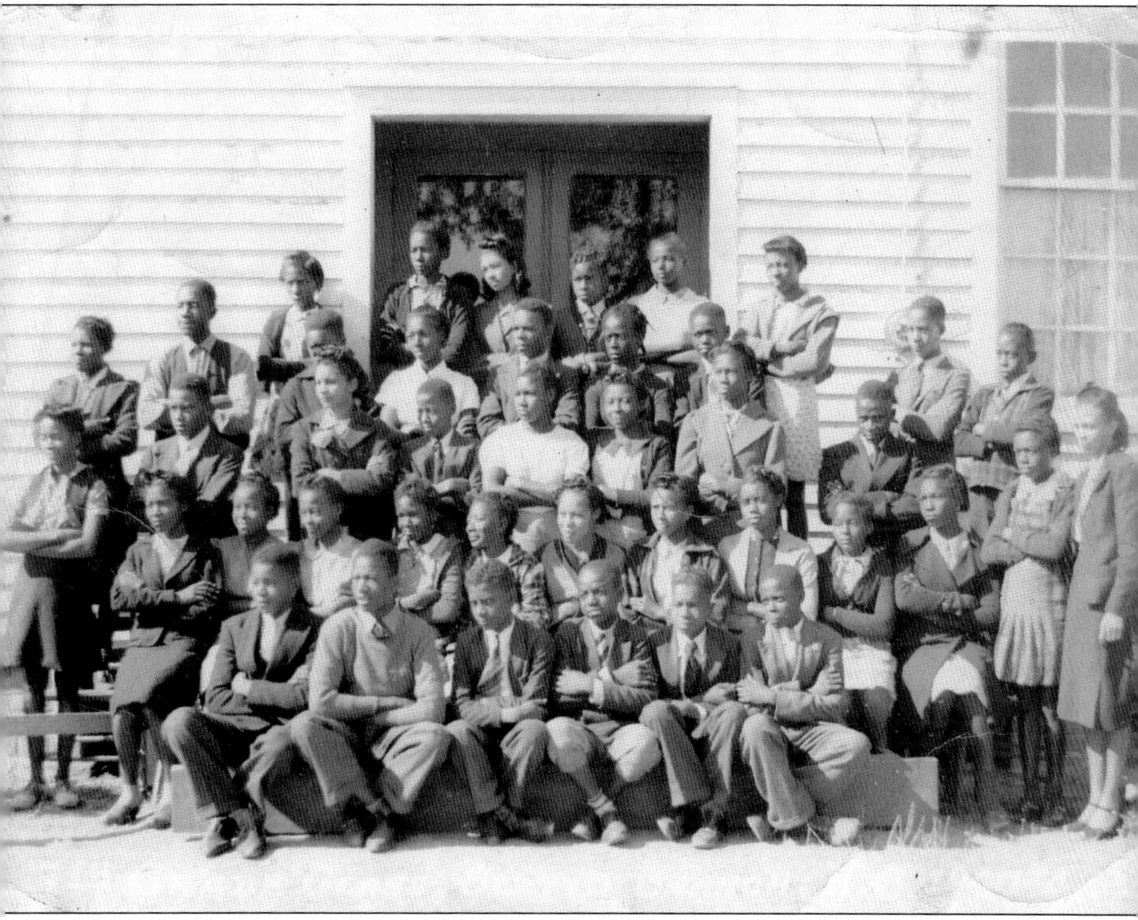

The 1940 seventh-grade class at the Scott's Branch School poses for a class picture at the side entrance of the school.

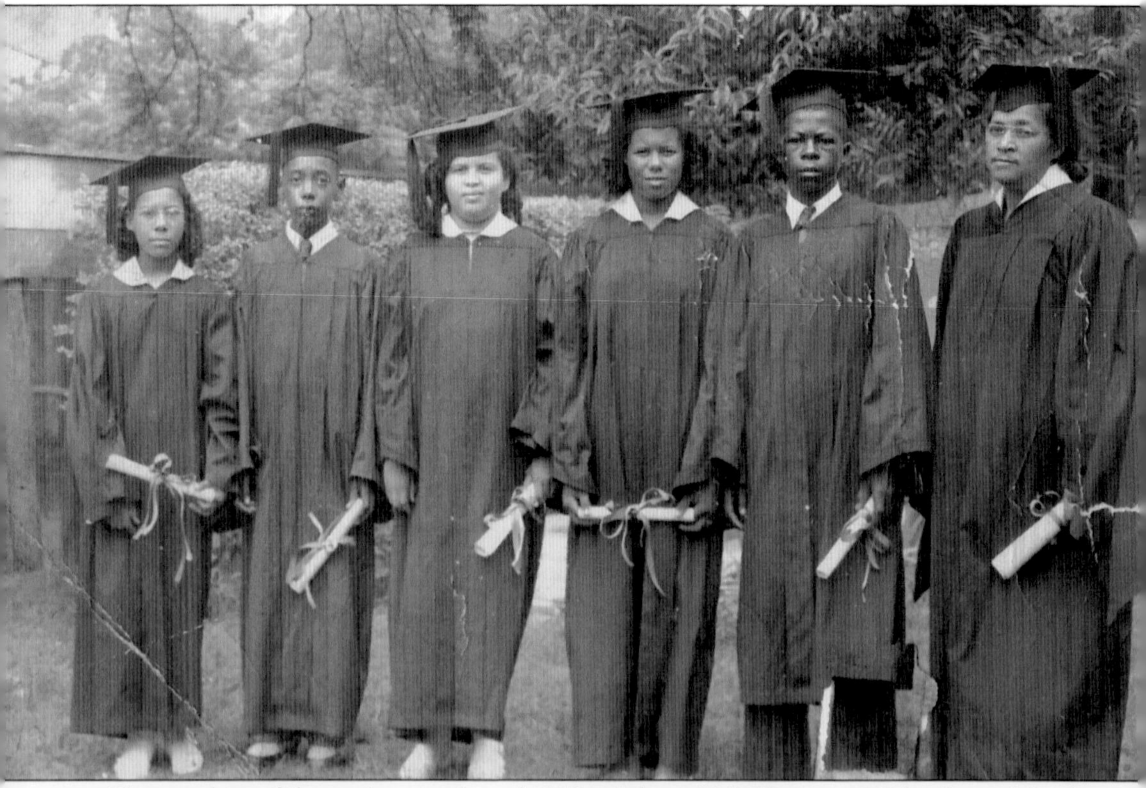

The members of the graduating class of 1948 at Liberty Hill Elementary School posed for this photograph. From left to right they are Shirley McDonald, Pinkney Wilson, Blondell McDonald, Dorothy Ragin, Charles E. Richardson, and their teacher, Carrie D. Martin.

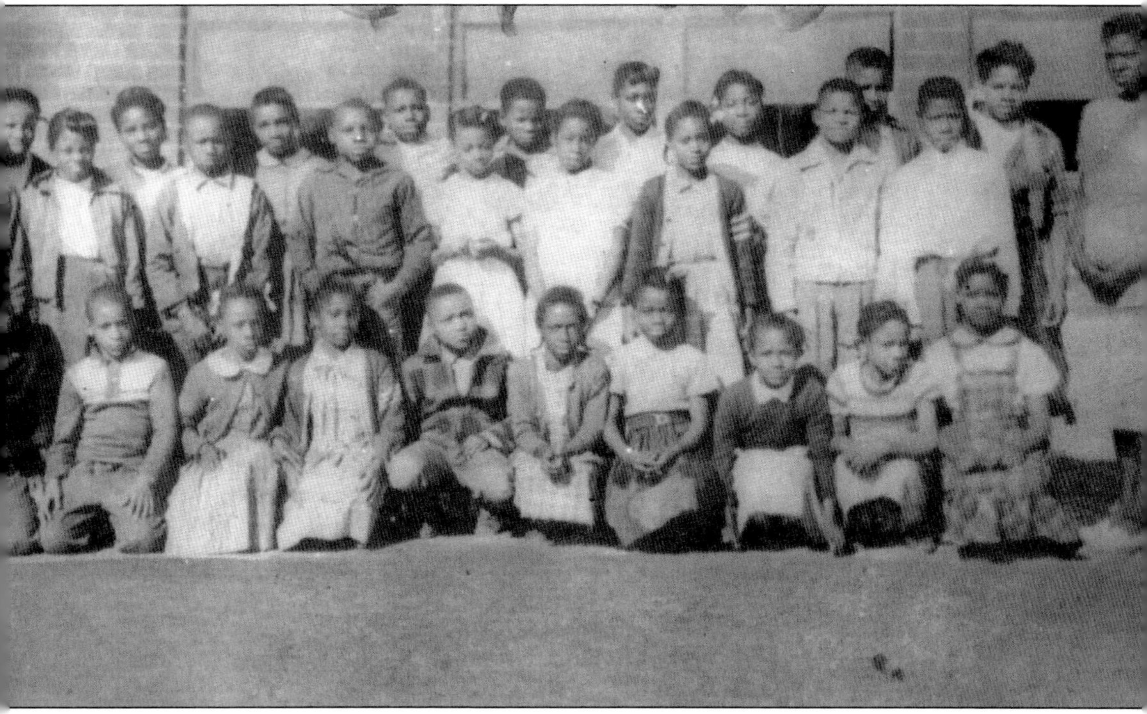

This 1955 group of fourth graders happily pose in front of the Walker Gamble School in New Zion for a class picture. Sadly, the boy with a dark shirt, fourth from left in front standing row perished in a house fire a few days after this photograph was taken.

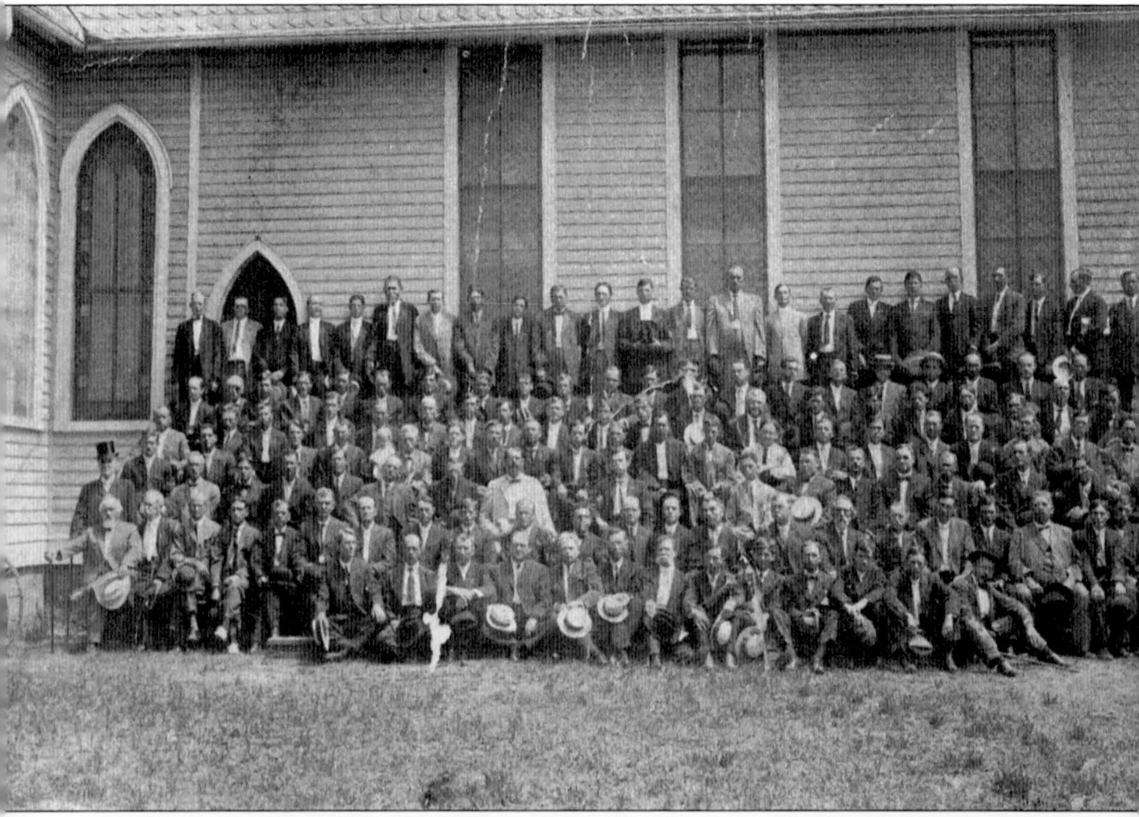

The 138 members of the Young Men's Bible Class pose on the side of Manning Methodist Church in 1915. The church is located on Rigby Street in Manning and is now known as the United Methodist Church.

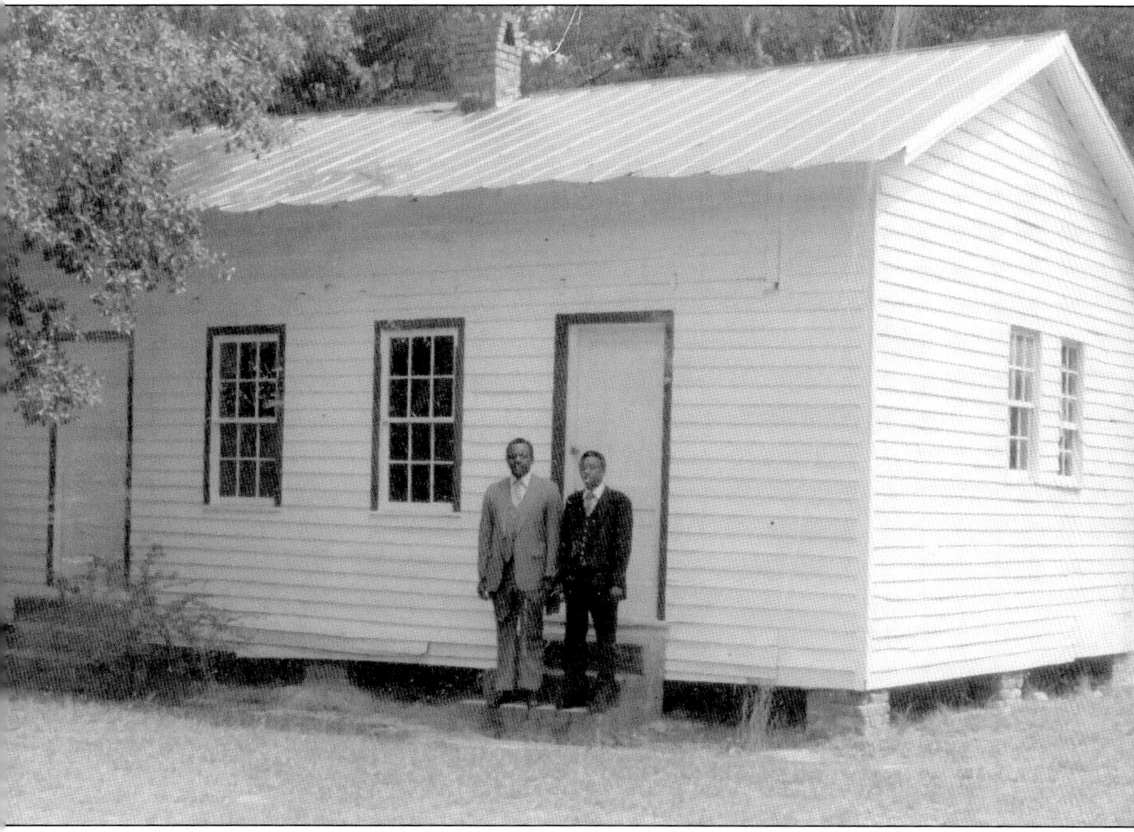

Lodobar Grammar School was founded and built in 1890. Parents in the New Zion community erected this structure because of their concern for the availability of an educational facility convenient to those within their community. The school closed in 1955

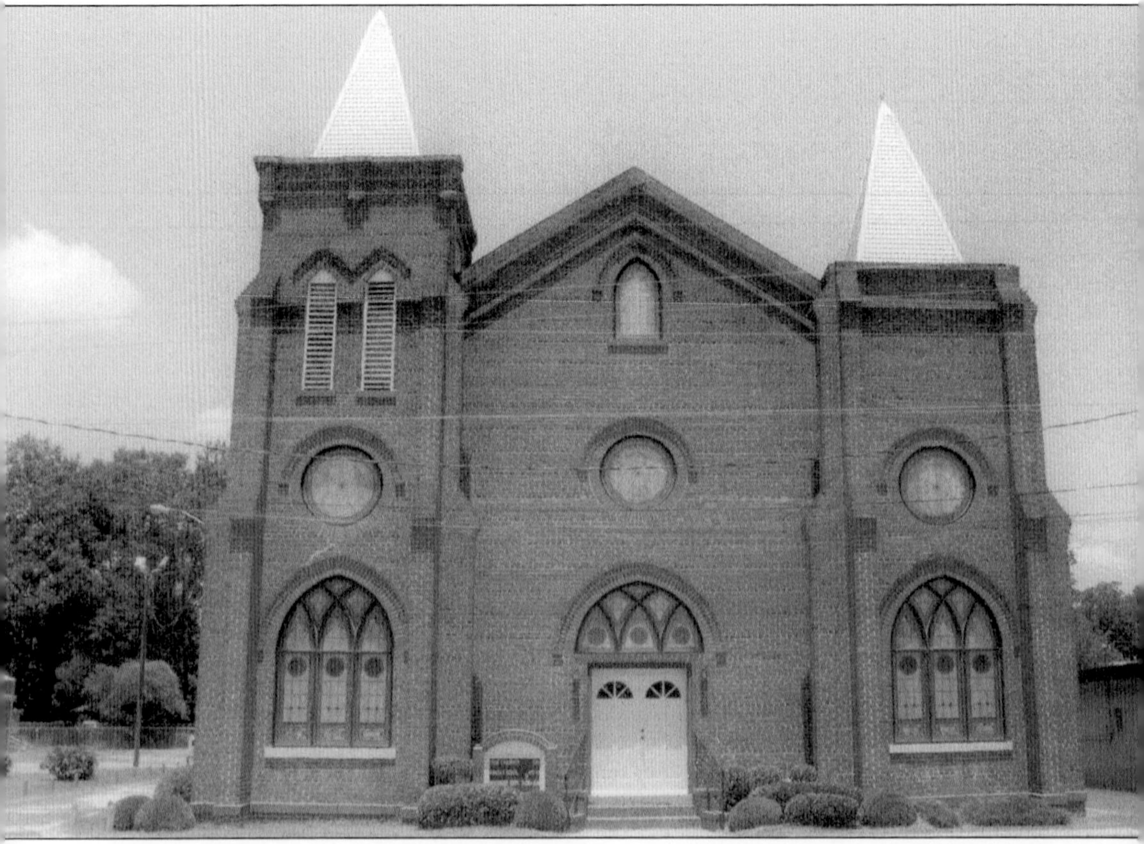

Trinity AME Church is located on Rigby Street in Manning. It is one of the oldest African-American churches in the Manning area. It was founded in the 1860s with a Reverend Watson as its first pastor. The church continues to be active in this community.

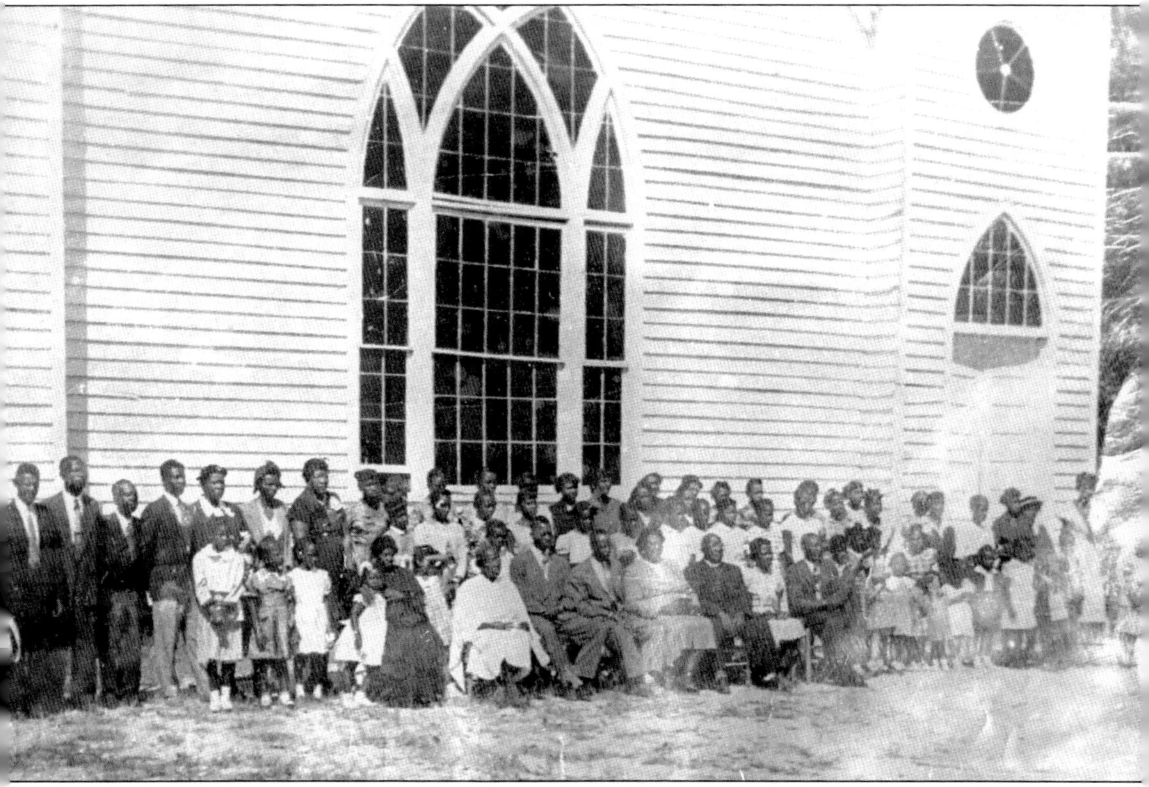

Mt. Zion AME Church was founded in 1865 near the Davis Station area. The original stewards were Frank Simmons, Scipio Mack, and I.S. Hilton. The founding trustees were Daniel Felder, Jack Lemon, Nero Miller, and Joe Simmons. Note that there are two entrances at the front of the church. Men and women were required to use separate entrances during bygone years.

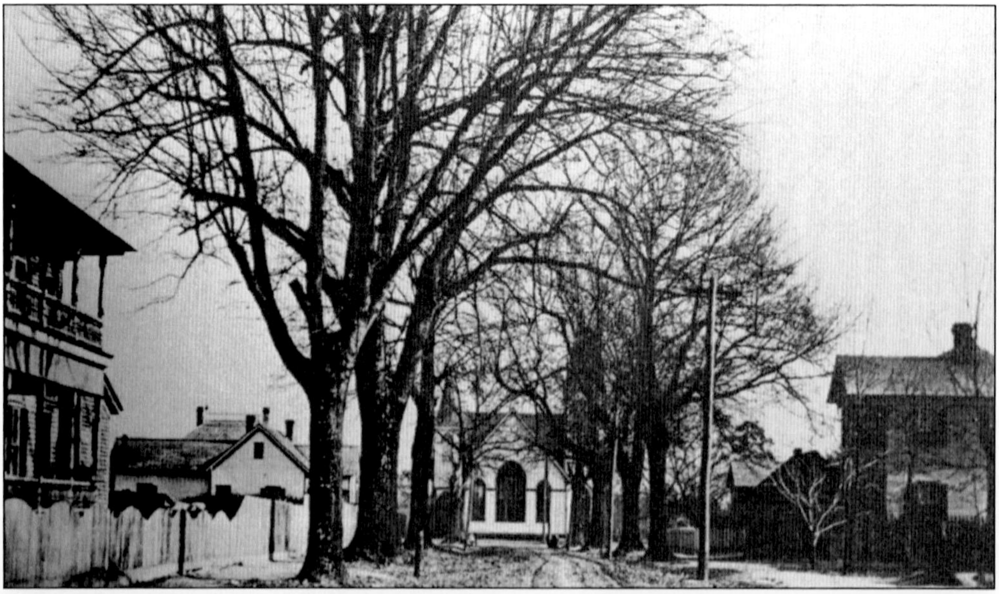

This photograph, taken before 1900, shows the Manning Methodist Church on North Church Street where it intersects with Oak Street. The church was later moved to its present location on Rigby Street by rolling it down the road on logs.

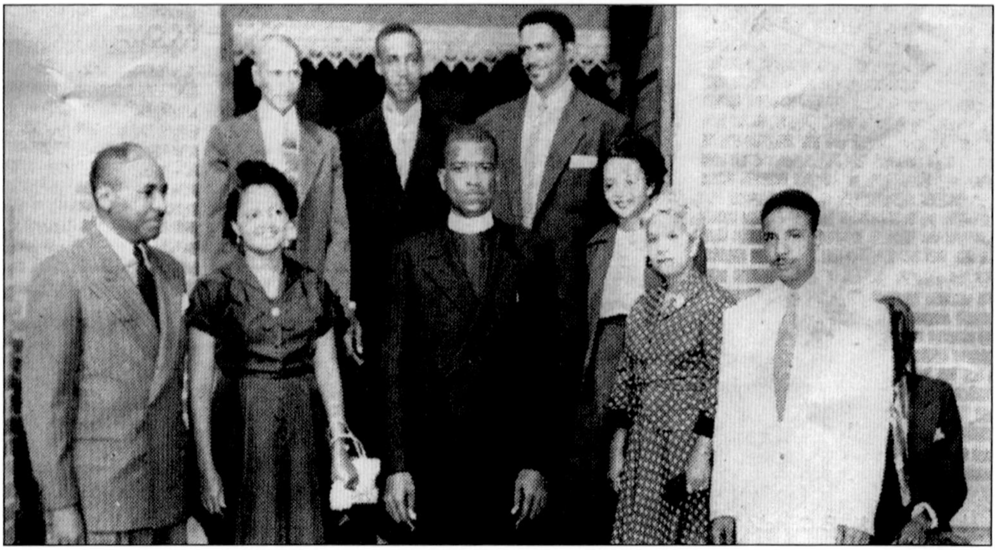

The Usher Board and pastor of Trinity AME Church in Manning are pictured at the church in 1950.

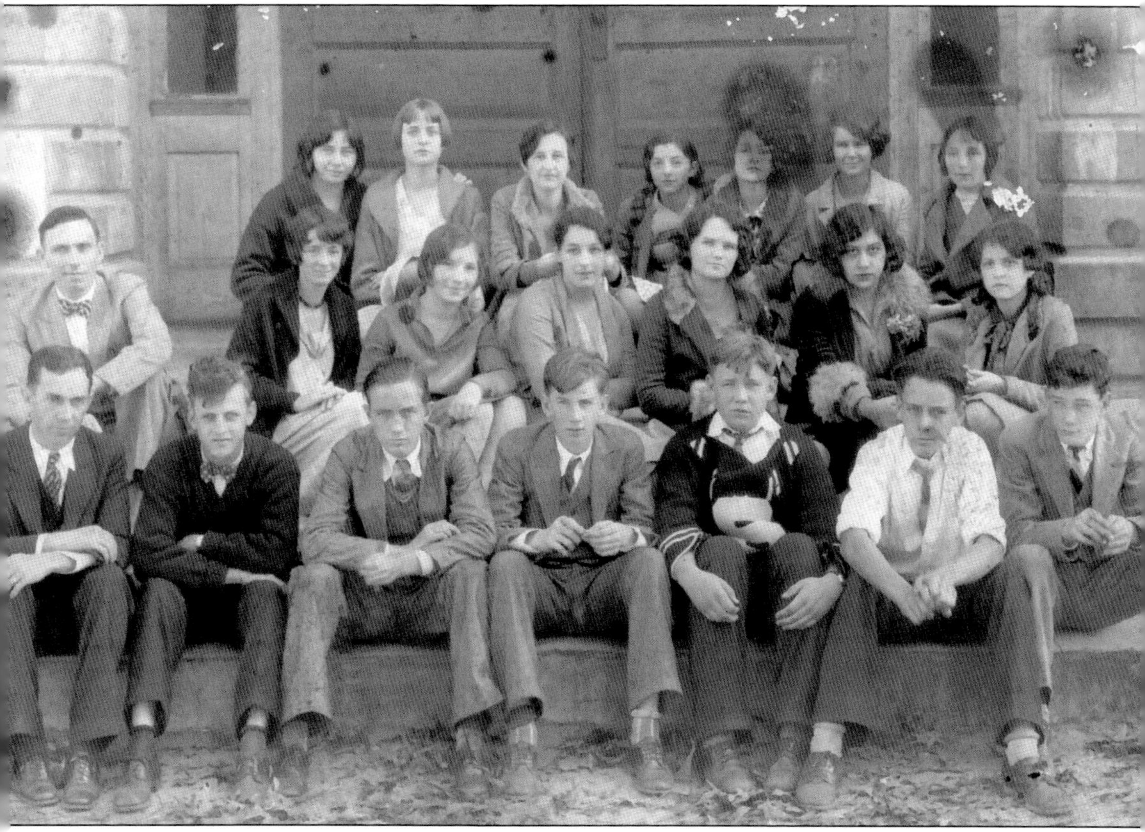

A group of students at Summerton High School pose for a class picture with their teacher, H.B. Betchman (seated far left). Betchman later became superintendent of the Summerton School District.

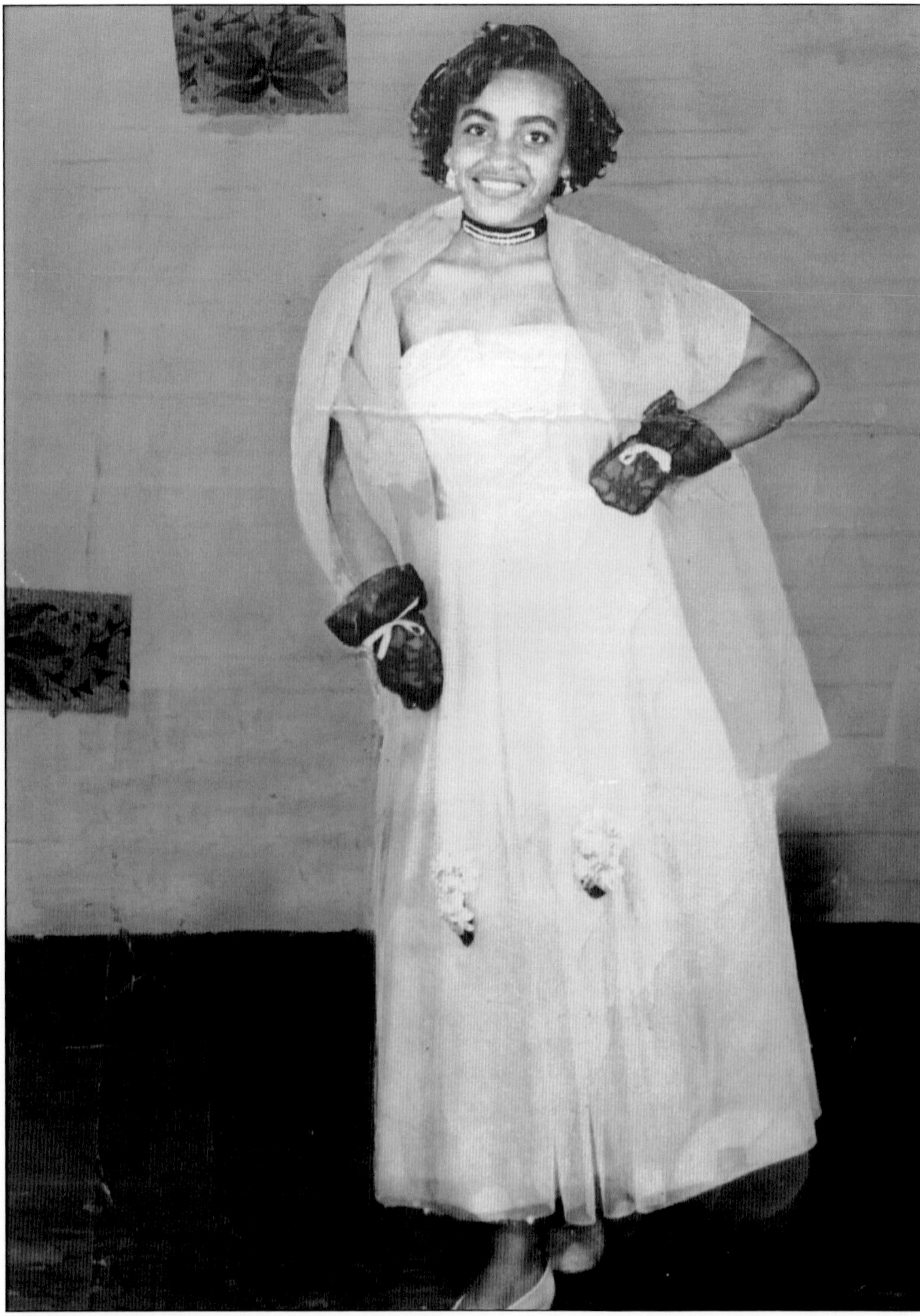

A bright, extremely ambitious, and friendly young lady, Vera Brown of Summerton poses at her high school prom in 1951. Unfortunately Vera's life was cut short by a criminal assault in 1952.

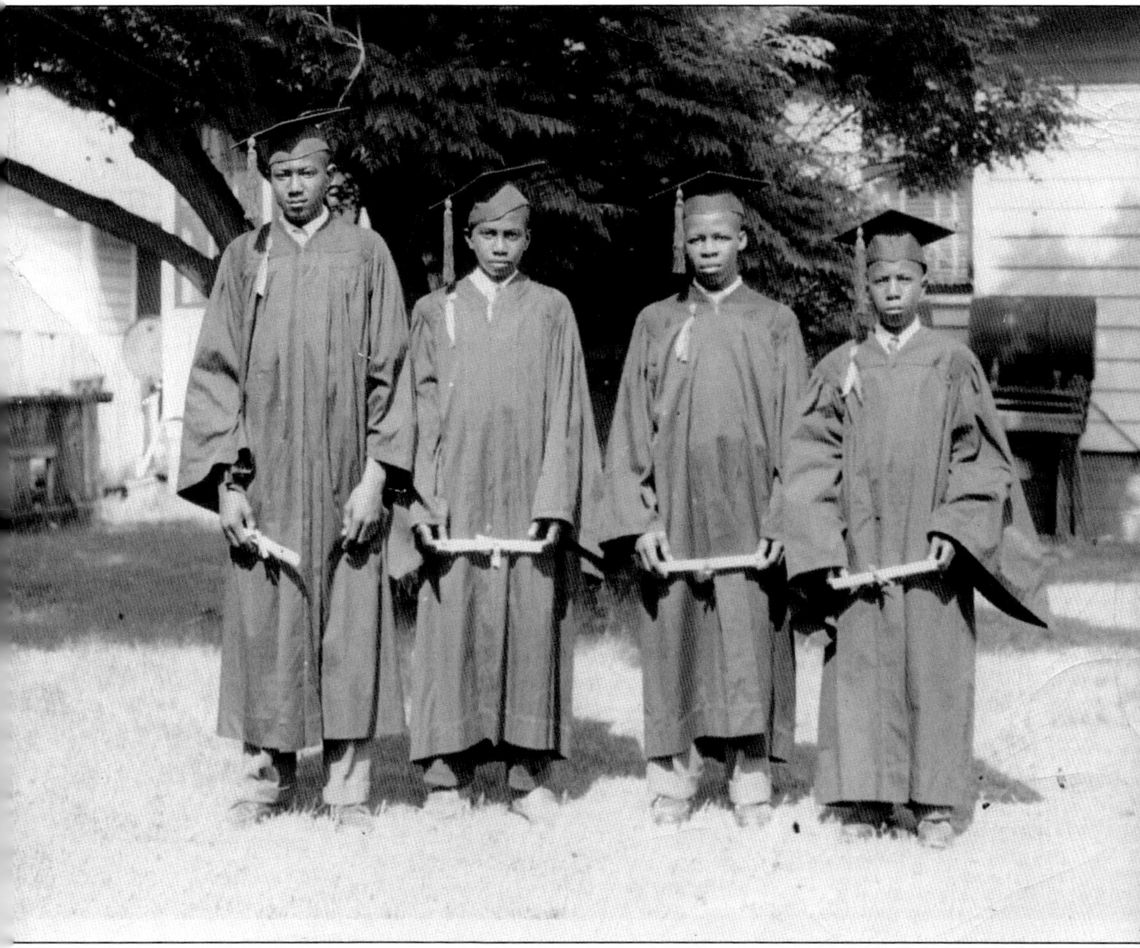

Four members of the class of 1950 at Liberty Hill Elementary School have their picture taken after graduation. Liberty Hill, a four-room school, housed grades one through seven with four teachers. The school was located between Summerton and St. Paul, adjacent to the Liberty Hill AME Church (see page 34).

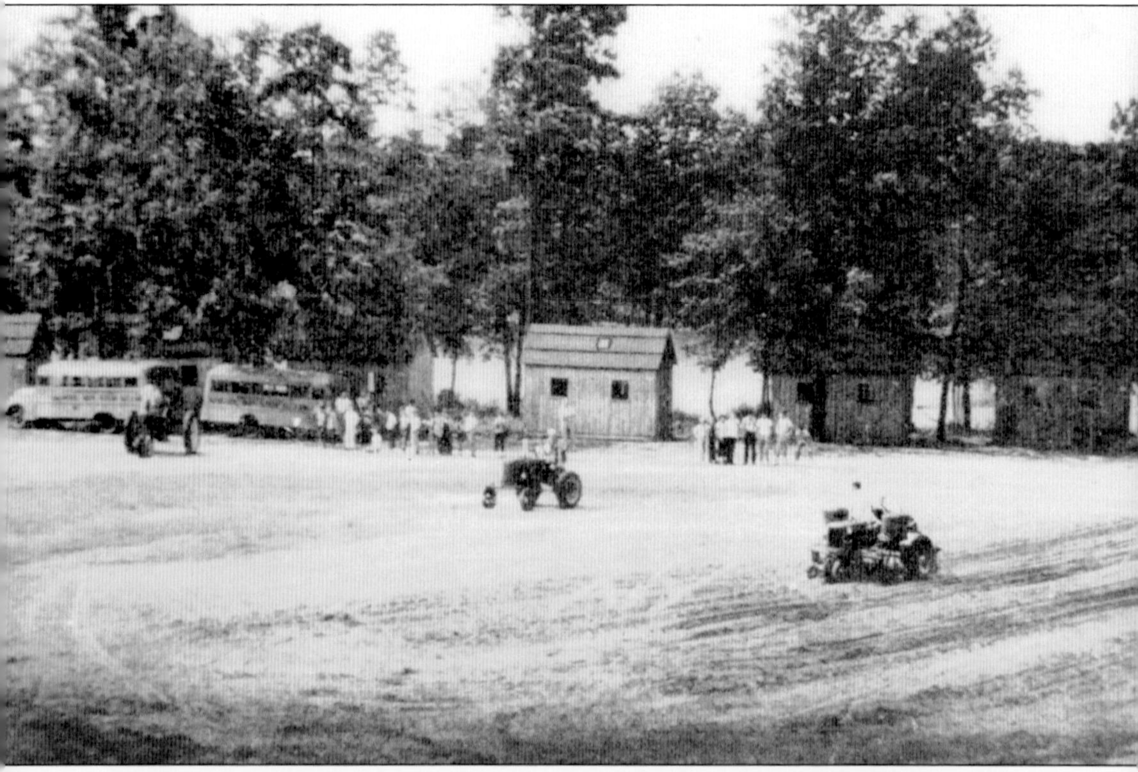

Students participate in a farm machinery instruction class at the 4H Club's Camp Bob Cooper around 1950. Instruction in the various aspects of farming and homemaking were critical elements in the training of rural youngsters. The 4H Club provided the experience and practical applications supporting theory taught in schools.

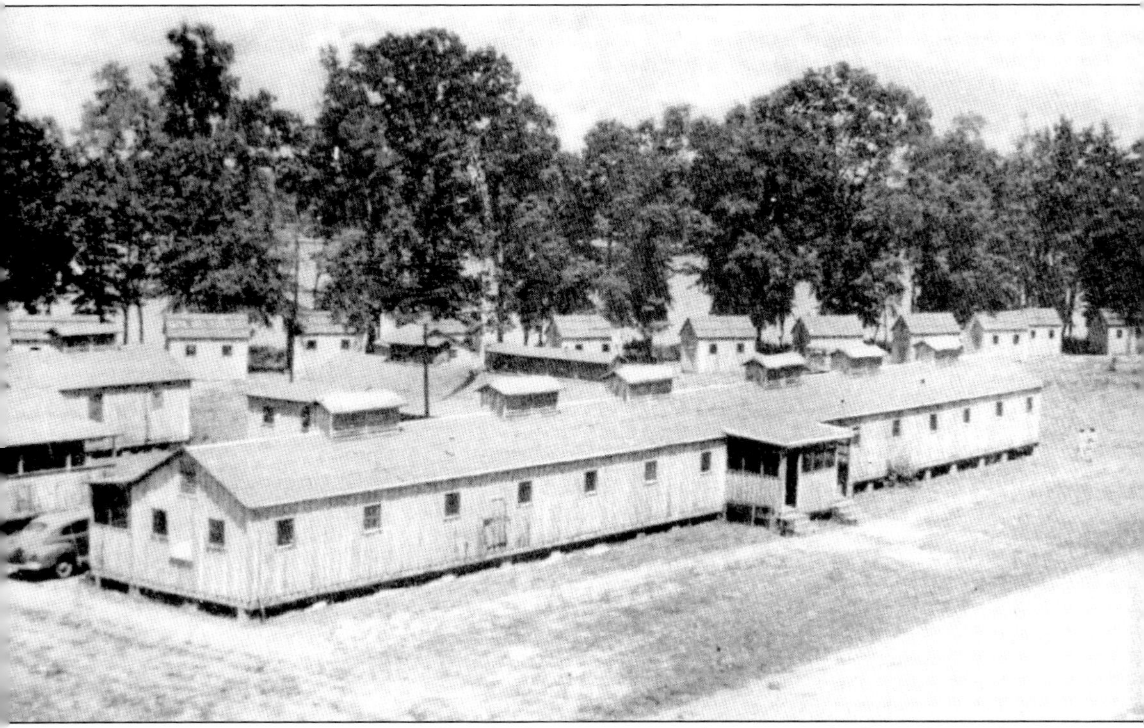

This photograph shows the dining hall and cabins at Camp Bob Cooper, which was located on Lake Marion. Photographed during the late 1940s or early 1950s, this camp provided training and practical experience by training the white youths of the county.

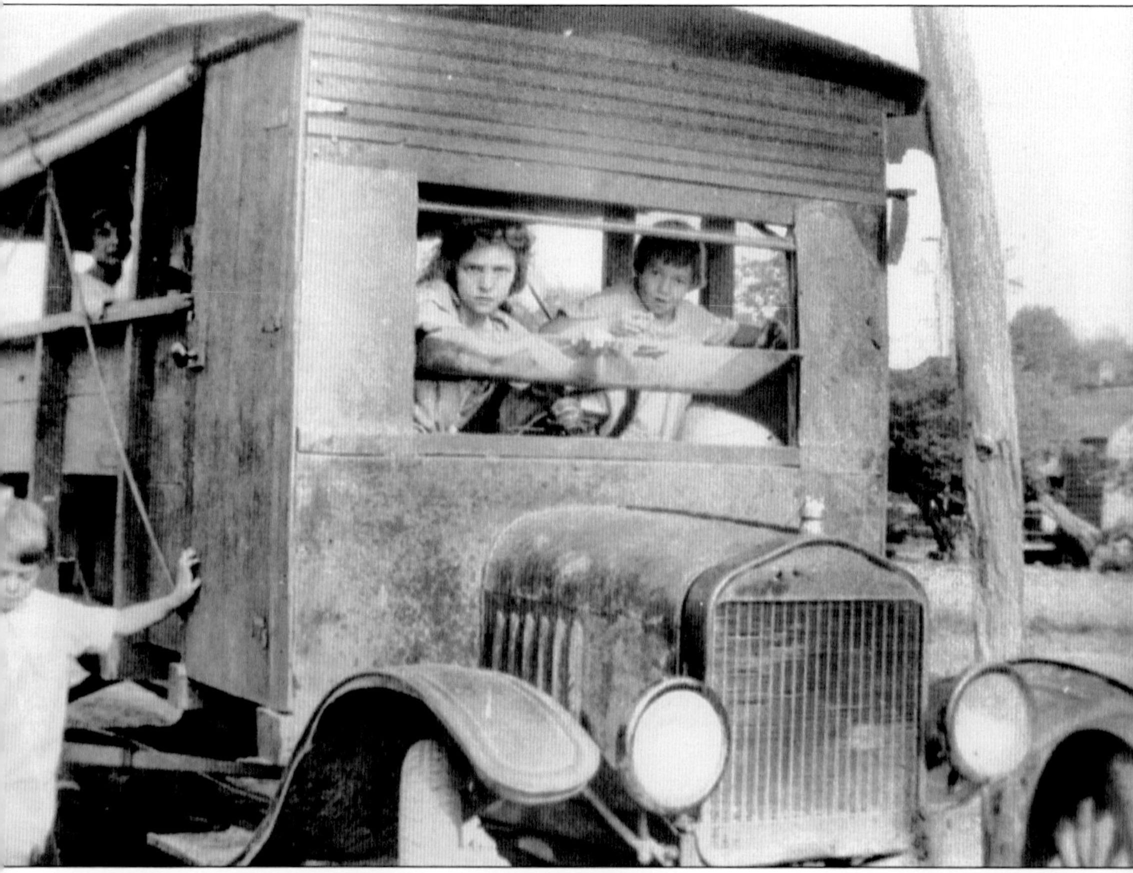

This is thought to be the first school bus in Clarendon County, in a photograph dated 1924. The bus appears to have been constructed with a wooden frame attached to a truck body.

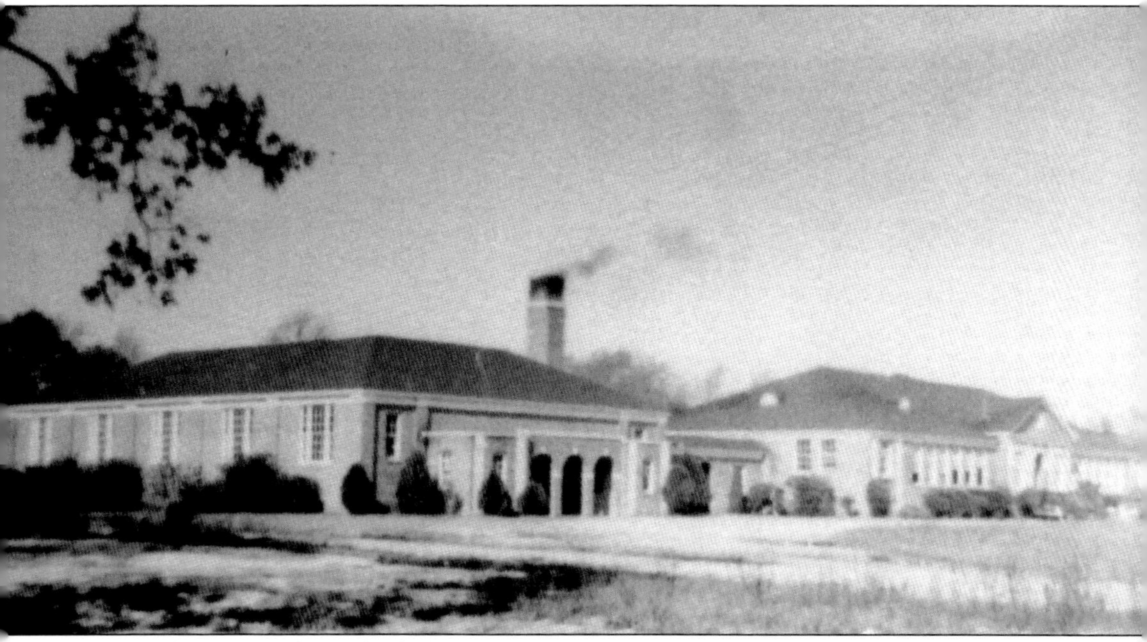

This 1950 photograph shows the buildings that housed Summerton High School. This facility was used as the basis for comparison between facilities available to whites and those available to blacks (see Scott's Branch School, page 20) in the *Briggs* school desegregation case. The structure was recently restored and now serves as the school district's offices.

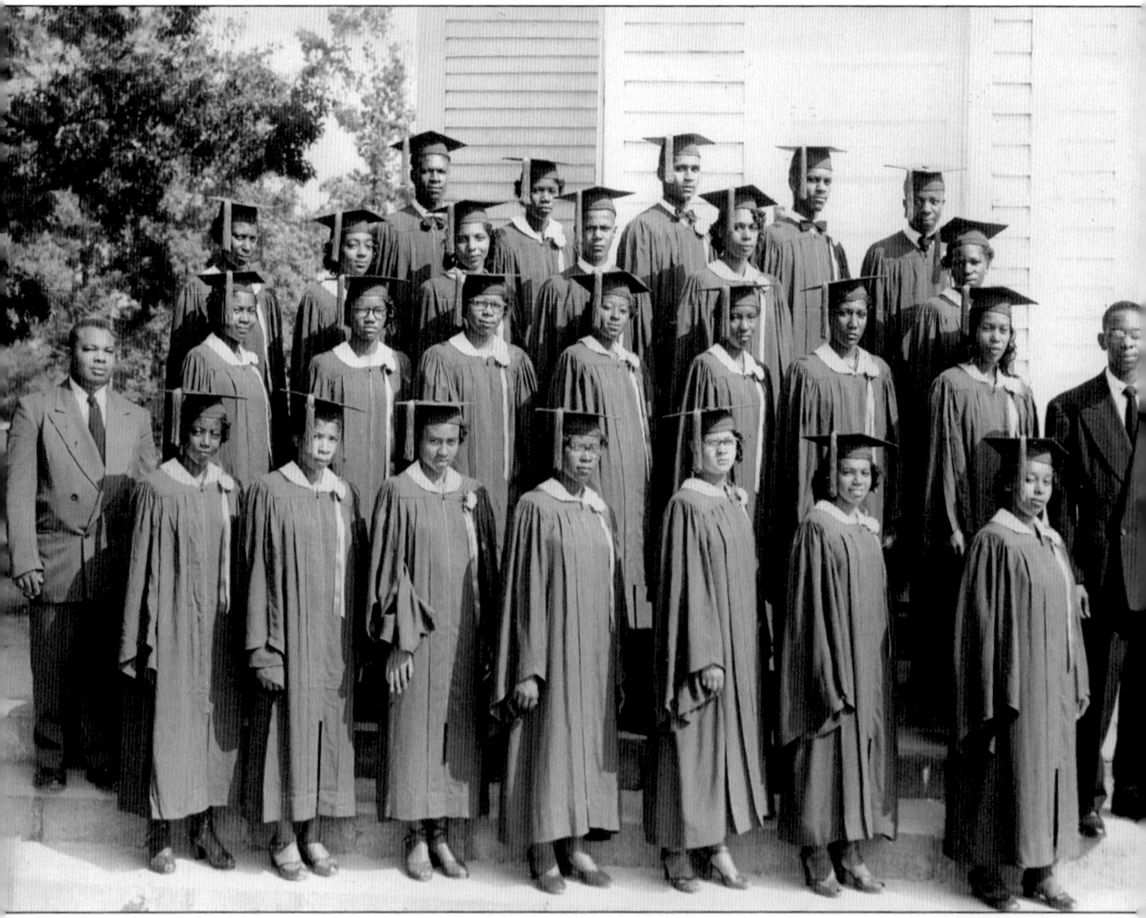

The 1952 senior class at Scott's Branch High School poses for a class picture. These students were among the first to enjoy the benefits of serious efforts by the state to improve the quality of education for blacks. These efforts were a direct result of the impact made in the *Briggs* case to outlaw segregated schools in the state.

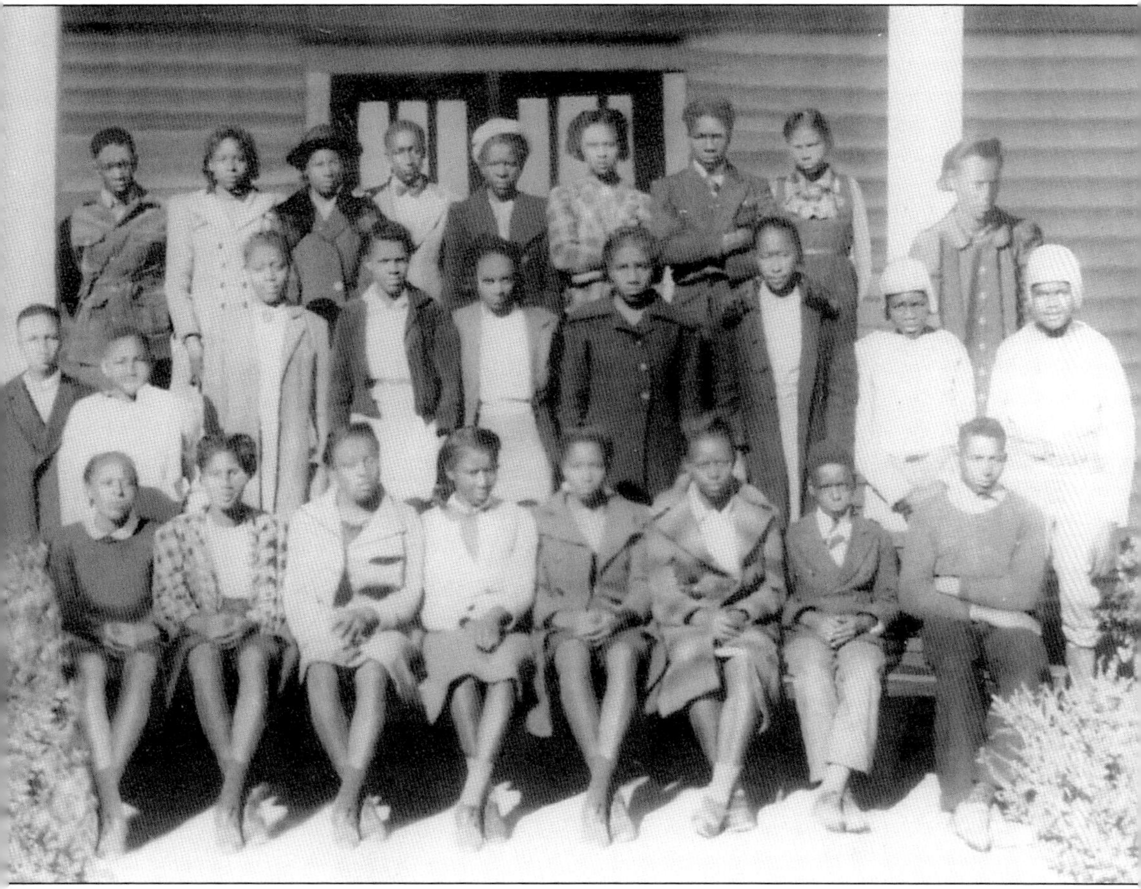

The eleventh-grade class at the Manning Training School poses for their class picture in 1939. Many black high schools were referred to as "training" schools instead of high schools. This school, a wooden structure with ten classrooms and an auditorium, served as the high school for blacks in the Manning area.

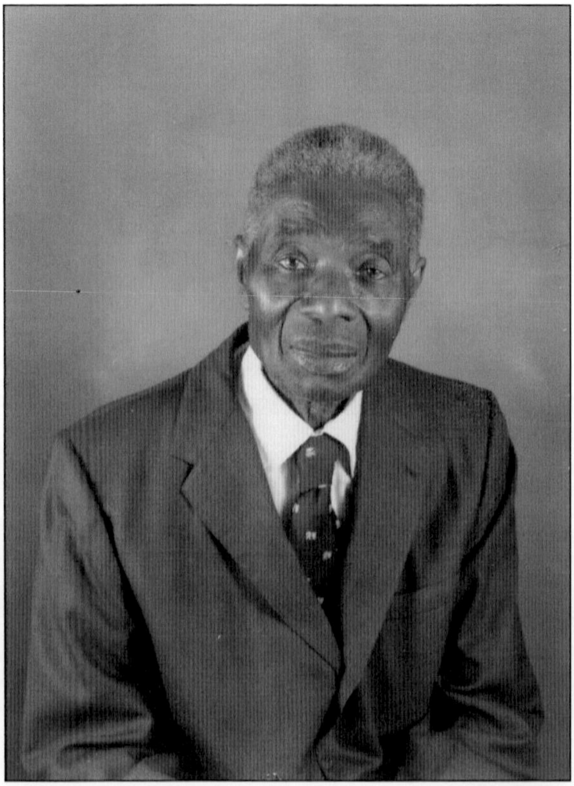

Charlie Gamble (1910–1990) and his wife (below) donated half of the property for the Walker Gamble School in the New Zion community. A need had been established for a school in that area; however, funds and a location for the school were not available. Through the joint efforts of the Gambles and Walkers, land was made available for the site on which the school now stands.

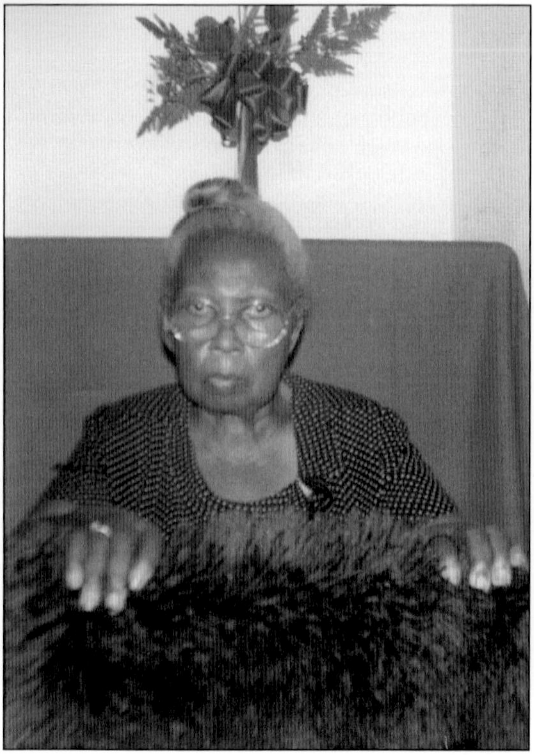

Edna Woods Gamble (1910–1995), wife of Charlie Gamble, wholeheartedly shared her husband's decision to contribute a part of their land wealth for the benefit of the neighborhood.

Silas Walker Sr. (1892–1987) was the contributor for the remaining property used for the creation of the Walker Gamble School site. He and his wife (below) were also lifelong members of the New Zion community.

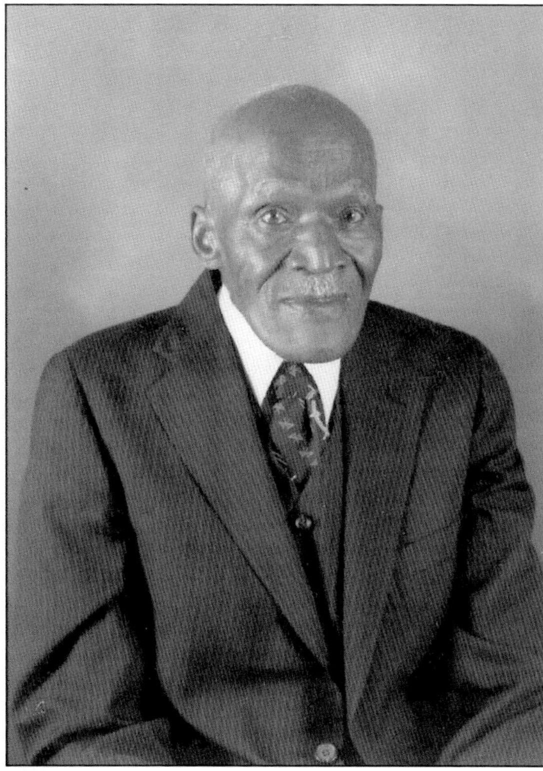

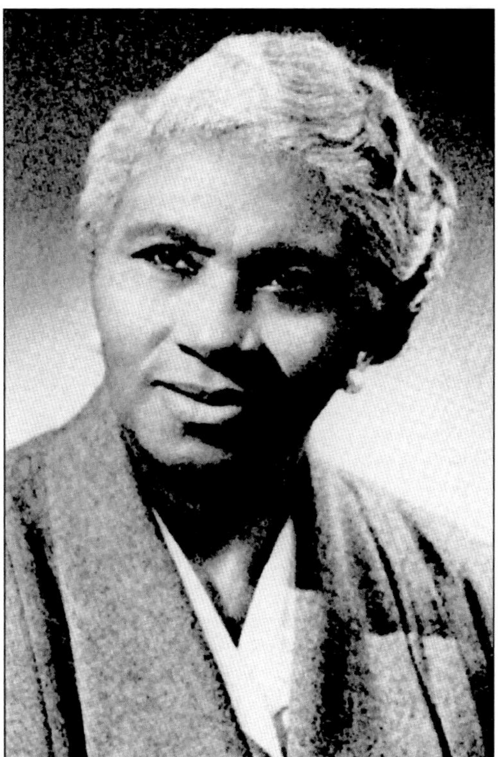

Carrie Walker, the wife of Silas Walker, also shares in the spotlight of the generosity of two families who have made a lasting impact on the community closest to their hearts.

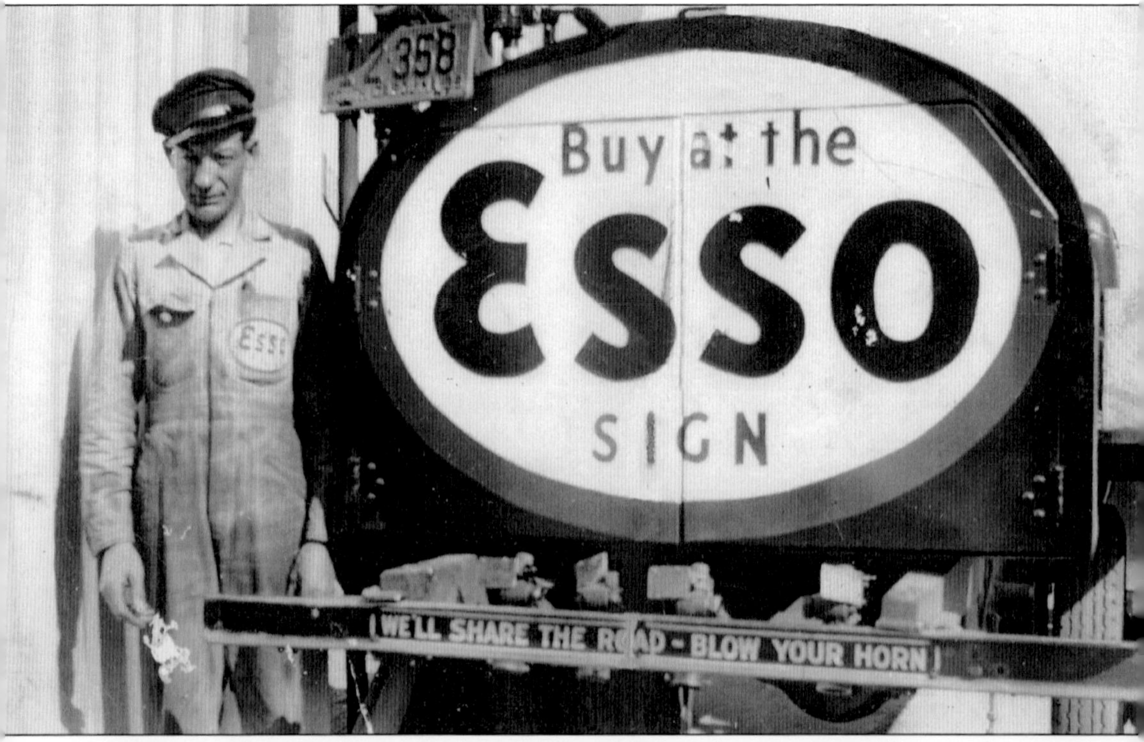

James Brown was the first African American hired to drive an oil truck in the county. In this 1933 photo, he poses beside the Esso oil truck that he used for the delivery of petroleum products. Brown, a petitioner in the first *Briggs* case (the equalization of educational opportunity in 1949) resigned from this job under pressure. The pressure was due to threats of boycotting those who employed blacks suspected of supporting Civil Rights movements within the county. The following year Brown moved his family to Detroit, Michigan, where he now resides.

Four

Personalities and Scenes of Bygone Years

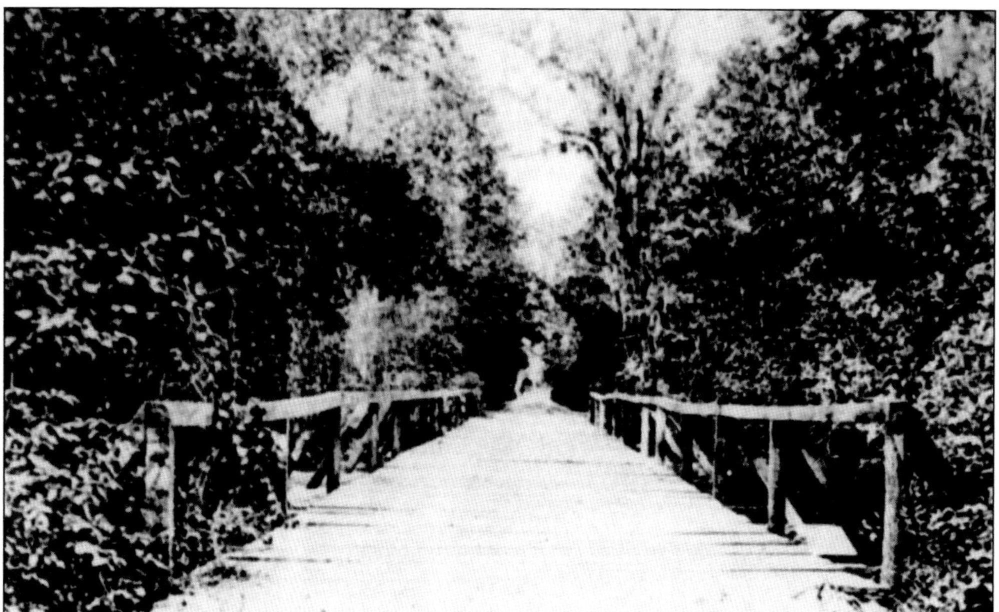

The wooden bridge on Black River Drive in Manning crosses the Black River and traverses the Pocataligo Swamp. This is the forerunner of the highway that now crosses Pocataligo Swamp, known as U.S. Highways 301 and 521.

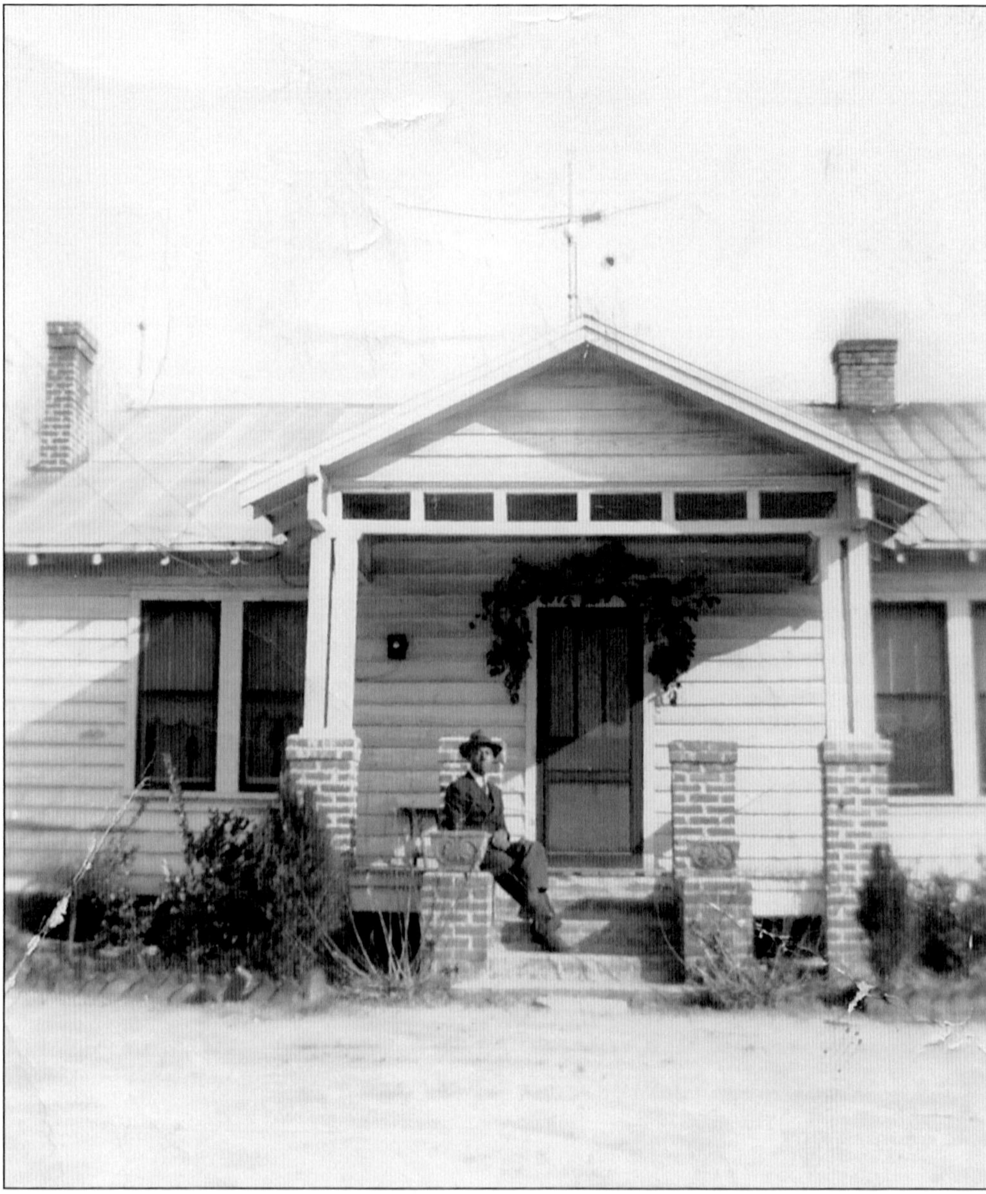

An unknown man is seated on the steps of a rural farm home. The structure of this house, wood frame and painted, with brick supports on the front porch would suggest an African-American family of above-average means by Clarendon County standards during the 1940s.

An unknown couple poses in a "picture booth." This backdrop was typical of the kinds of props used by photographers at temporary locations such as county fairs in the early 20th century.

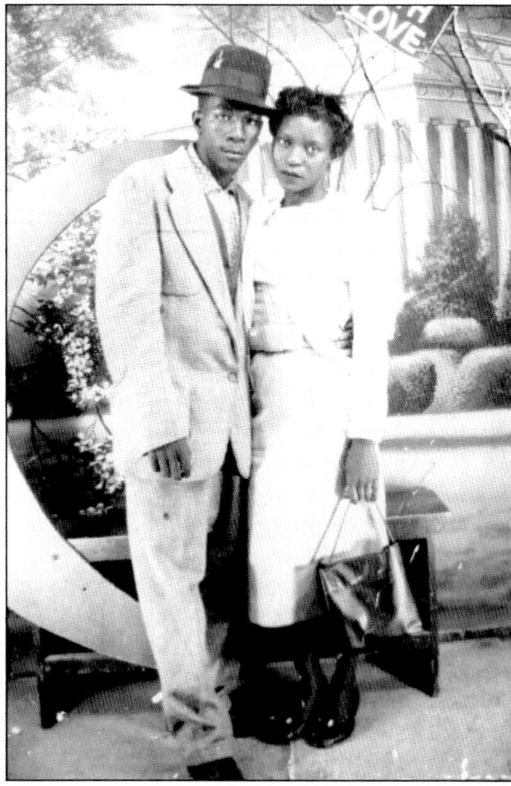

The primary mode of transportation before the popularity of the automobile was the horse and buggy. This scene is believed to have been captured in Manning around 1900.

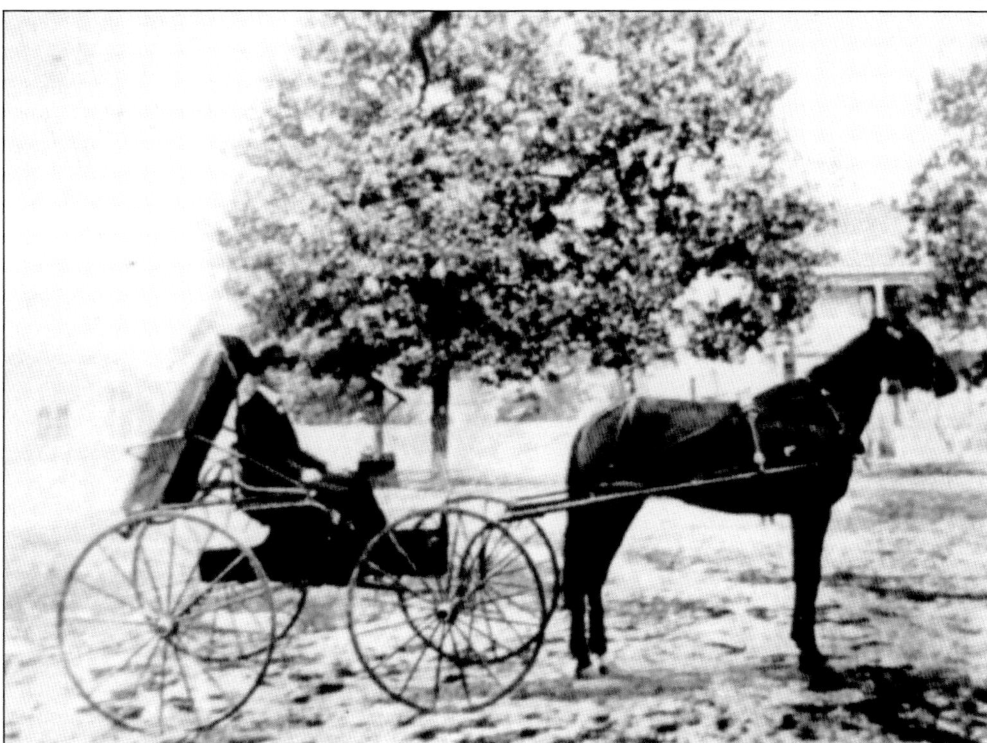

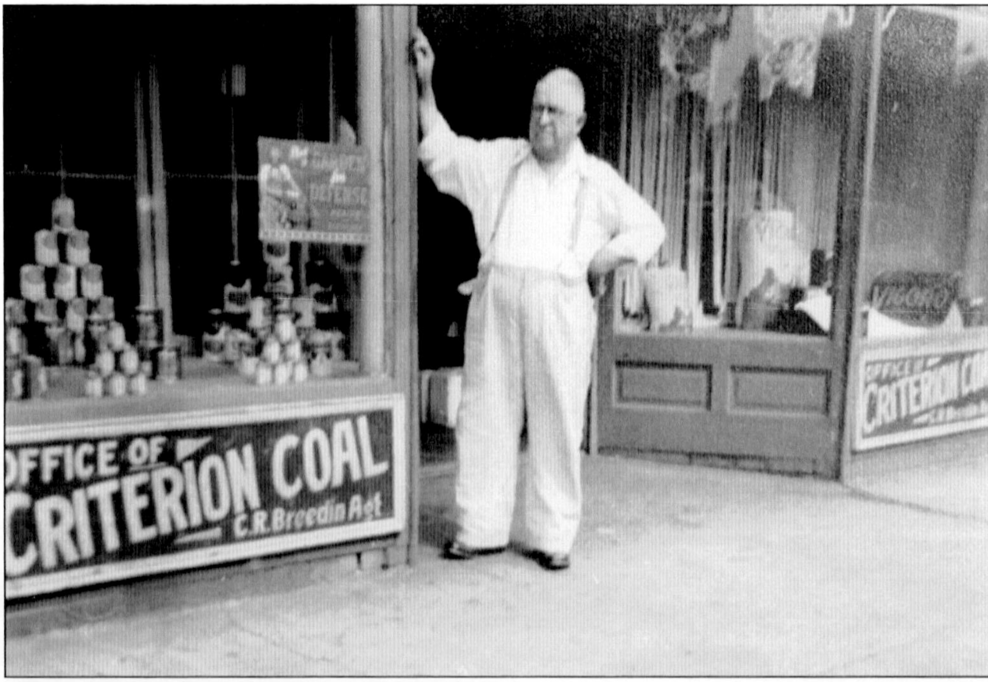

C.R. Breedin awaits customers at his general store in Manning on South Brooks Street opposite the courthouse. Stores of this type sold everything from coal to dry goods to food.

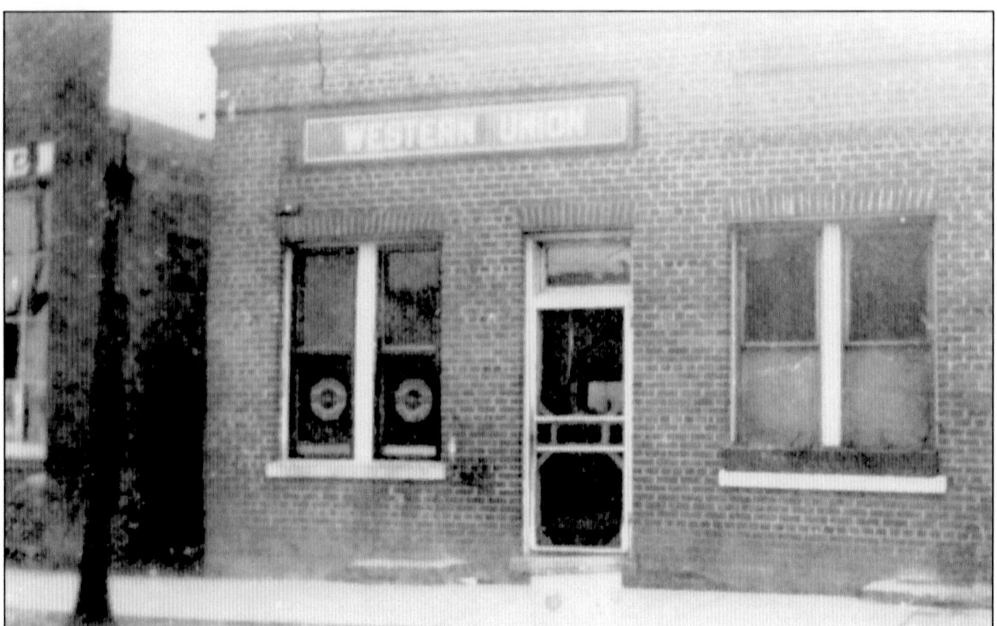

This Western Union office operated in Manning for many years on East Boyce Street.

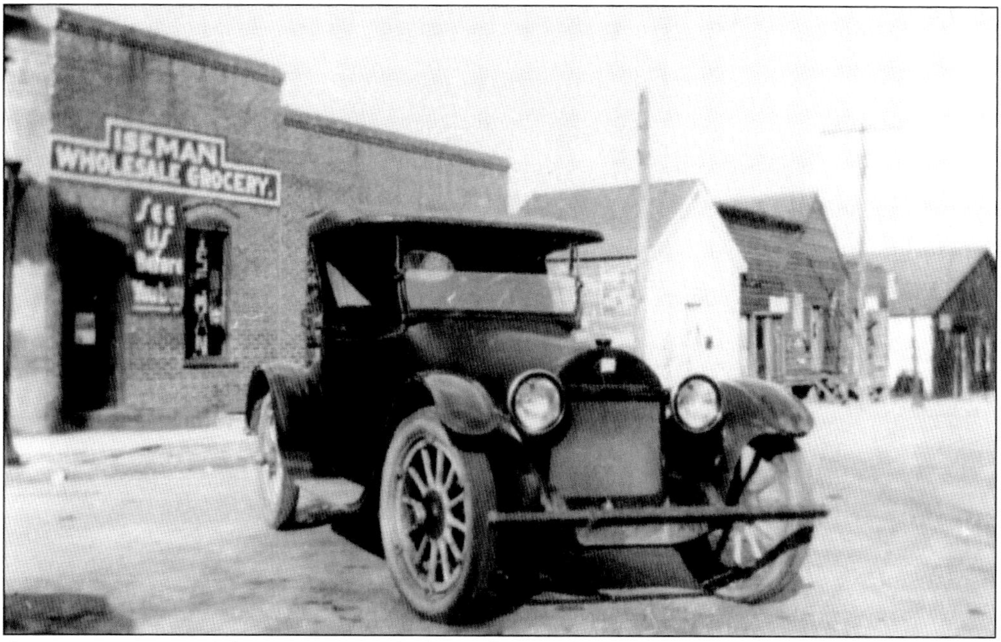

A vintage automobile is seen parked in front of Iseman Wholesale Grocery on East Boyce Street.

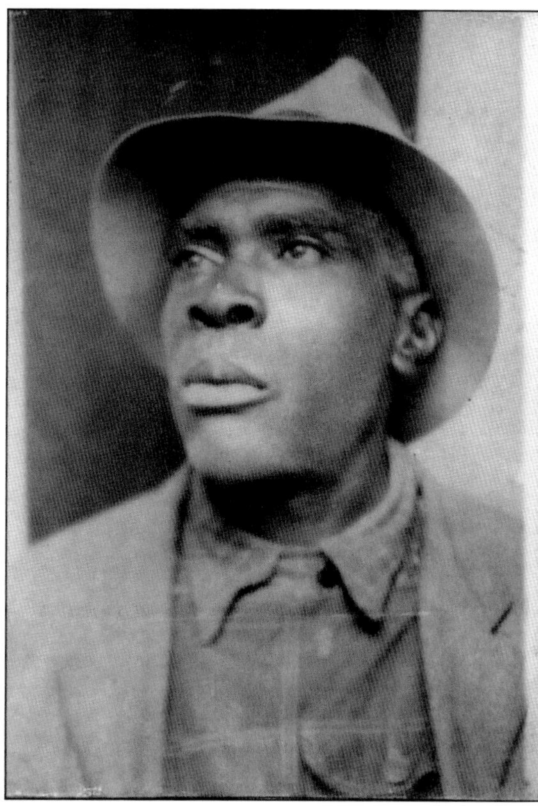

Quincy Dyson, a farmer in the Summerton area, is dressed in his work attire. Hats were important to county people to provide protection from the elements. For protection in hot weather, leaves were often placed in the hats to provide additional insulation from heat.

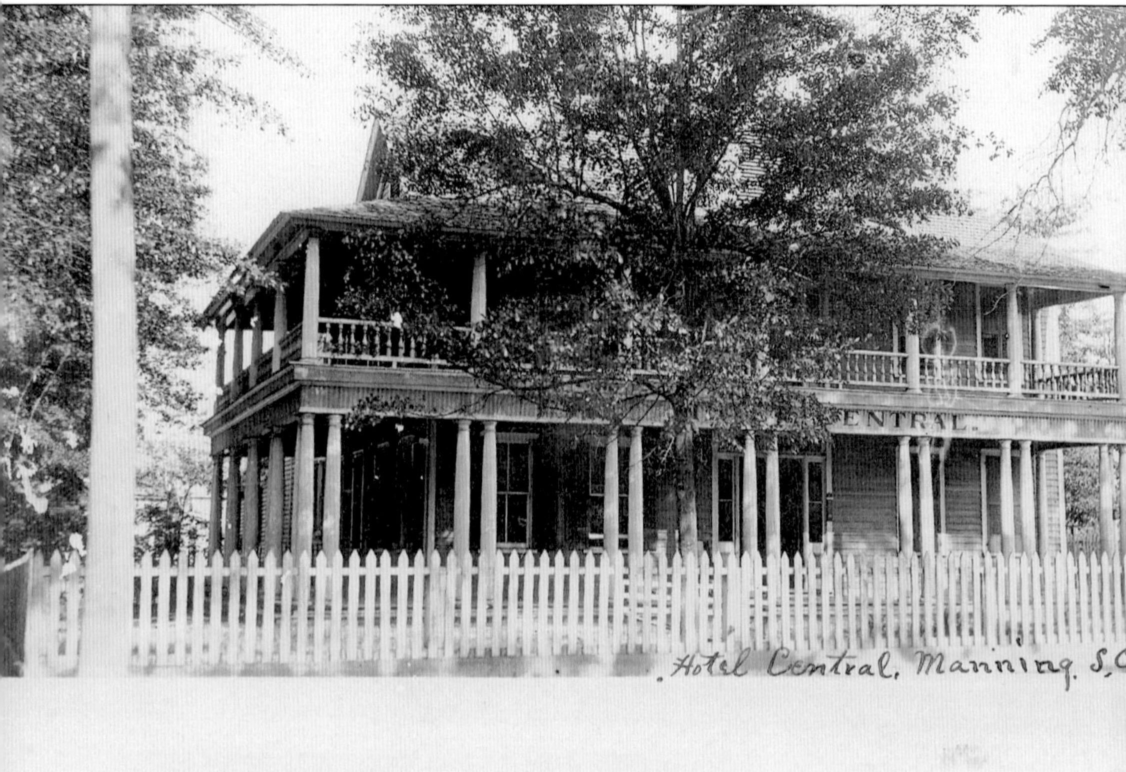

The Hotel Central operated in Manning during the early 1900s. The extensive porch served as a respite on hot and humid days to capture whatever cool breezes might occur.

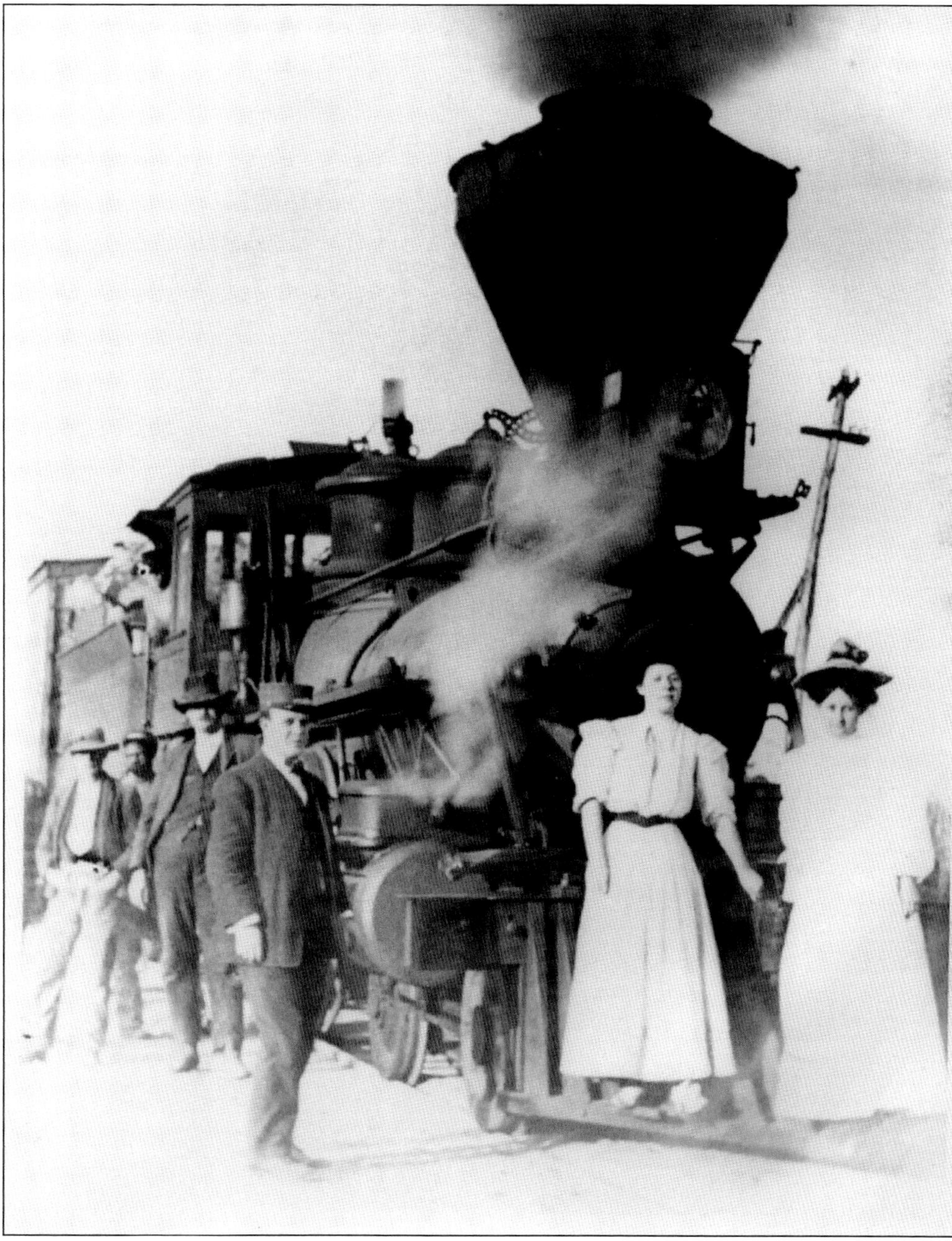

This is a photo of a Northwestern train taken in Paxville. Pictured here, from left to right, are Jim Pack, unidentified, Larry Barwick, Alvin Curtis (train conductor), Madge Cregg, and Eva Curtis Gunter.

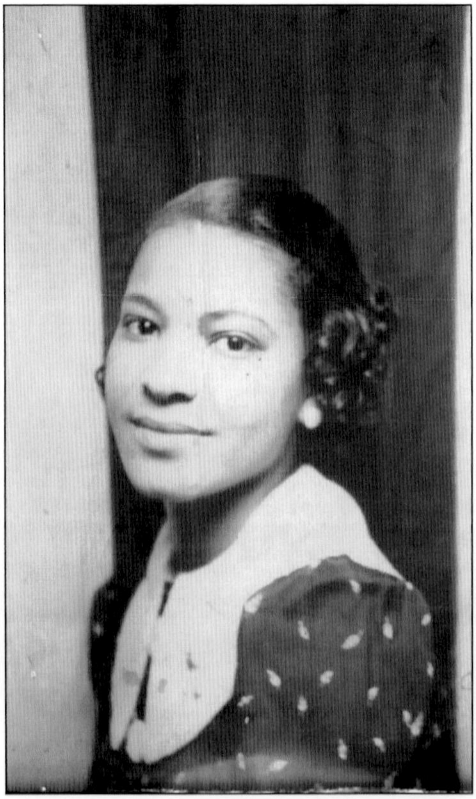

Inez Sumter Keith resided in Manning most of her life. For many years she taught at Scott's Branch School in Summerton. This picture was taken in 1933.

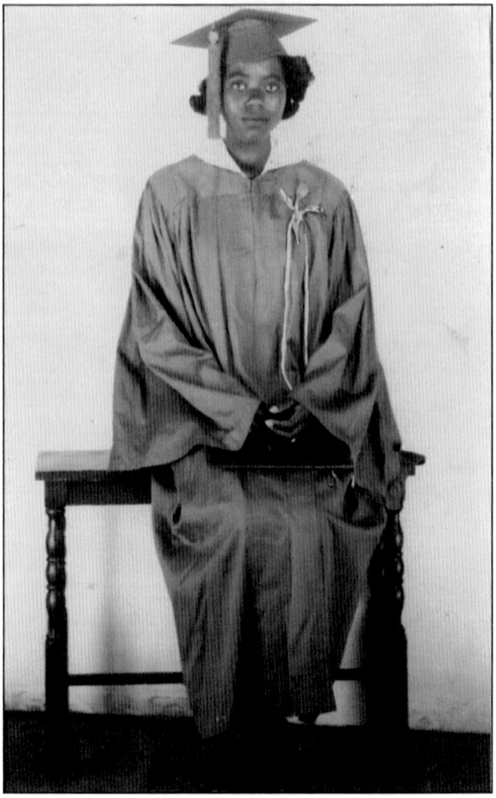

Inez Jones poses at her high school graduation from Scott's Branch High School in 1945. Inez later married Jessie Pearson. She is the "beloved" mentioned on his picture in the military section of this book.

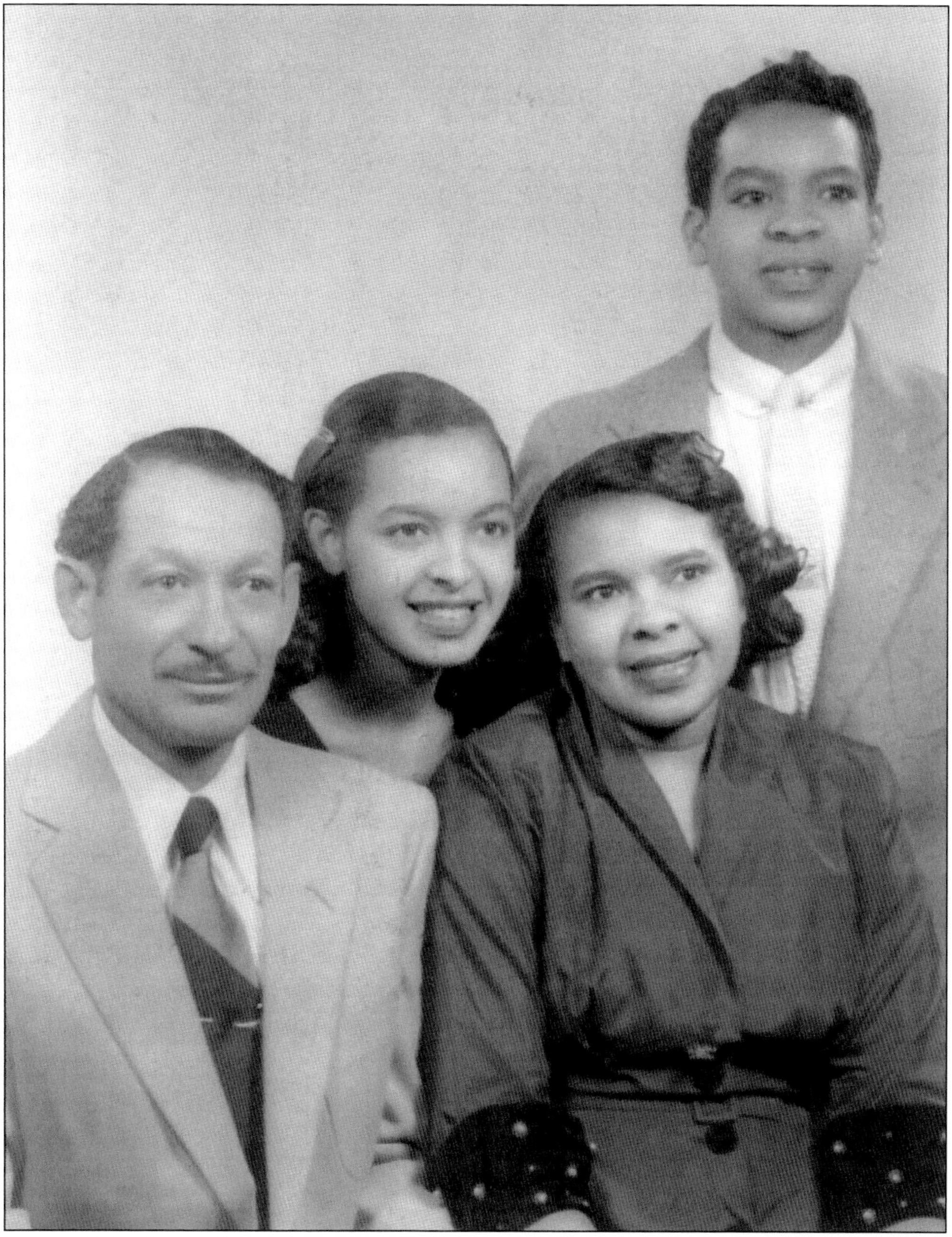

Mr. and Mrs. James Brown are pictured with two of their children, Euralia and Joe Morris. Brown, the former Esso truck driver (see page 56) poses with the family during a visit to Summerton in 1955.

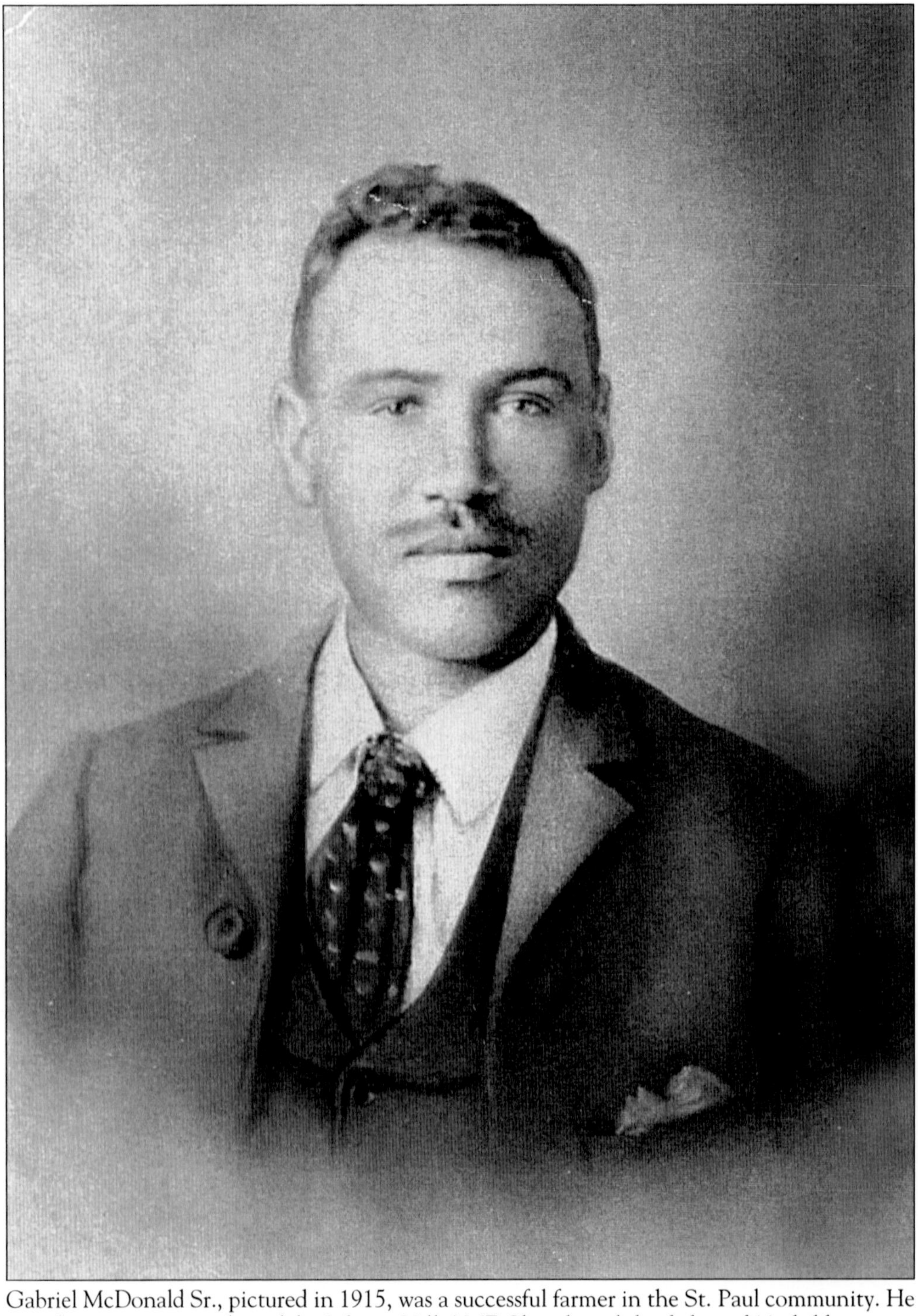

Gabriel McDonald Sr., pictured in 1915, was a successful farmer in the St. Paul community. He was also an active member of the Liberty Hill AME Church and the father of 11 children.

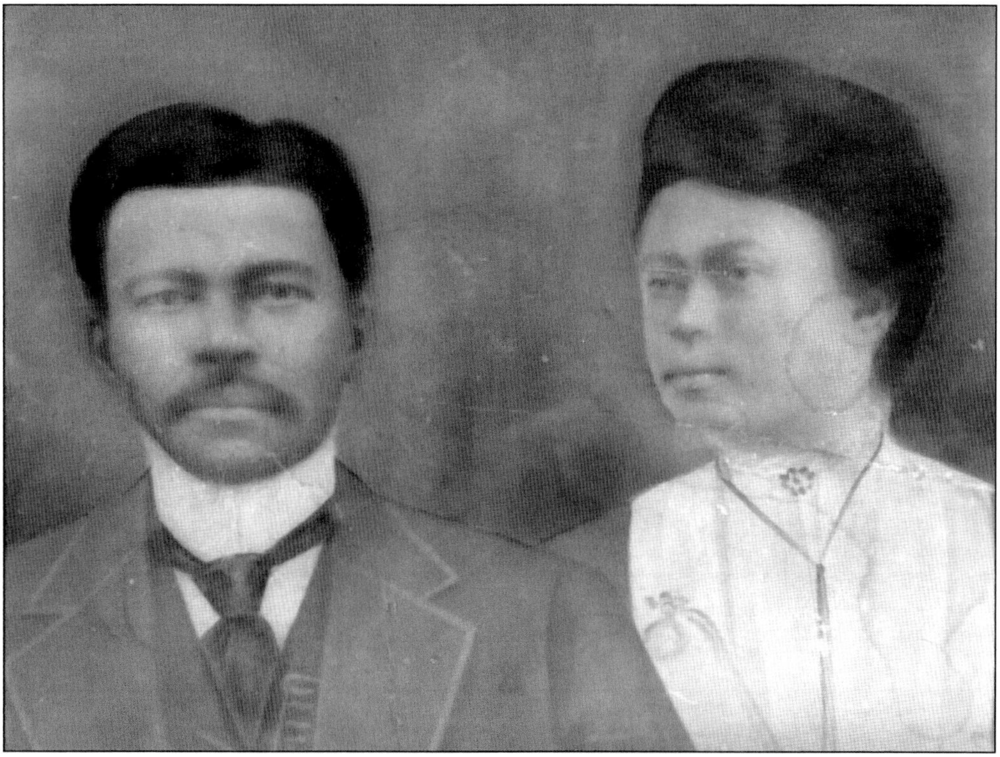

Gip and Mamie Ragin of Summerton are shown in this 1910 photograph. Gip, a popular individual and a successful farmer, was the father of at least 21 children.

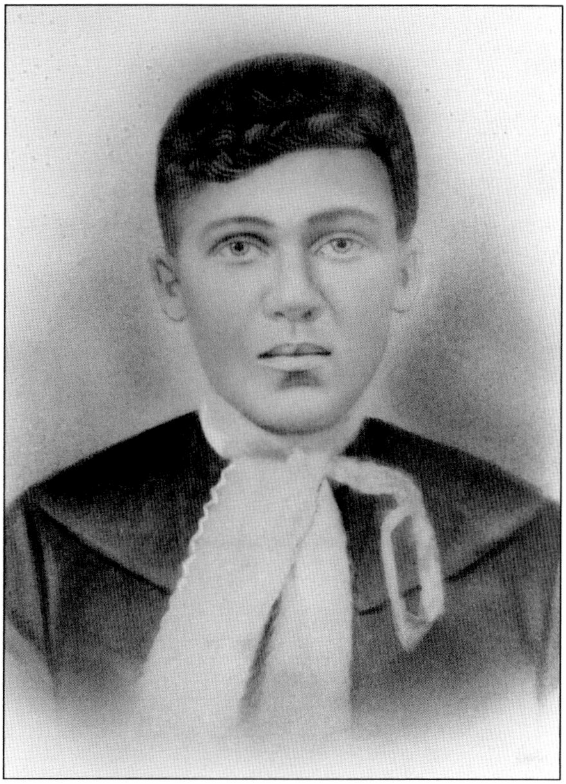

Mary Martin Weston is dressed in an outfit typical of the 1910 era. Neck carves were considered an integral part of a "dress" ensemble.

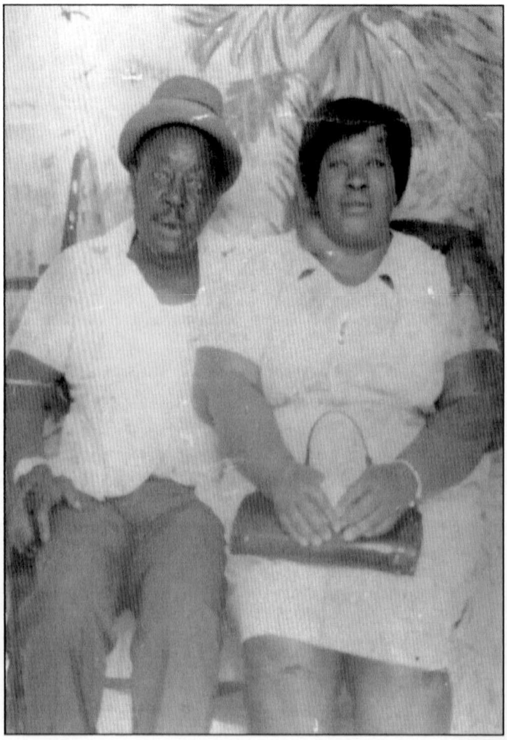

Laurence and Mary Elizabeth Cooper of New Zion take pride in their affection in this 1944 photograph. The background props were common during those days.

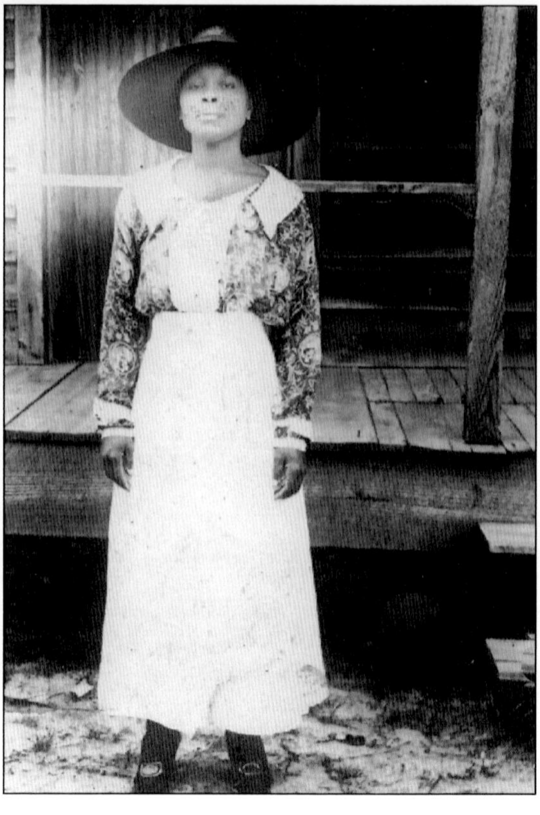

Fannie L. Kennedy McFadden is dressed in her Sunday best for this 1930 picture. Mrs. McFadden became a public school teacher in the New Zion area.

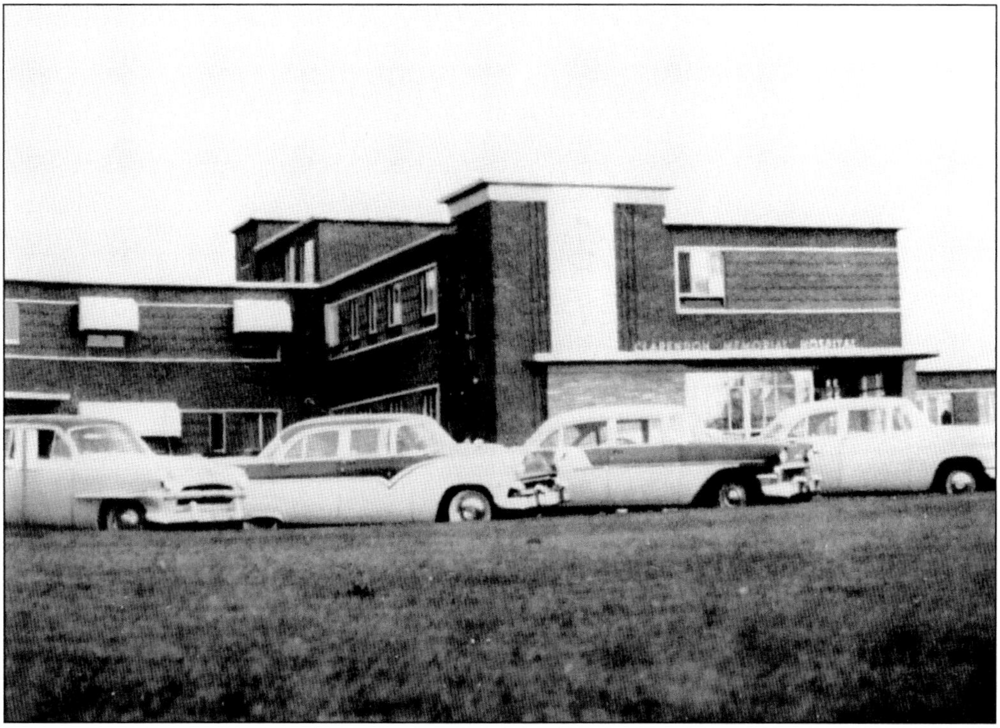

This 1955 view of Clarendon Memorial Hospital shows the front entrance to the hospital and is representative of the architecture of the late 1940s and 1950s.

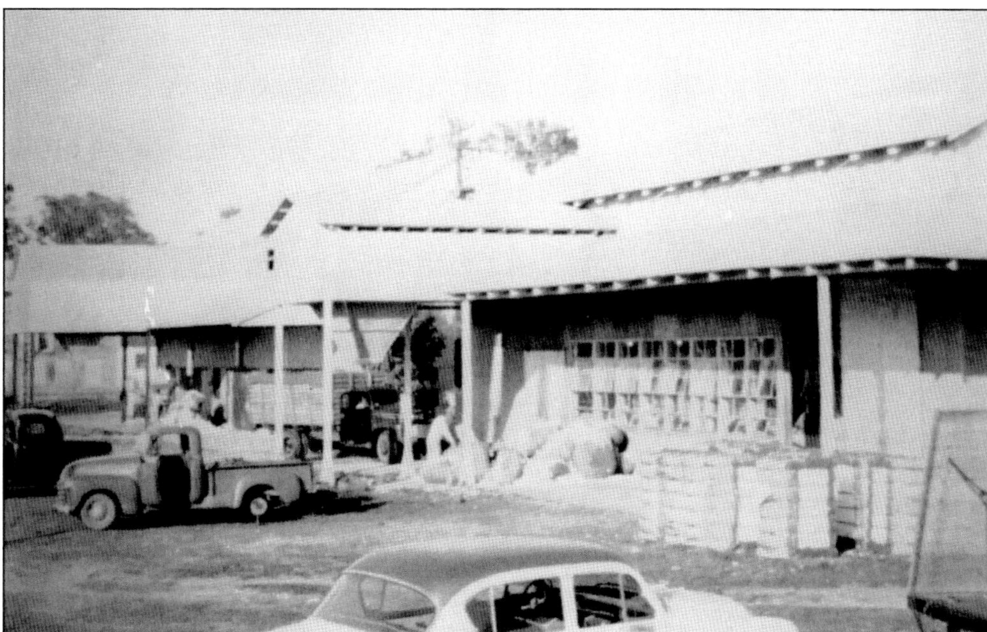

Elliott's Cotton Gin in Summerton was a beehive of activity during the fall months when cotton was king. It was common for the gin to operate far into the night during the height of the season. This photo, *c.* 1950, shows several bales of cotton waiting for removal.

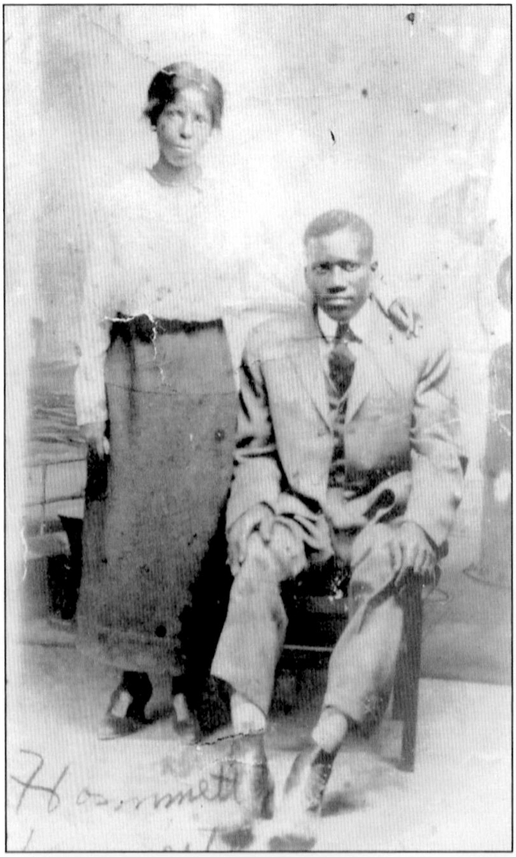

Hammitt and Viola Pearson, farmers in the Davis Station area, are posing in their dress attire in 1917. Hammitt and his second wife, Charlotte, were instrumental figures in the decision made by Thurgood Marshall to take the Civil Rights case from Clarendon County, which became known as *Briggs v. Elliott* in 1949.

Amy Tindal Ragin, a native of Summerton, taught at the Scott's Branch School for 43 years. During the 1949–1950 school year she served as one of the acting school principals. She is standing at the front of her home with the Scott's Branch School in the background.

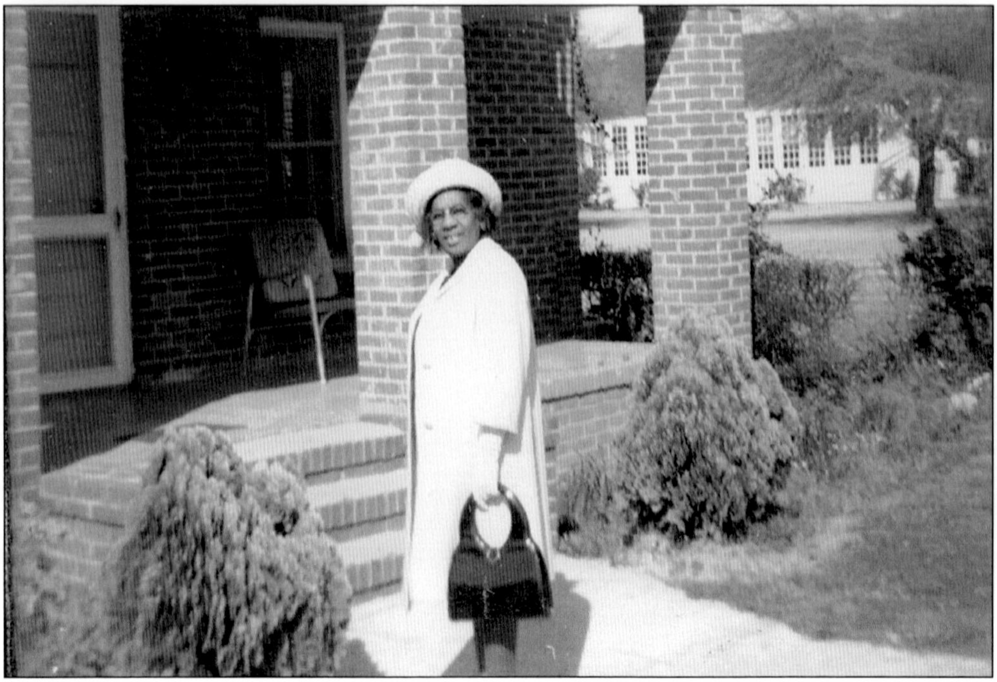

Walter Kennedy and his son are shown here in 1947. This mode of dress was typical of rural folk. Note the length of the child's trousers and his high-top shoes.

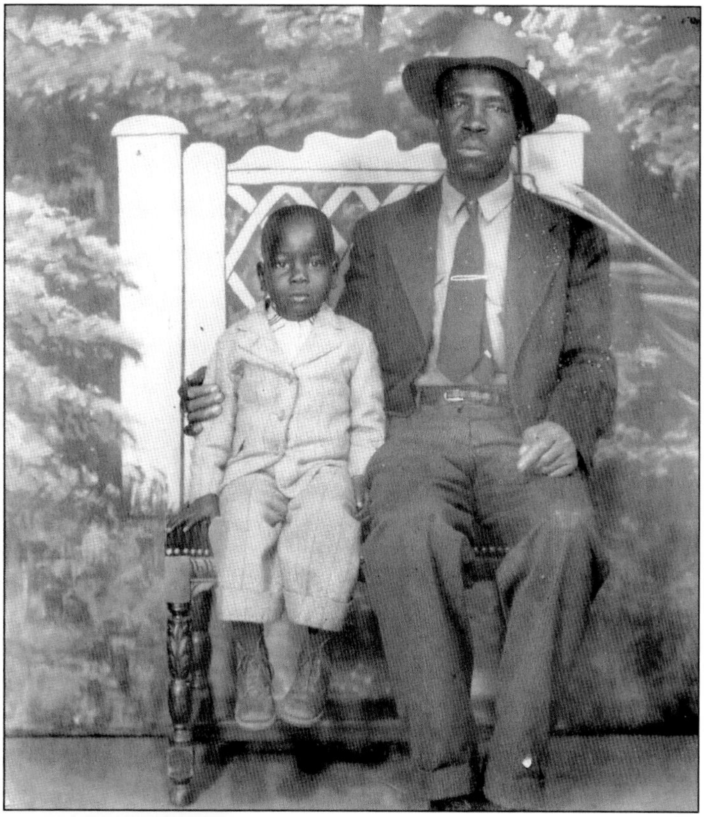

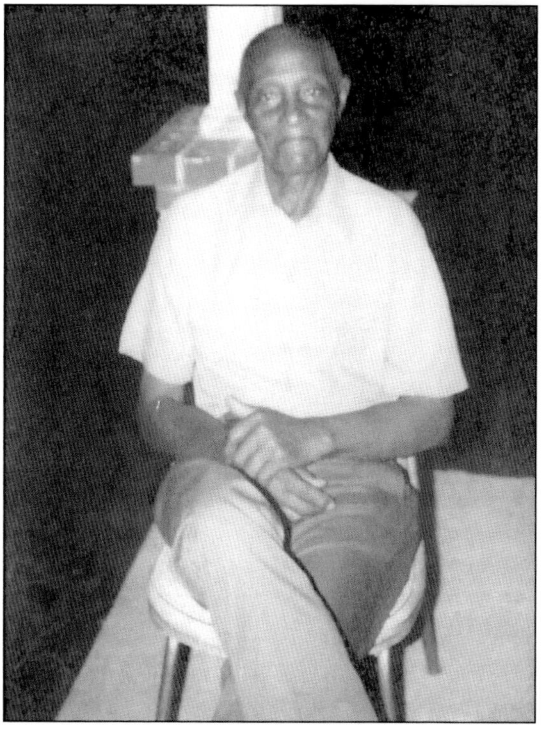

Robert Georgia of Summerton relaxes on his front porch. He was one of the plaintiffs in the *Briggs v. Elliott* desegregation case. He was also active in the Parent Action Committee for responsible leadership at the Scott's Branch School and a member of Taw Caw Baptist Church.

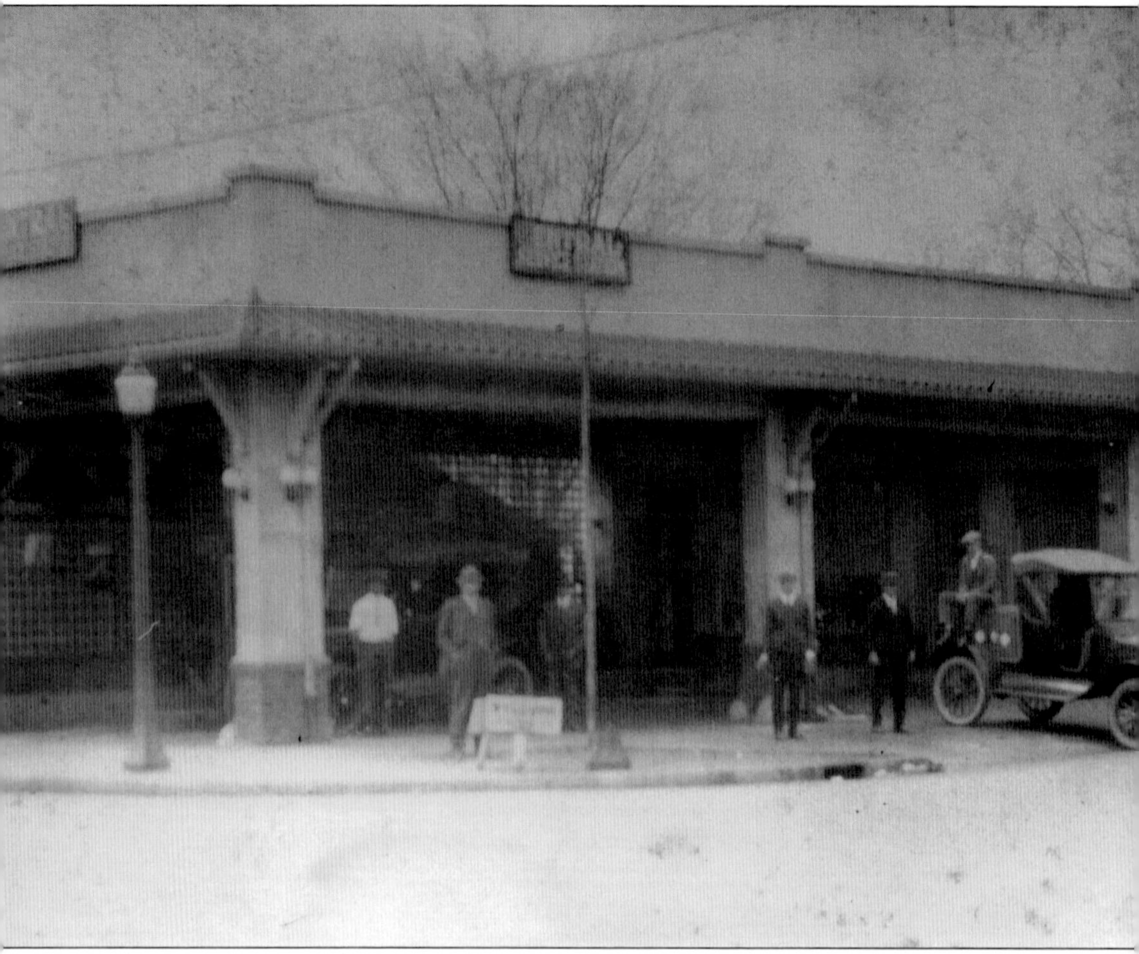

This *c*. 1920 picture of the Central Service Station in Manning is typical of this era. Note the street lamp and the lamps on the columns.

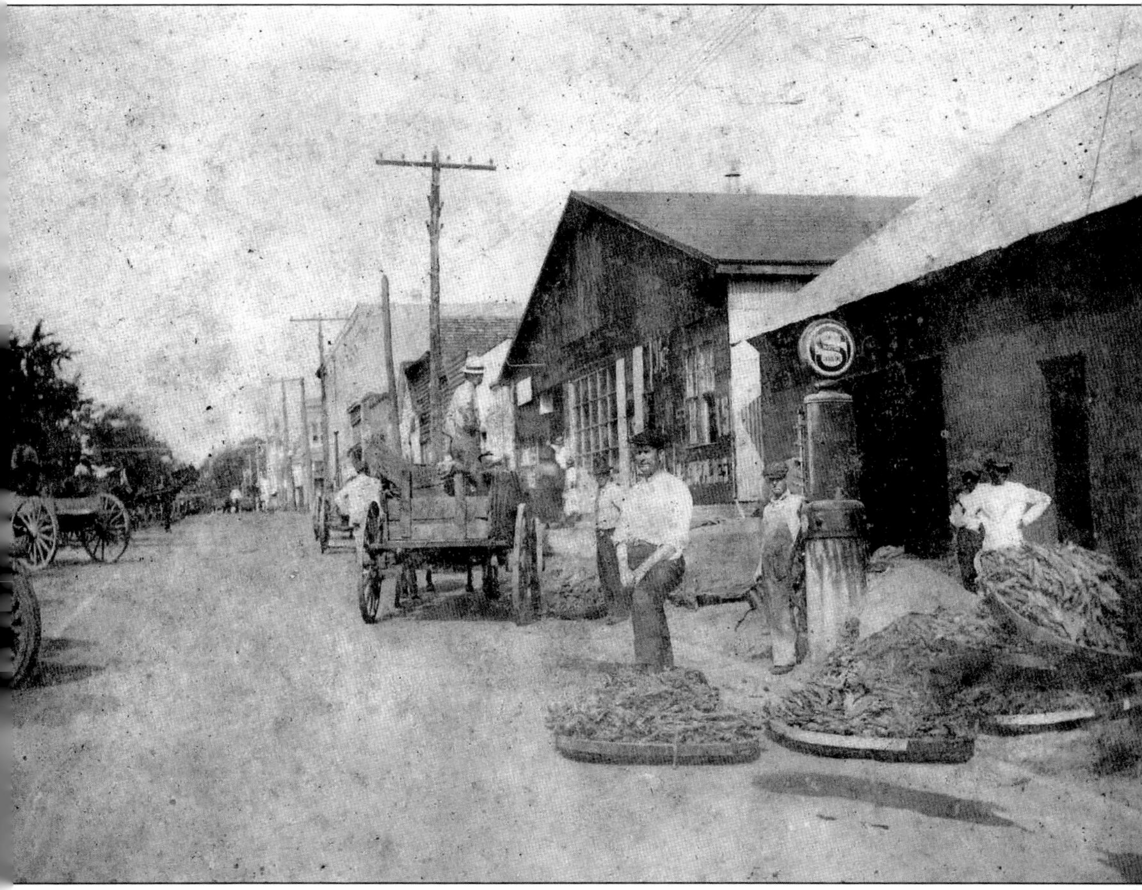

This is the Manning tobacco warehouse operated by R.D. Cothran c. 1920. The view is looking west on Boyce Street from the corner of Church St. See the same street from the other end in the photo on the top of page 61. The tobacco was piled on baskets after being sorted by quality grade. The farmers then awaited the auctioneer who received bids for each basket. The highest bid determined the price that the farmer would receive for his product.

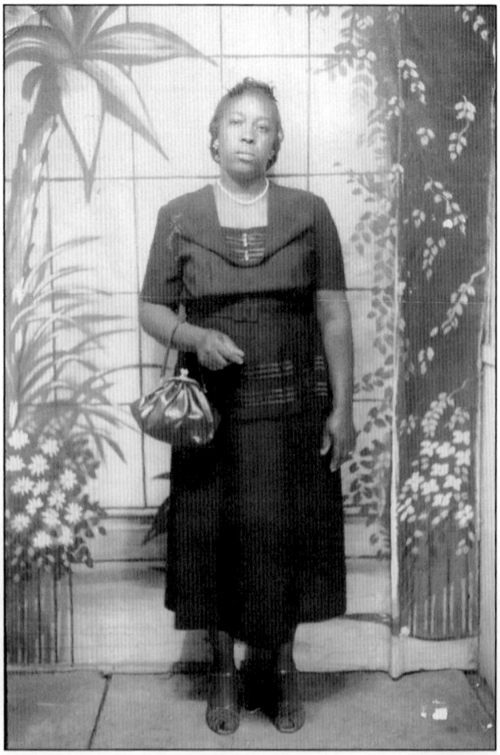

Eva Gamble, shown here in 1955, was a midwife from New Zion. She is credited with the delivery of many newborns in the New Zion area. Physicians were almost nonexistent in many rural areas and people relied on the midwife to attend the chores of birthing.

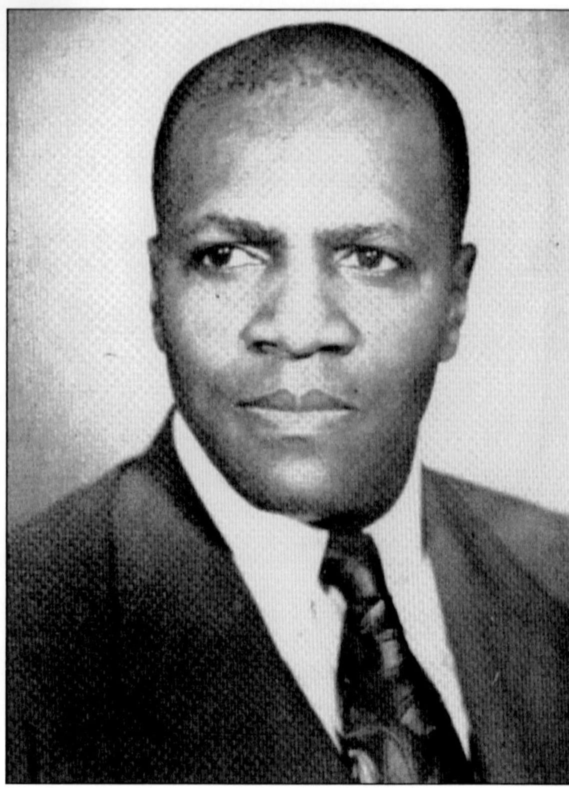

Rev. J.W. Witherspoon, a native of Manning, once served as the official historian of the African Methodist Episcopal Church and taught at Allen University. He died in 1993 at the age of 100.

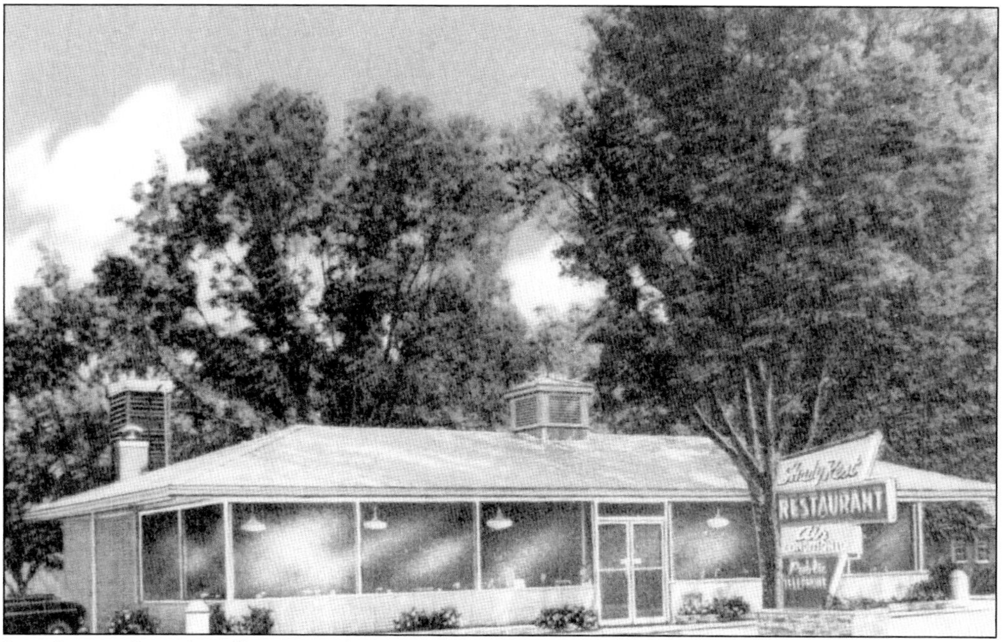

Residents of Turbeville enjoyed many delicious meals at the Shady Rest Restaurant. The contemporary construction of this building was unusual in the Turbeville community in the 1930s.

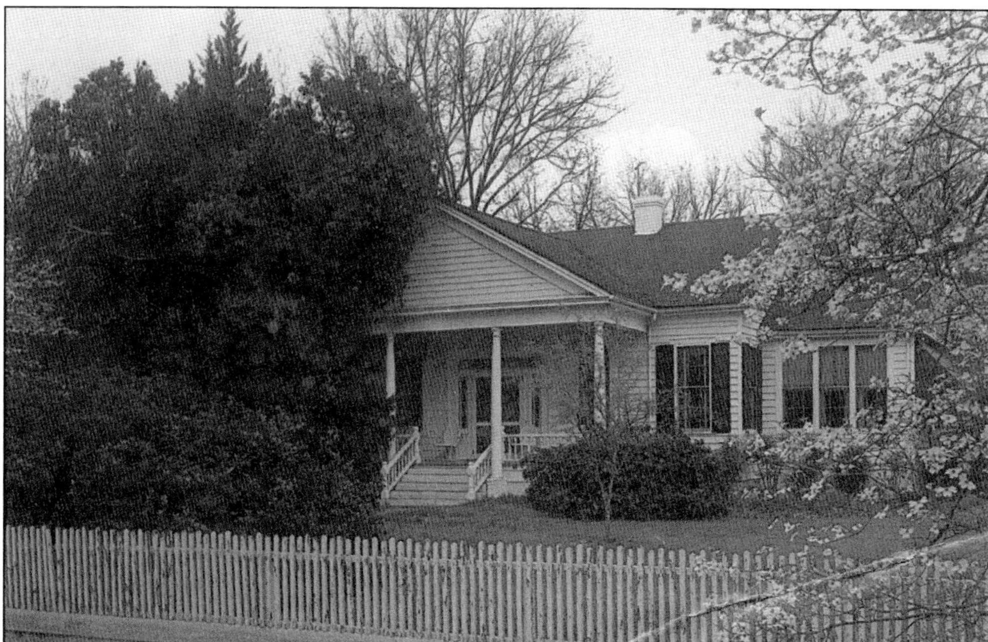

The Manning residence of Judge Taylor Stukes seems to nestle itself in the arms of the trees at the time of this early spring photograph. Note the dogwood tree in bloom on the far right.

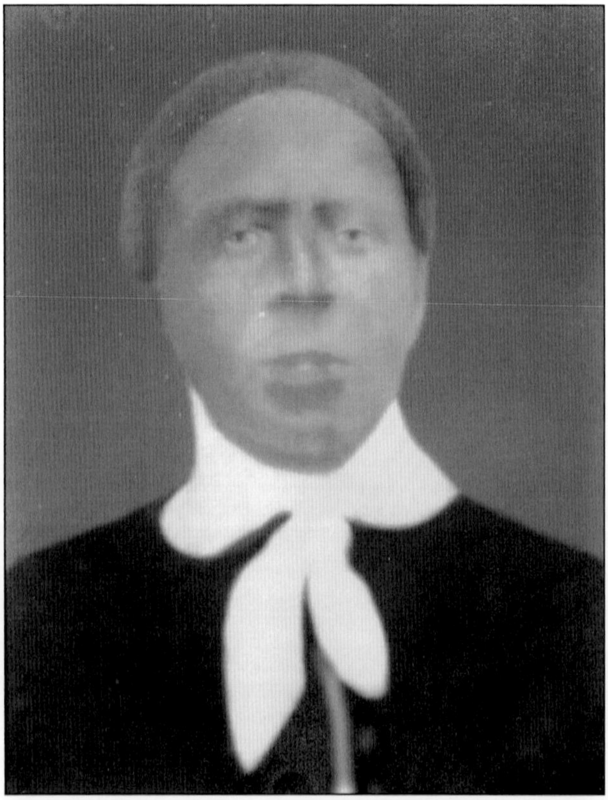

Dinah Beshet Bowman lived 33 years as a slave. She was a part of the initial organization of the Liberty Hill AME Church when their congregation met under a local bush arbor. This image is from the 1880 era.

An early scene shows Brooks Street in Manning. Formerly Main Street, Brooks Street is part of U.S. Route 301. Prior to the initiation of interstate highways, Route 301 was a major north-south artery.

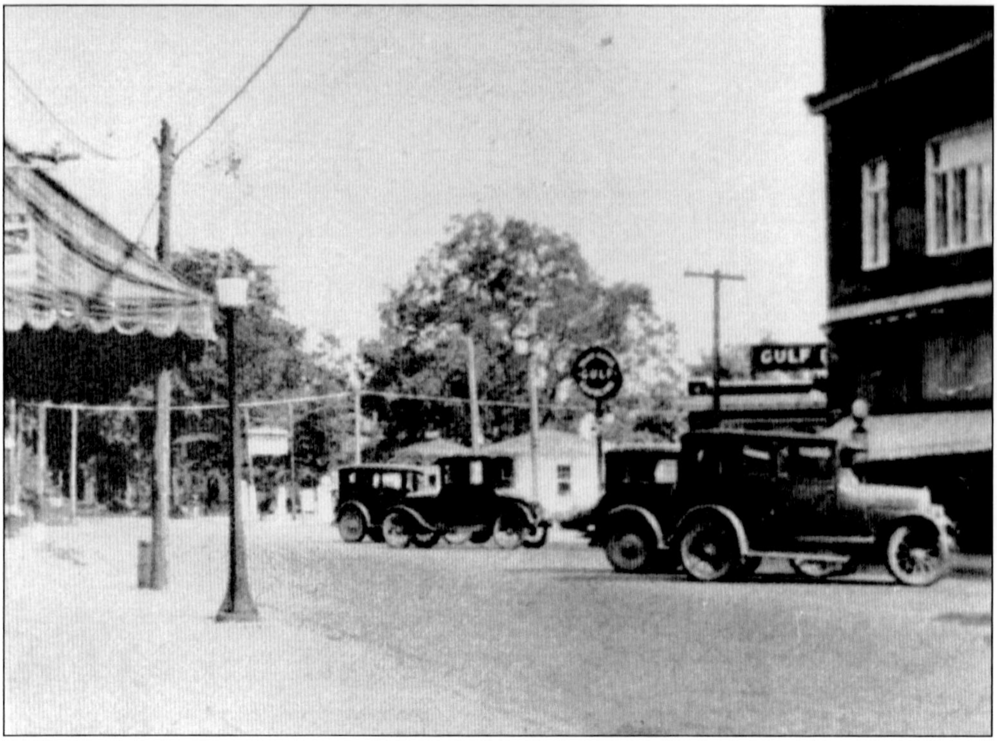

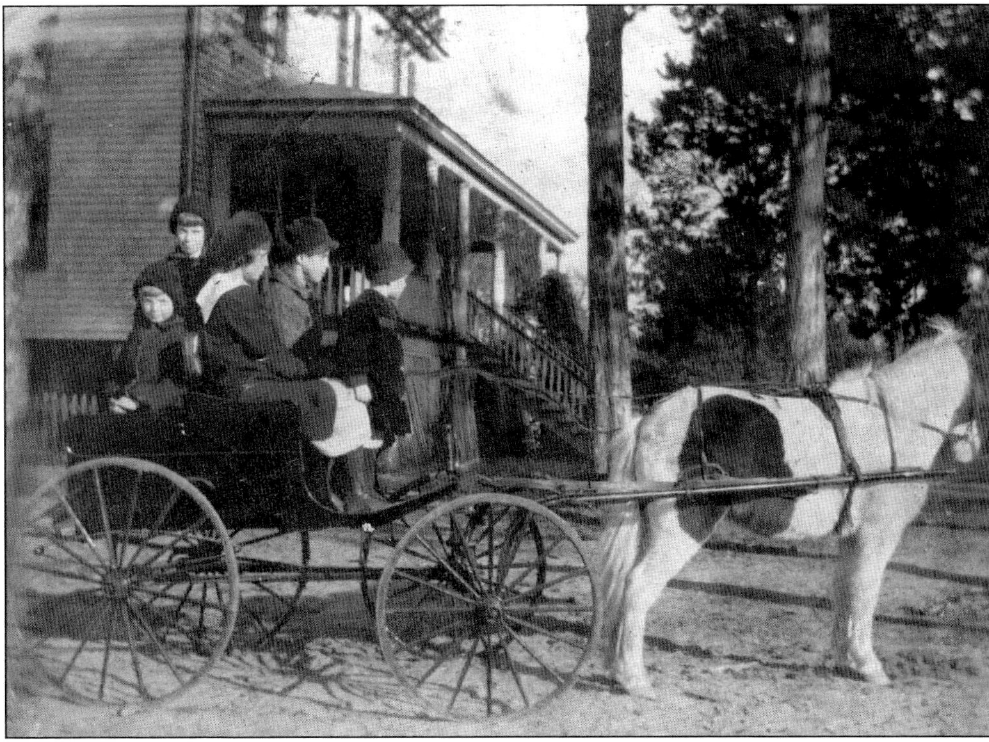

The children of J.M. Cantey are seated on a horse-drawn buggy in front of the Cantey home in 1916. The full picture of this house is shown before and after restoration on pages 108 and 109.

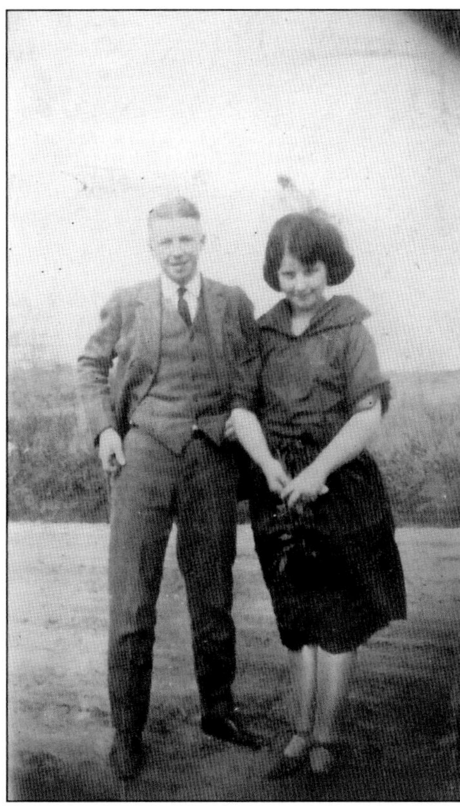

This unidentified couple from Summerton was photographed in 1923.

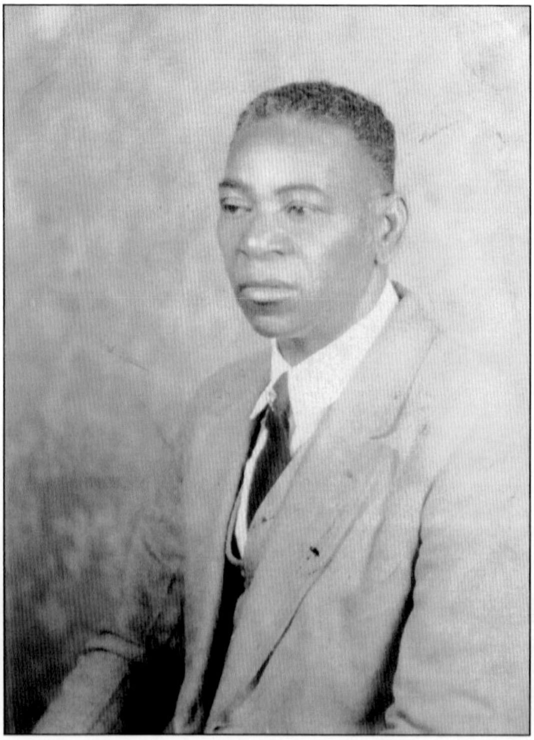

Jared D. Warley Jr. of the St. Paul area is pictured *c.* 1930. St. Paul is a community about three miles south of Summerton on Route 301.

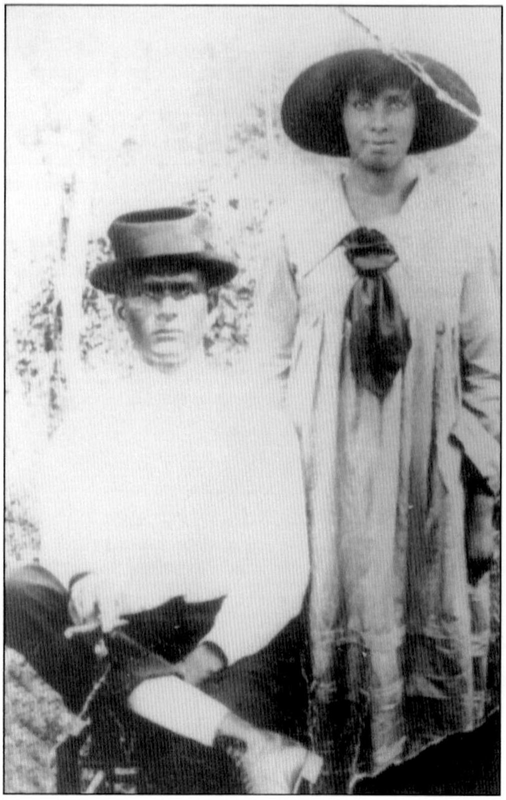

Gilbert and Willie Henry of Summerton pose for this photograph around 1920. They were among the 20 petitioners involved in the *Briggs* case for the desegregation of schools.

The three siblings pictured here are, from left to right, Lottie, Evelyn, and Oliver Sumter of Manning. They were photographed in 1914.

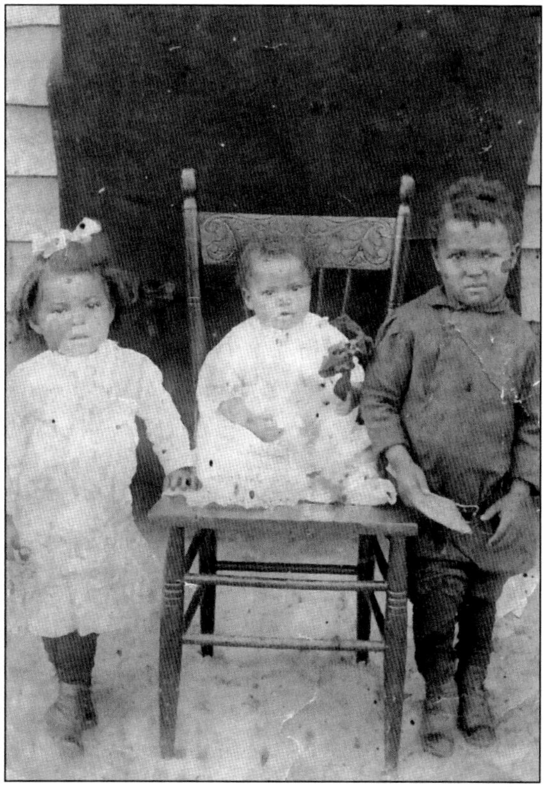

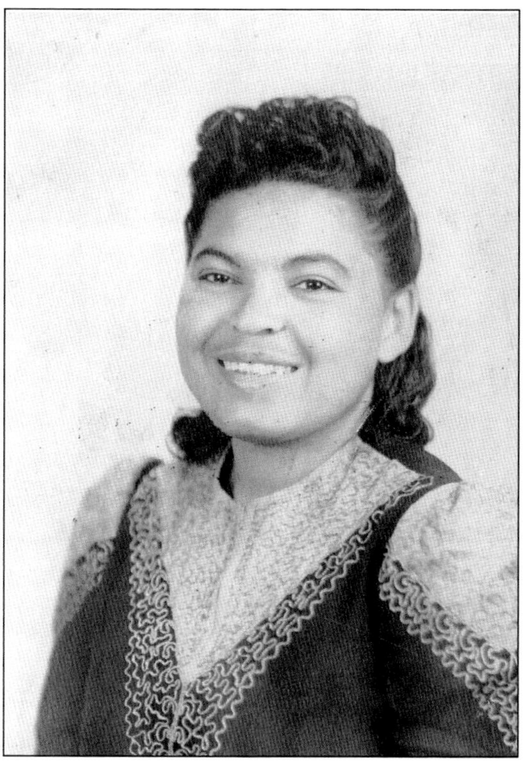

Lottie Sumter, all grown up, is shown here as a young lady in 1932.

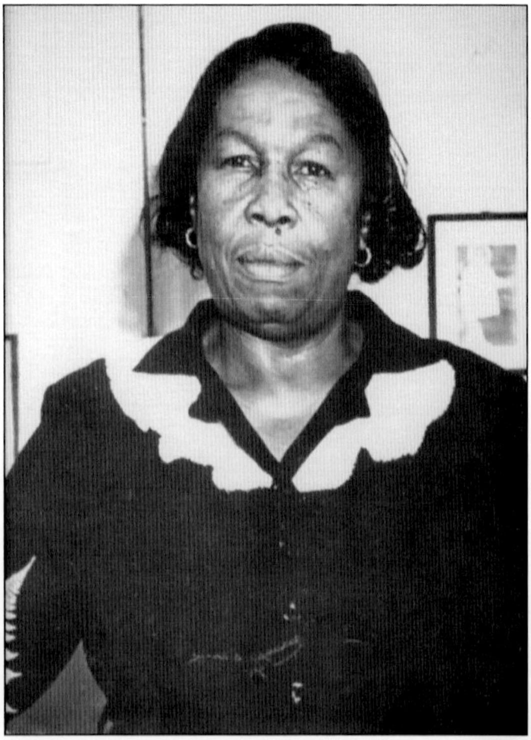

Margaret Smith Ragin, the wife of Rufus Ragin, is pictured in 1948. She and her husband were farmers in the Summerton area.

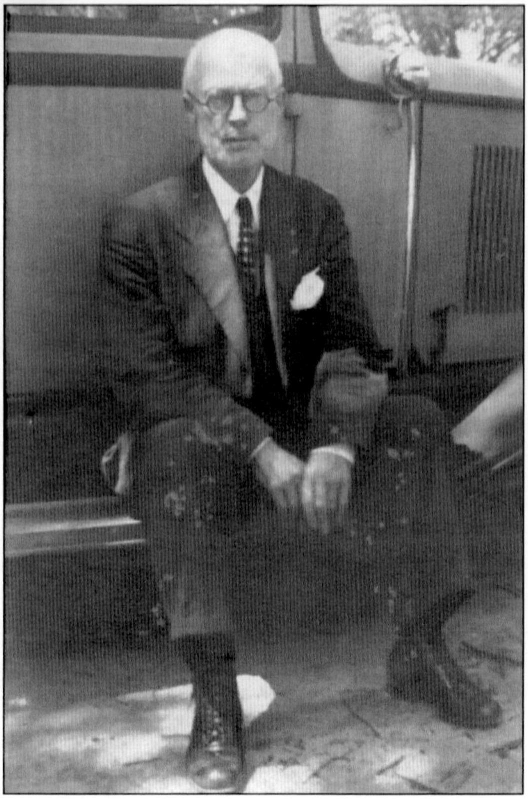

John James Cantey, a prominent resident of Summerton and a descendant of the Richardson family, is seated on the running board of his automobile. The Richardson family is known for the number of members within their clan that served as governor of South Carolina.

Hampton Anderson and son of Summerton are shown here in 1920. The ties suggest that they were probably dressed for a special occasion.

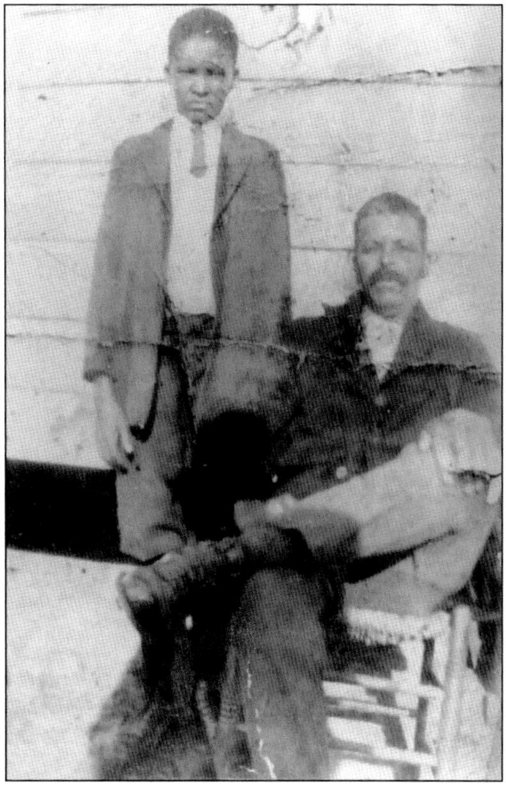

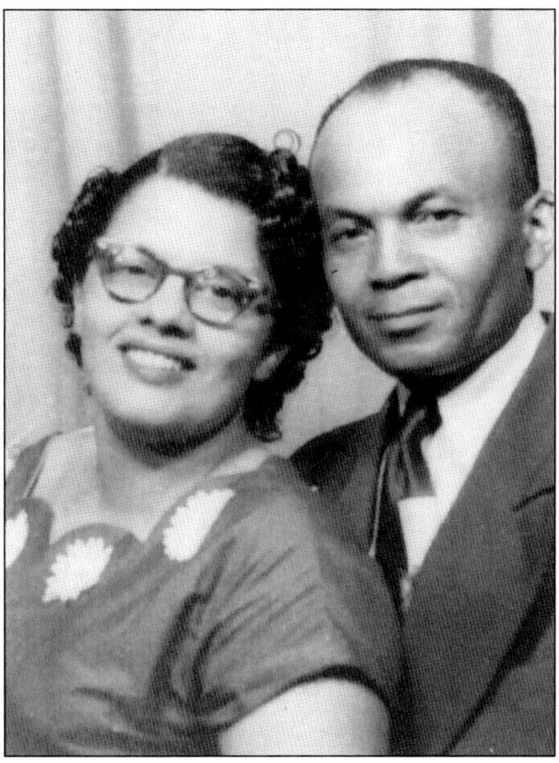

Gussie and Anthony Palmer, a loving couple from Summerton, posed for this picture in 1945. The couple was instrumental in efforts to raise funds in New York City to aid the black citizens of Clarendon County. This was necessitated by the economic pressures blacks were subjected to during the height of the Civil Rights Movement.

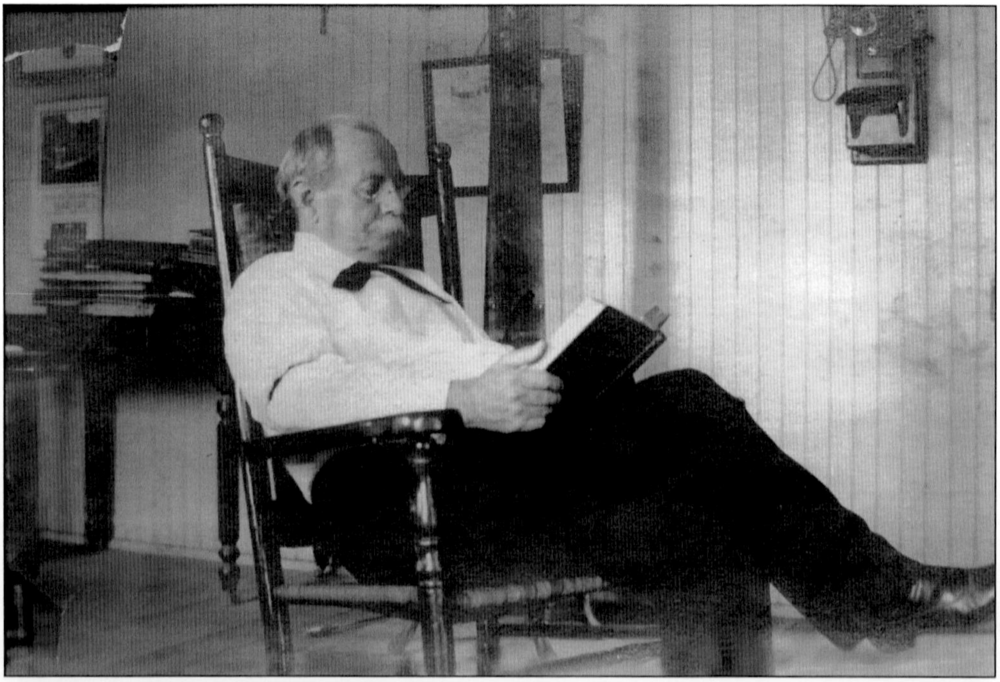

Dr. William Wallace Anderson, shown here in 1915, was a resident of Summerton. Physicians in this part of the state had difficulty earning a decent living because of the inability of patients to pay with cash. Therefore, Dr. Anderson augmented his income through activities related to the farming industry.

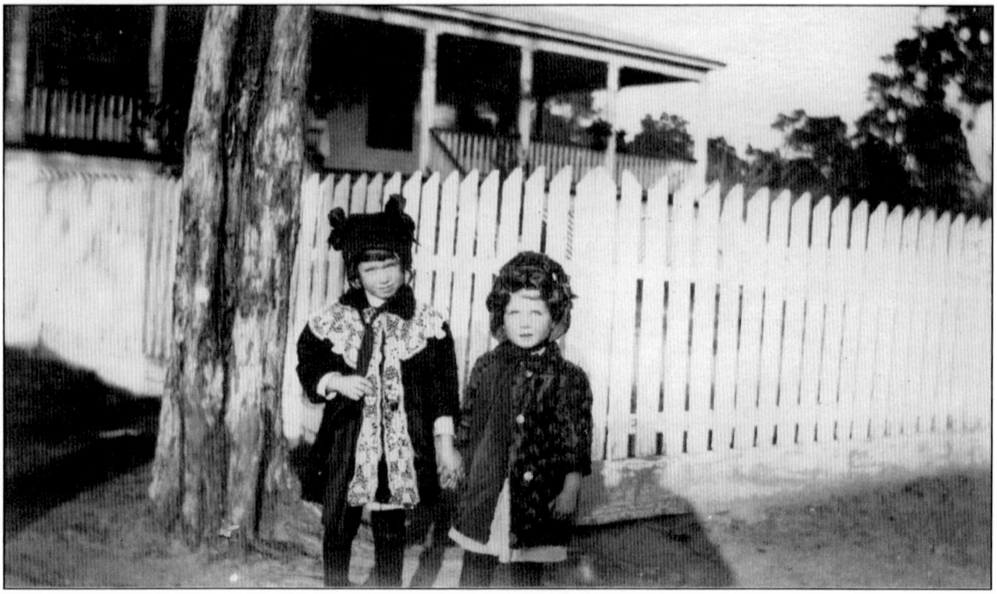

Julia Anderson Cantey and Kate Converse Cantey posed for this photograph in 1915. The Canteys were a prominent family in the Summerton area.

Margaret Stukes and "Sis" Smith are seated on the steps of the first Scott's Branch School building in 1924. This is the original Scott's Branch located near the St. Mark Church.

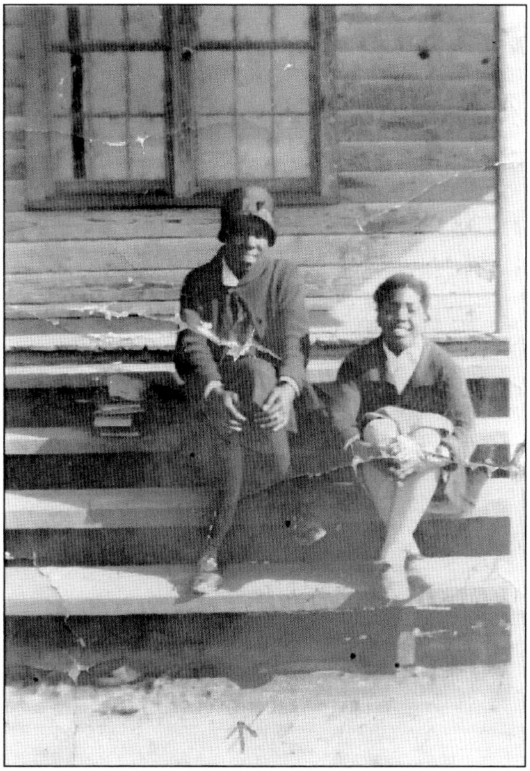

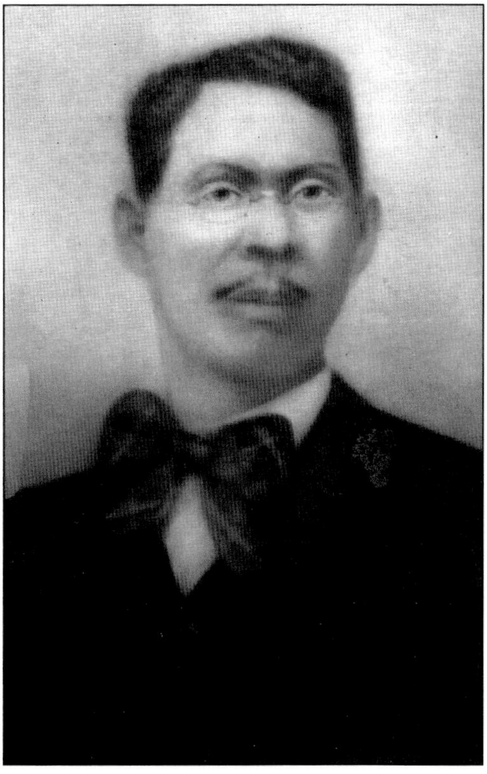

James Brown, a native of Summerton, operated a butcher shop in the town for many years. This photograph was taken in 1919.

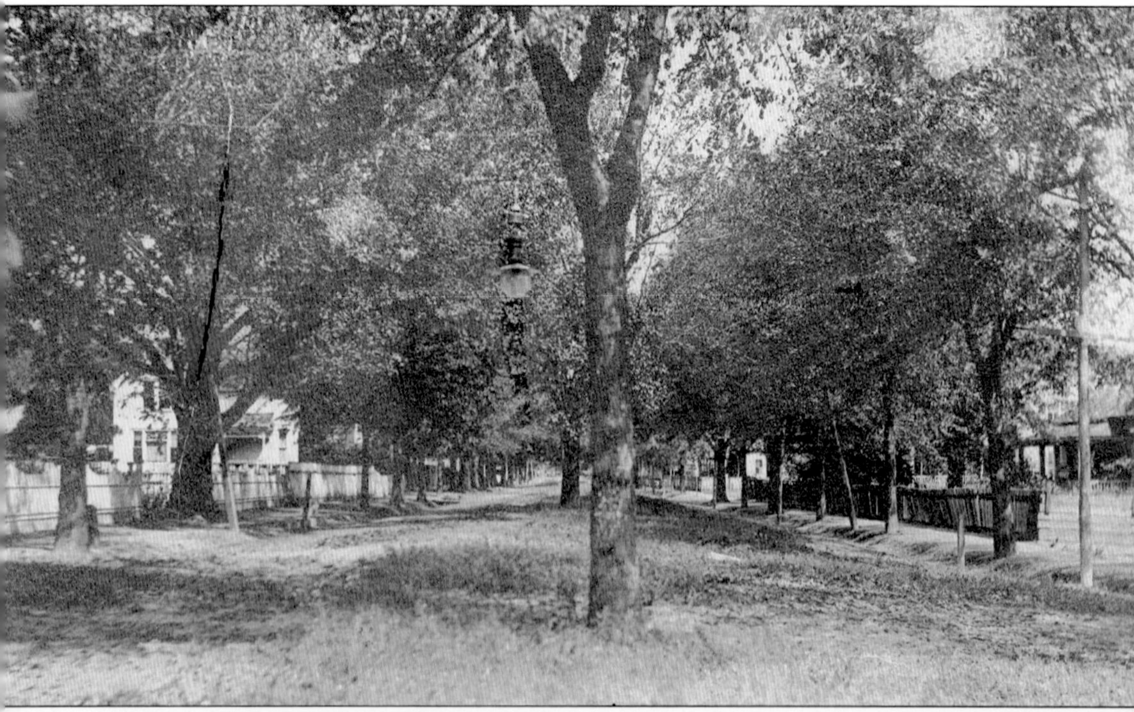

This is South Main Street in Manning before the advent of paved roads. Note the trees dividing the center of the street as well as lining the curb areas. This street is now known as Sunset Drive. The trees in the center of the street have now been removed and those that line the curbside of the street are still in existence.

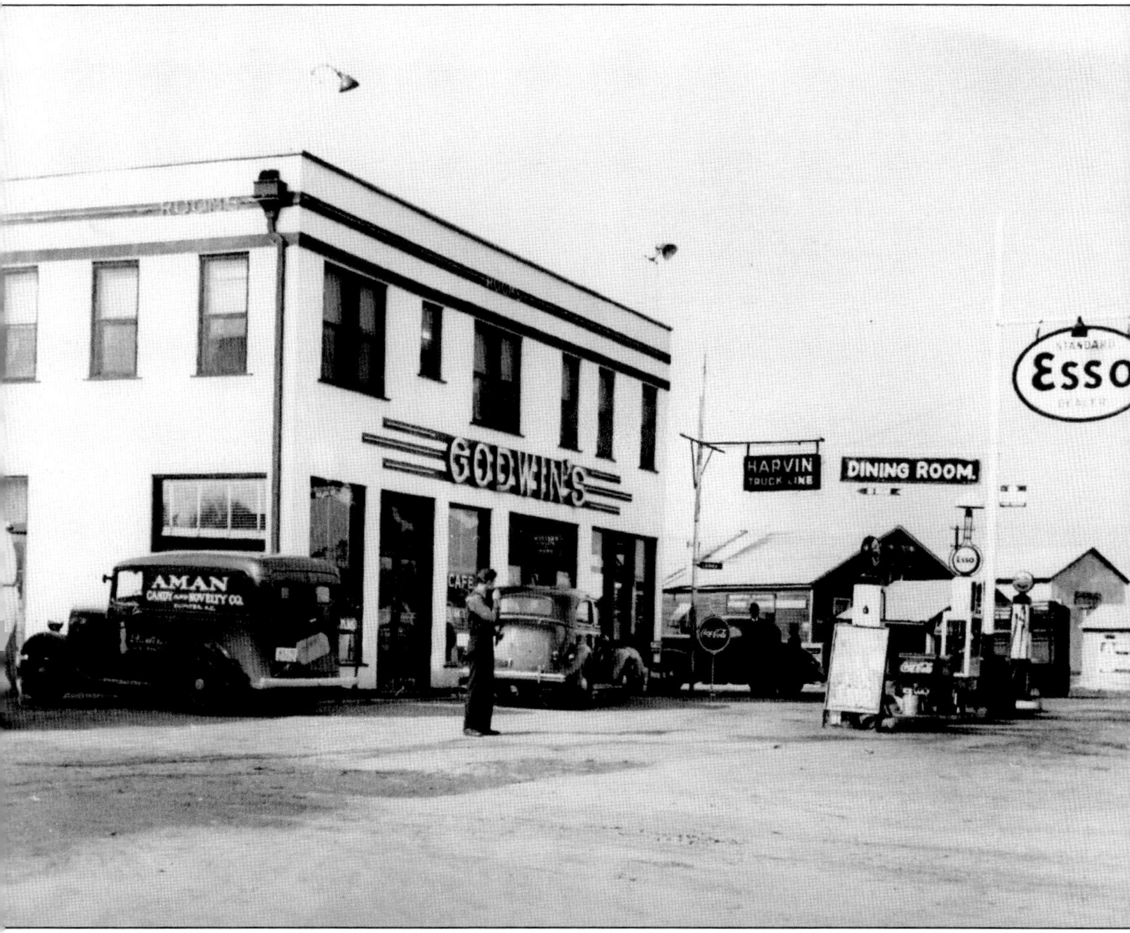

This is a 1938 view at the junction of U.S. Routes 301 and 15 in Summerton. Godwin's Esso Service Station and the Dining Room served as a haven for many tourists traveling along this major north/south highway.

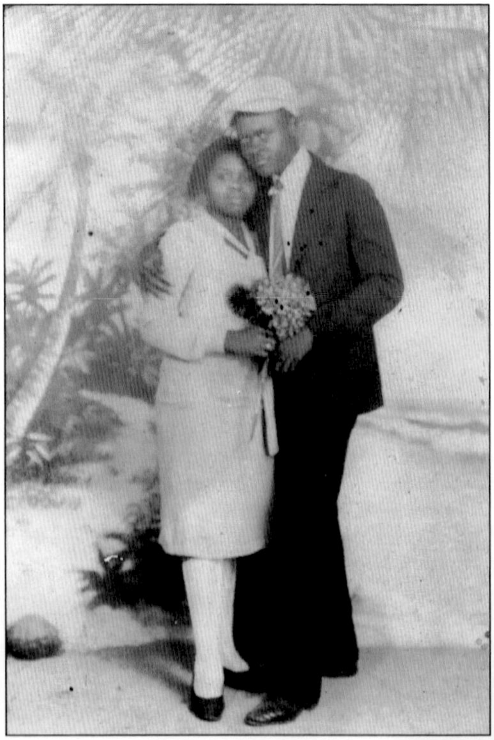

Edward and Mattie Bowman III of Summerton are photographed celebrating their marriage, *c.* 1929.

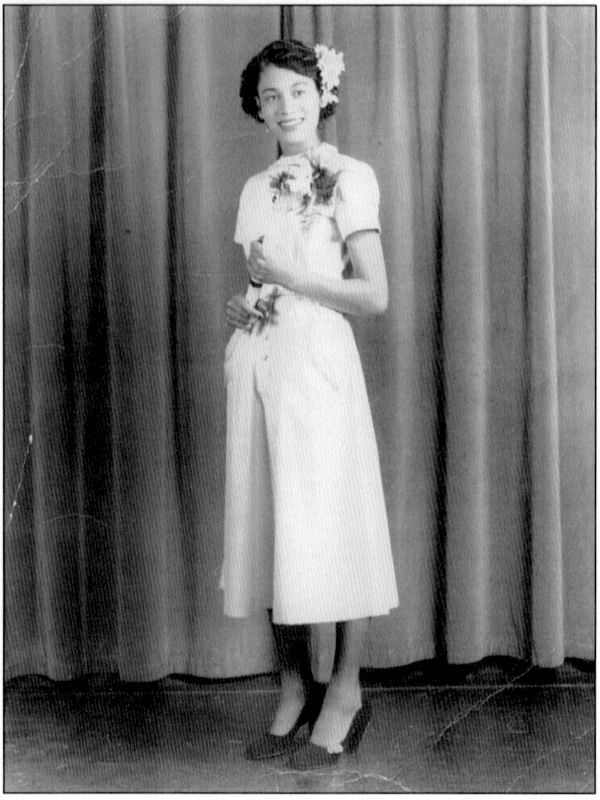

Annie Lee Palmer, granddaughter of James Palmer, poses for a photograph in 1930.

In this 1936 picture, Christine "Sister T" Bowman, wife of Edward Bowman II, is standing beside her home in Summerton.

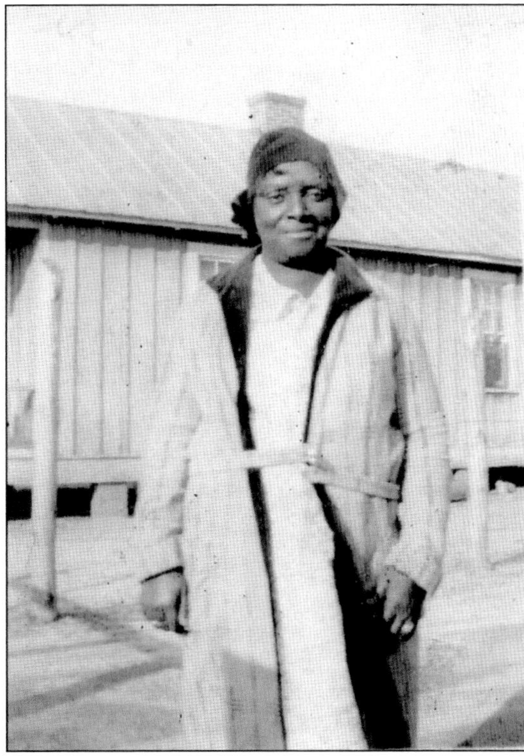

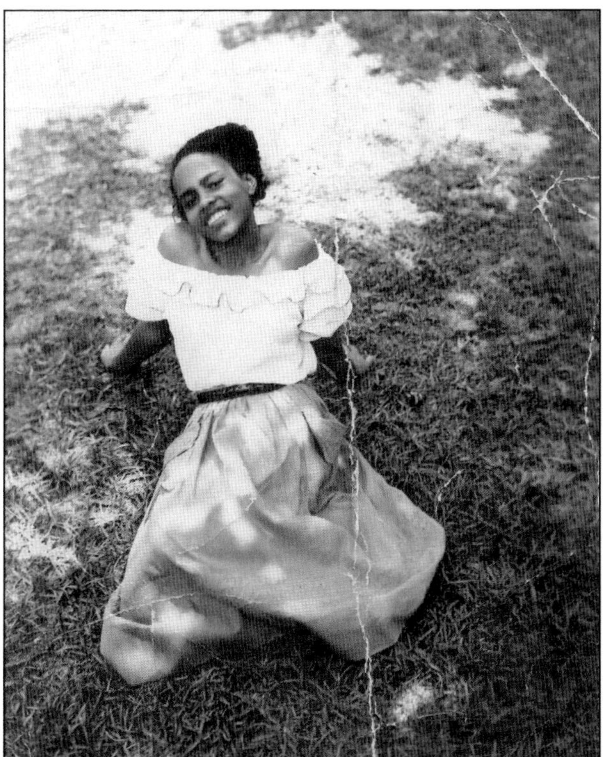

Myrtle Robinson, niece of Richard and Madge Miller, relaxes in this c. 1950 photograph.

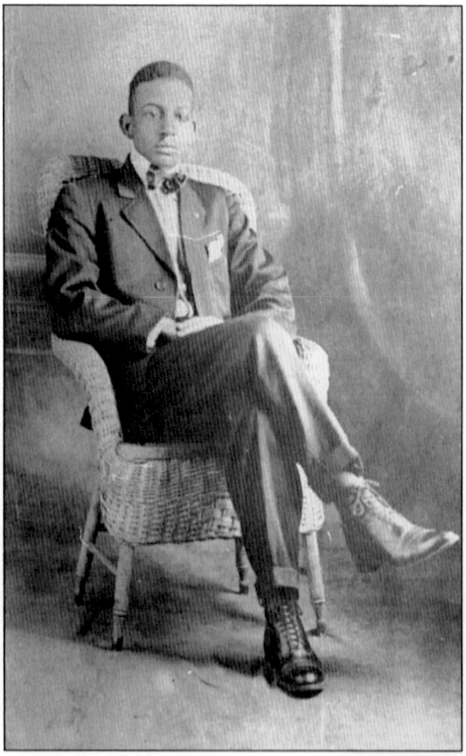

Henry Brown, a native of Summerton, poses for this 1920 photograph. He was one of the original petitioners in the case that became *Briggs v. Elliott*.

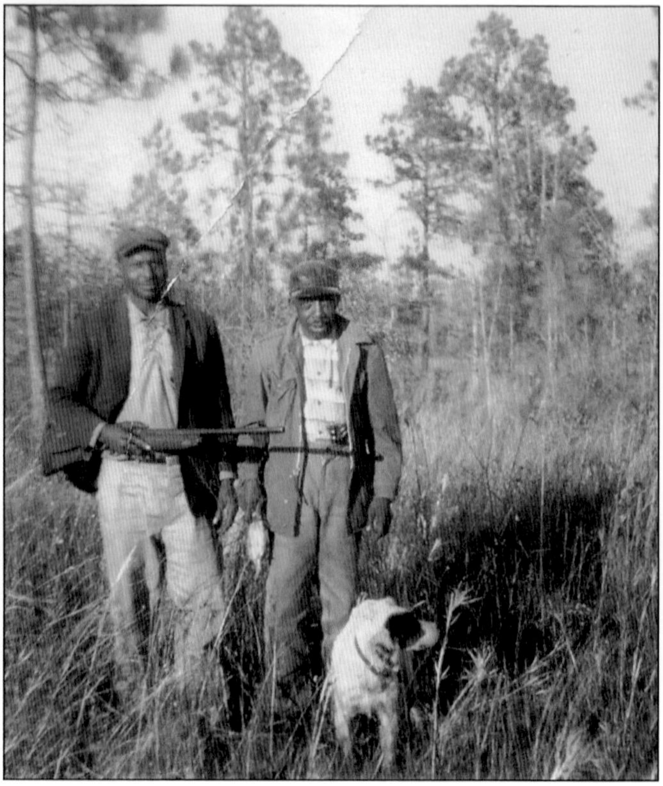

A popular sport activity in this area is hunting. Wade Smith is shown with a friend as they prepare to hunt for wild game in 1944.

Davis Brown, a native of Summerton, poses for the camera in 1940.

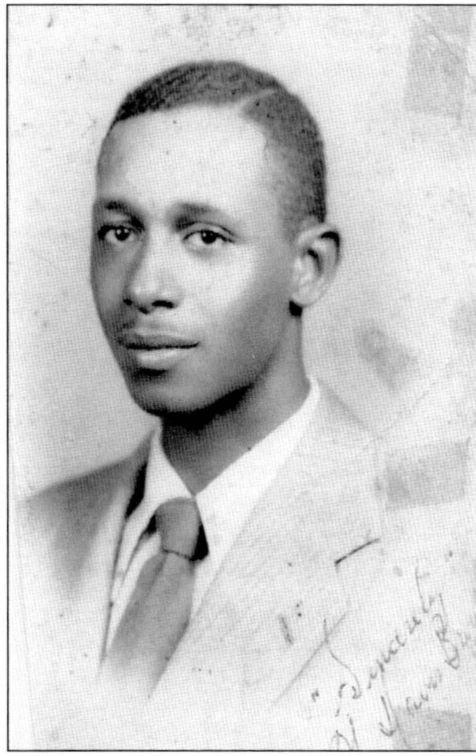

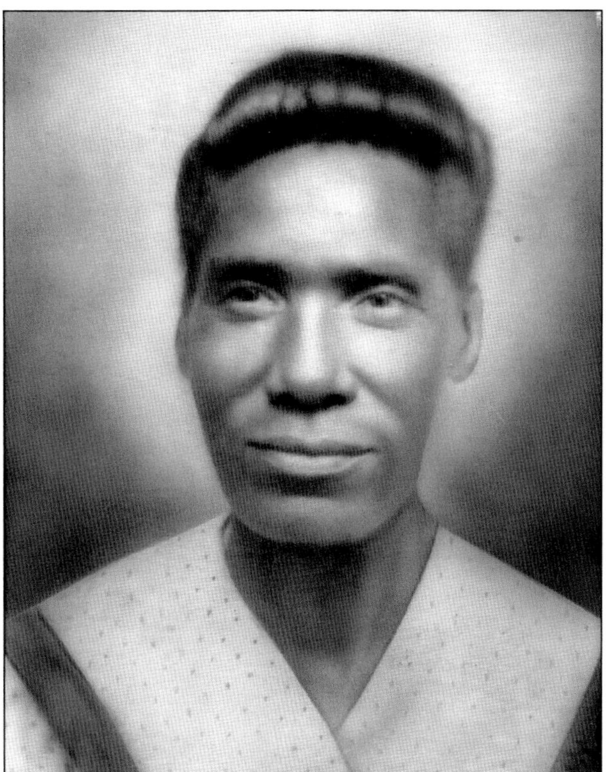

Rose Dow Green of Summerton is seen in a photograph believed to have been taken around 1915.

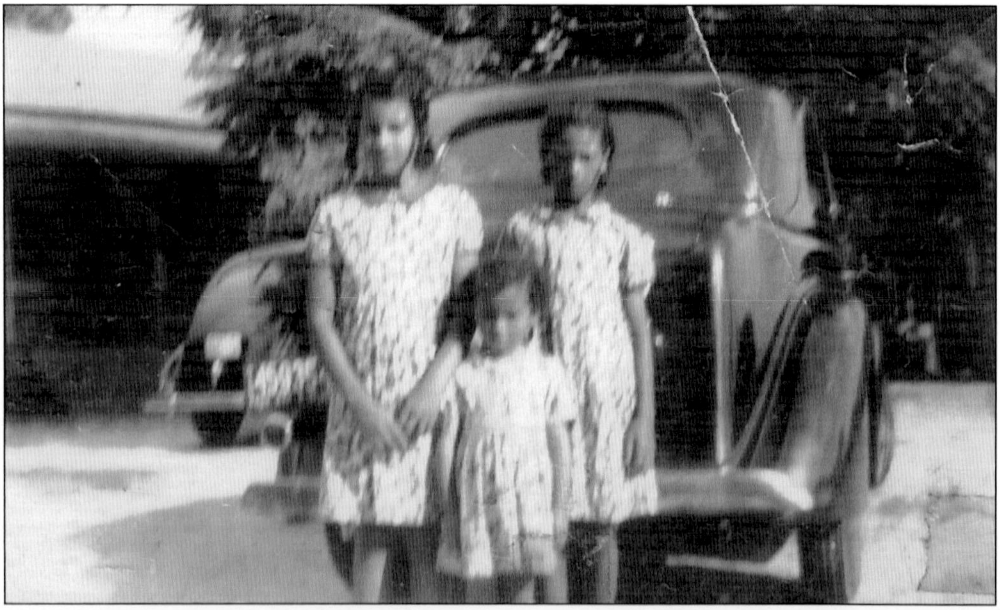

The three sisters in this 1939 photo are, from left to right, Vera Miller, Blondell McDonald, and Beatrice Miller. The family house in the background still stands near Summerton. Their father, Charlie McDonald, was a cotton and tobacco farmer.

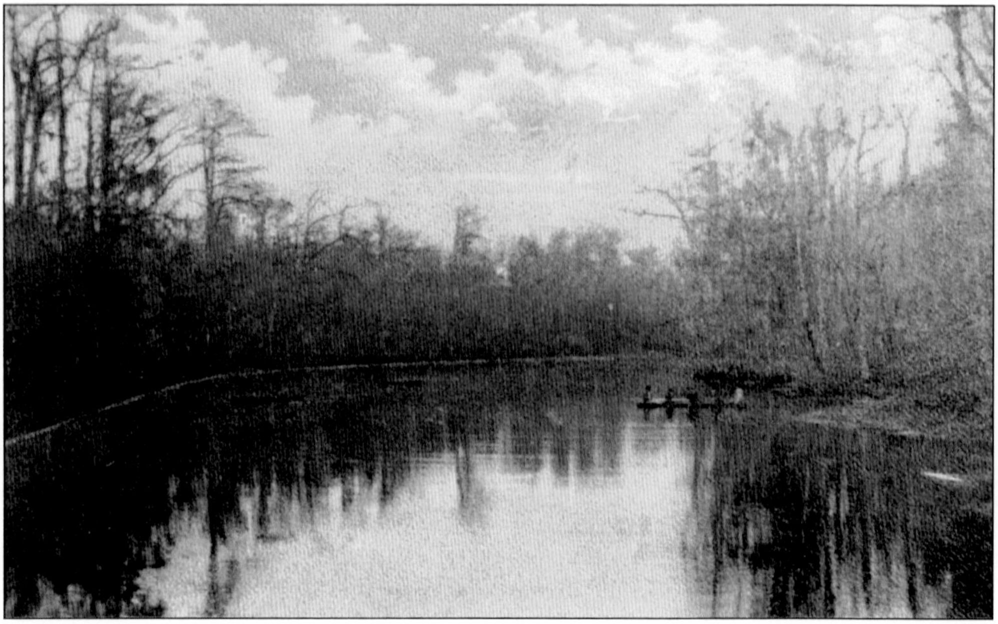

This early view of Brewington Lake shows boaters enjoying an afternoon of fishing around 1935. This lake continues to be a popular fishing spot

Margaret Harvin Stukes, the daughter of Dinah Beshet Harvin, resided in the Summerton area. This picture was taken around 1890.

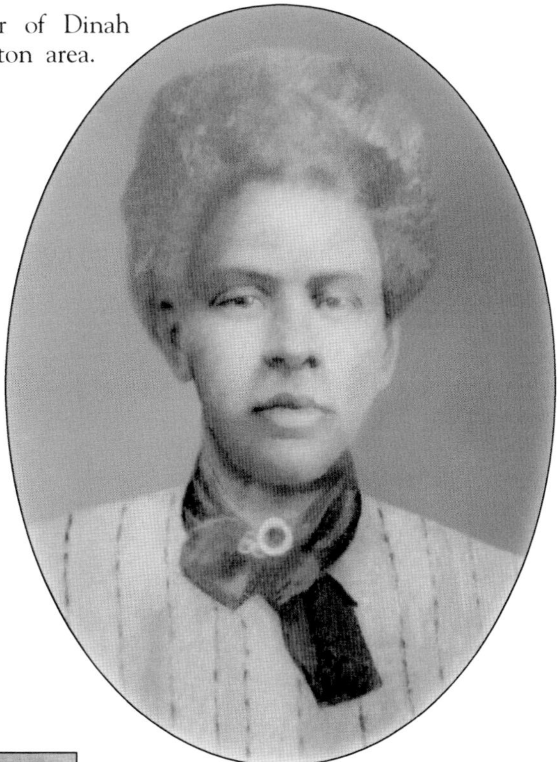

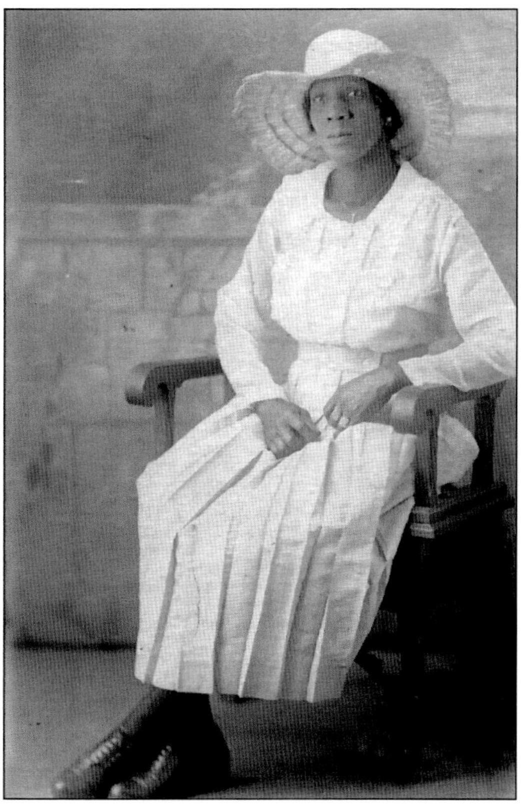

An unknown lady from the Summerton area sits for a formal photograph in her white crocheted hat and white dress.

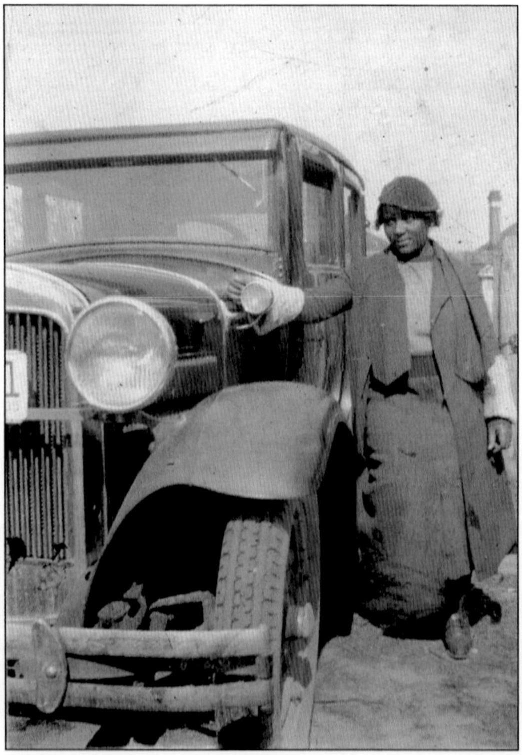

As automobiles became more popular, women also learned to drive. Christine Bowman is about ready to go for a spin.

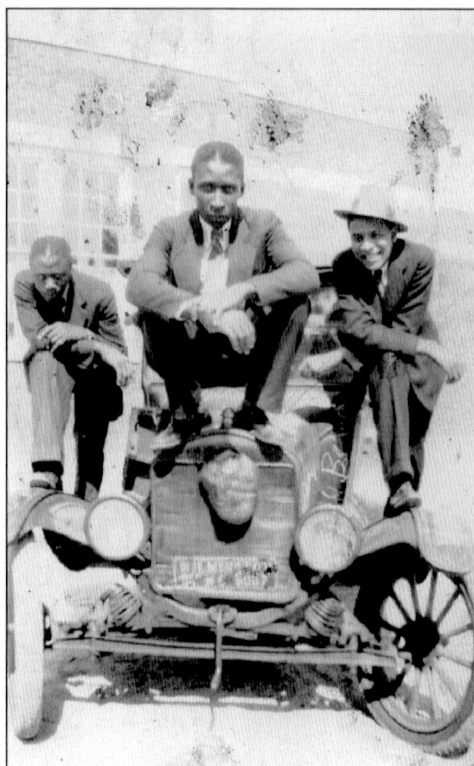

"Have car, will travel" was the motto of many young men. These three, ready to take off, attract the attention of all the pretty girls.

Henry and Thelma Brown of Summerton are photographed as they return home from church, c. 1926. Henry was one of the plaintiffs in the first *Briggs* case against the Clarendon School System. His name was removed to minimize any threat of employment retaliation against him.

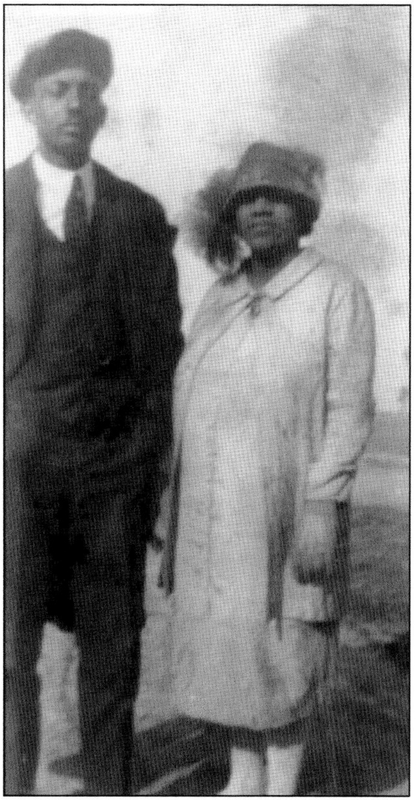

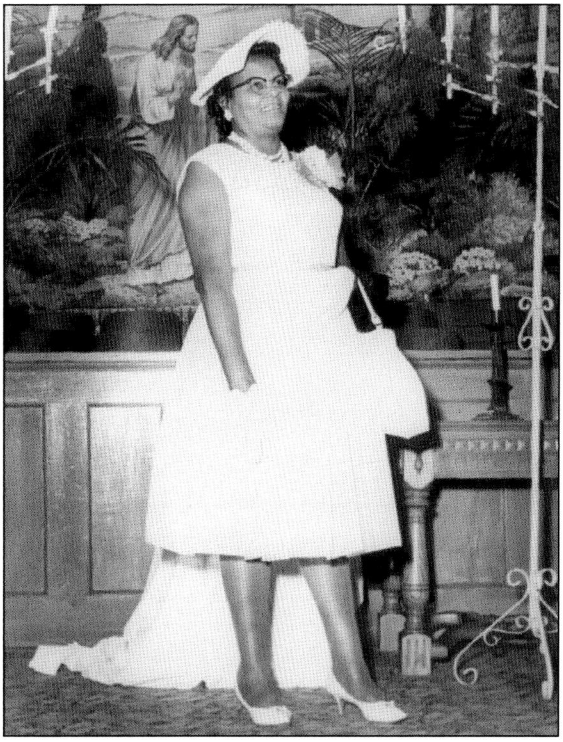

Mary Oliver was the owner/operator of Oliver's Café in Summerton. She was also a plaintiff in the *Briggs* case from Clarendon County.

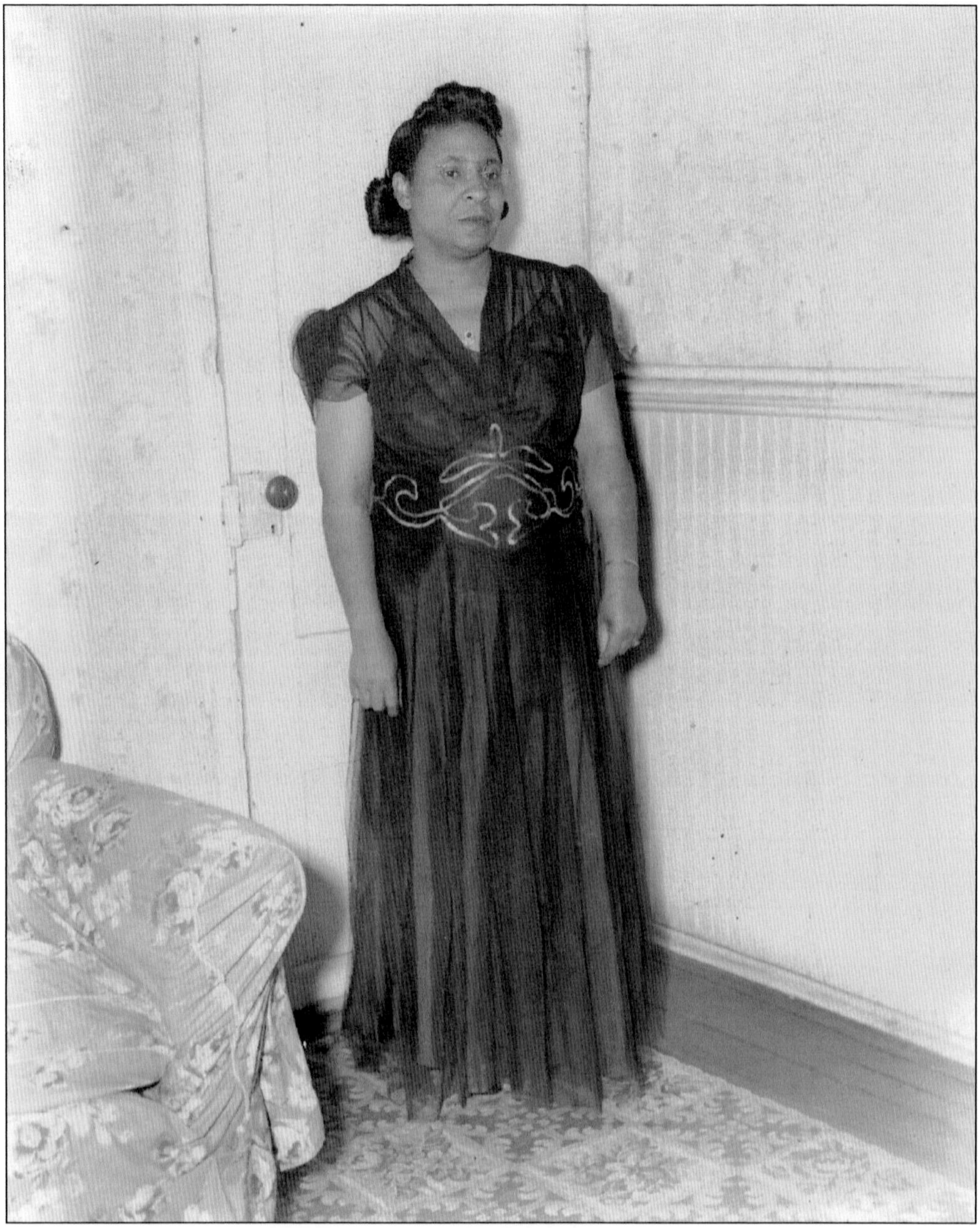

Julia Witherspoon is pictured in 1940. During those years there were not many events for African-American women to dress in evening attire; the occasion for this formal wear is not known.

James and Geneva Brown Mays married in 1951. They taught at the Scott's Branch High School during the 1950s. They were both terminated from their teaching positions in the Summerton school because of her father's support of the Civil Rights Movement.

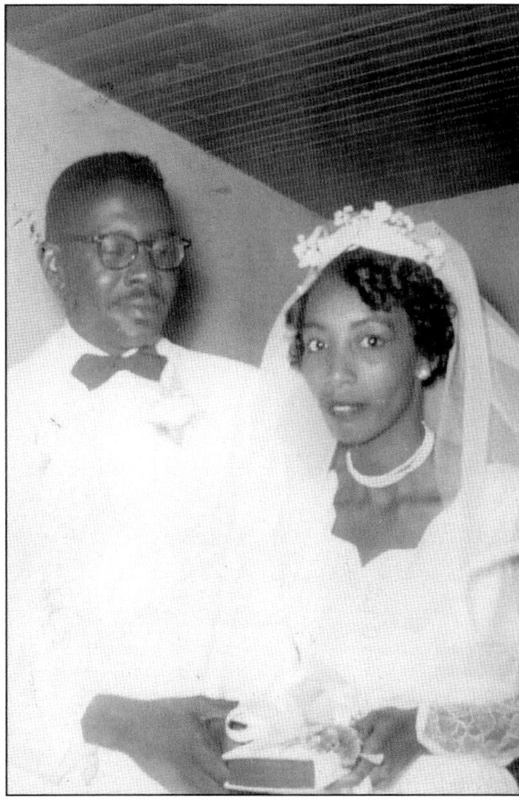

One hundred and thirty-one patrons at the Parkhill Theater on East Boyce Street line up for the showing of *The Ten Commandments*.

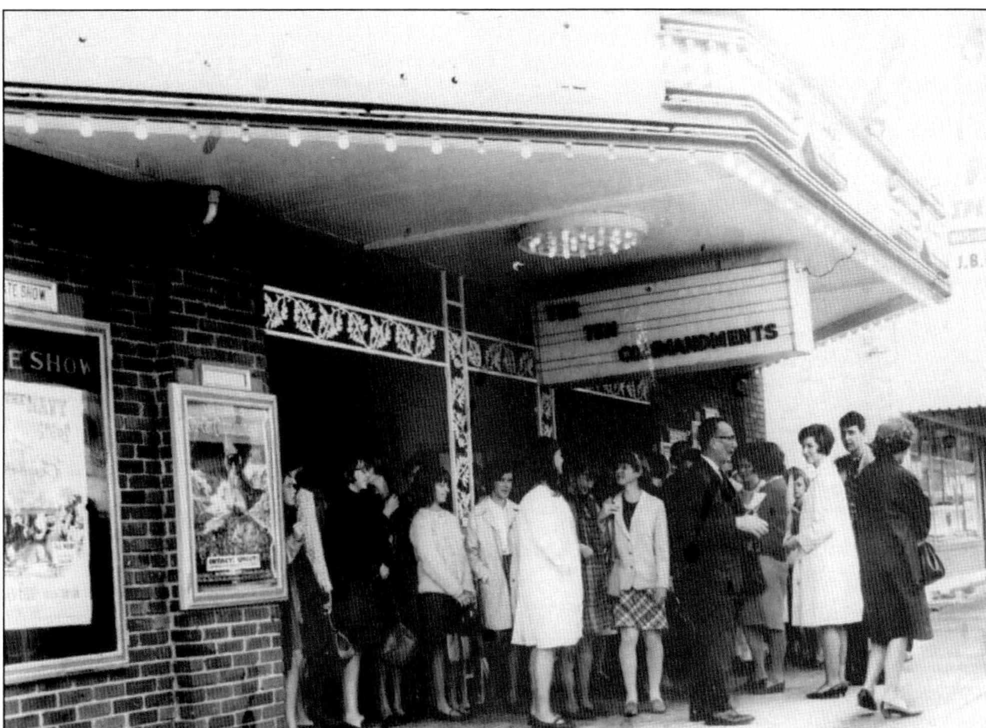

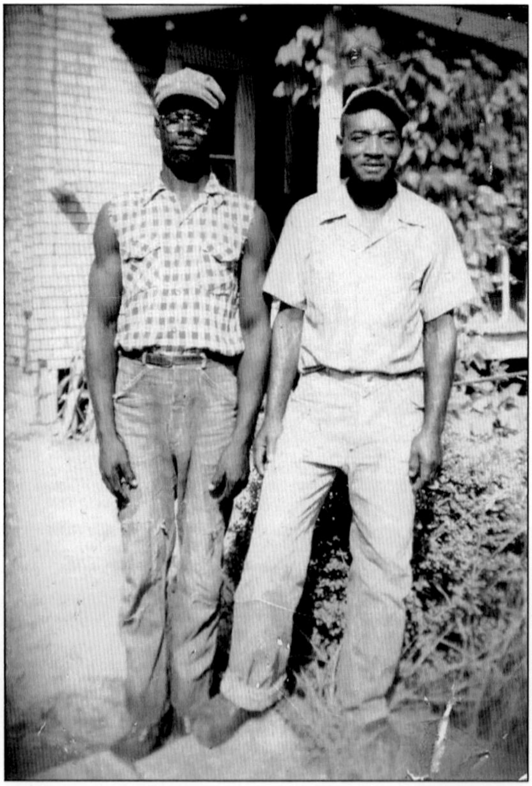

James A. Bethune and his friend, Moultre Hayworth, pose for the camera around 1950.

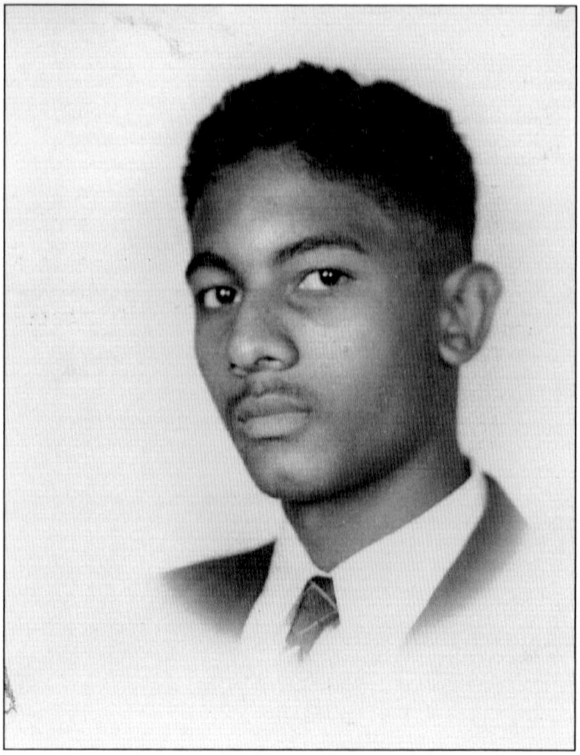

Reverdy Wells was the valedictorian and president of the class of 1949 at Scott's Branch High School. As president, he assumed the leadership role for the class and proposed the removal of the school principal.

Beatrice Brown and her daughter Vera of Summerton are seen in 1910. Beatrice was a loving mother of eight children. Her home was a gathering place for the children of the community.

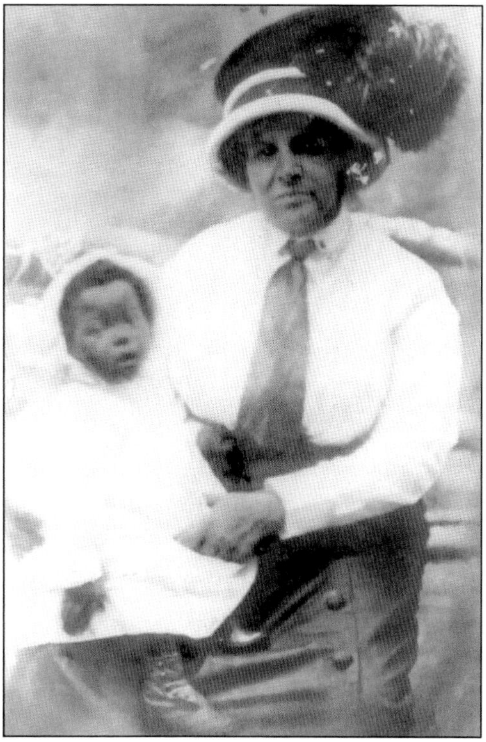

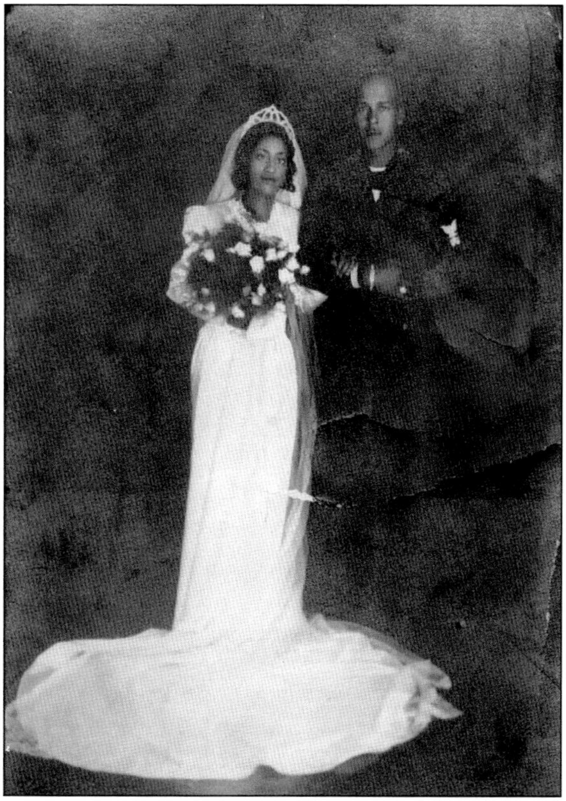

William and Thelma Ragin were married in 1941. The both taught at a public school in the Summerton area.

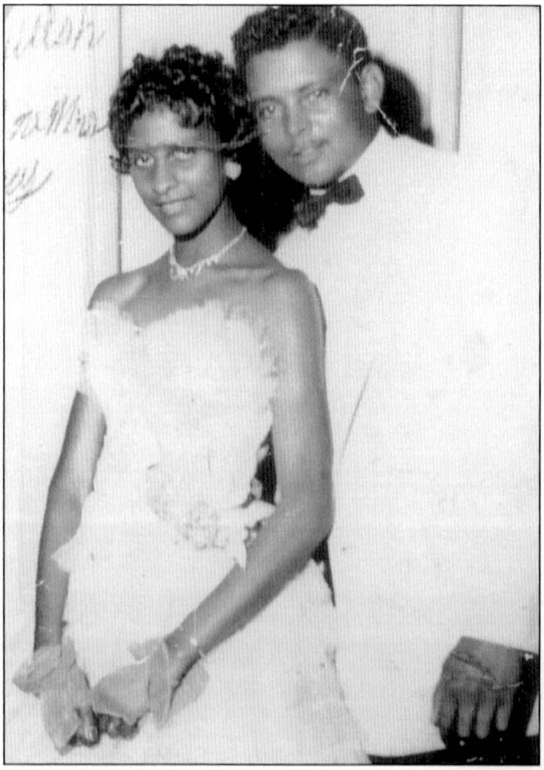

Joe and Susie Anderson Henry attended her high school prom in 1950.

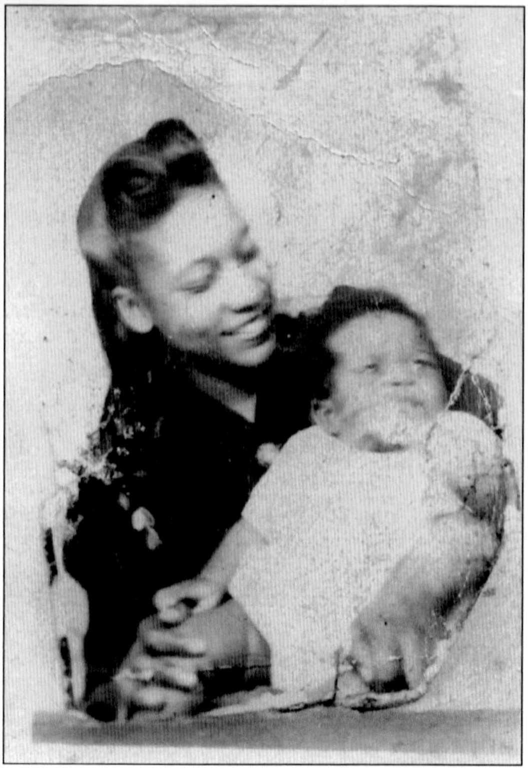

LaNelle Samuels shows off her infant son, Hayes Jr., in this 1940 photograph. She taught for many years in the Clarendon County schools.

This formal picture, evidenced by the hat and gloves, is typical of the 1940s. African-American women wore hats with flair and distinction.

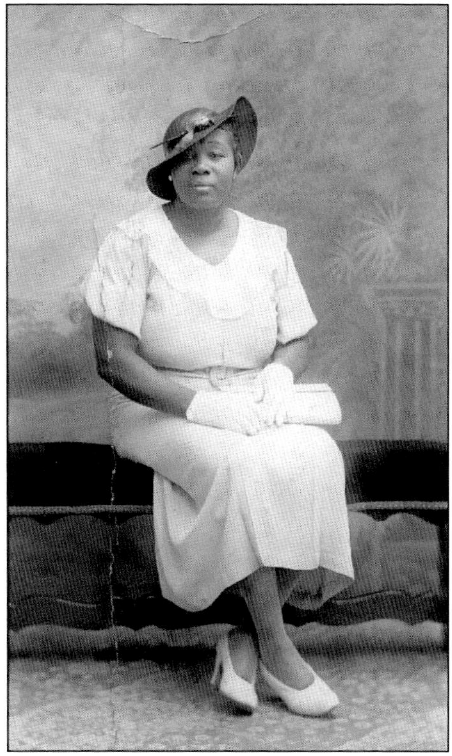

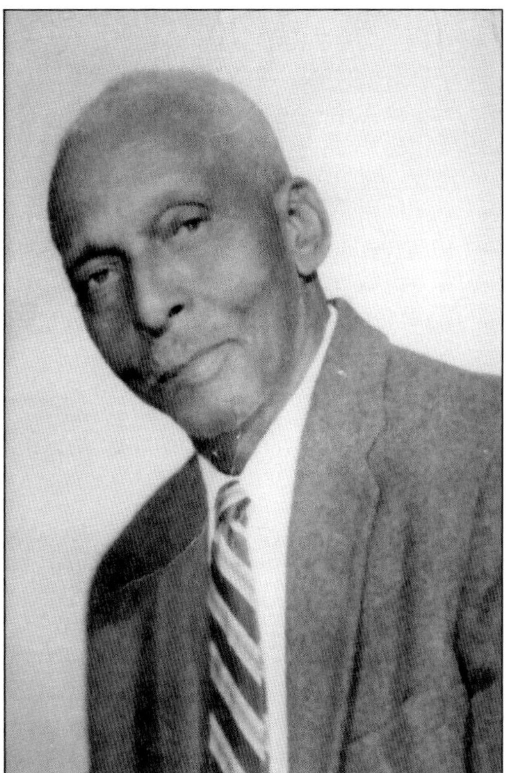

Rufus Ragin, a farmer and native of Summerton, is pictured c. 1948. His wife is pictured on page 80.

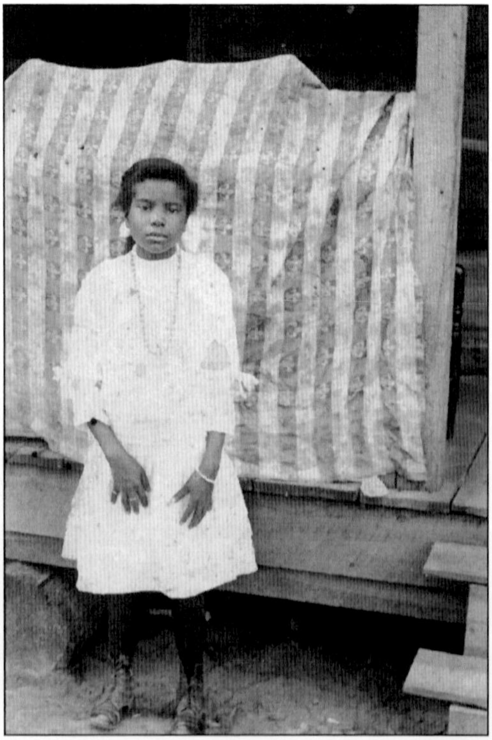

An unknown girl is pictured standing in front of her home.

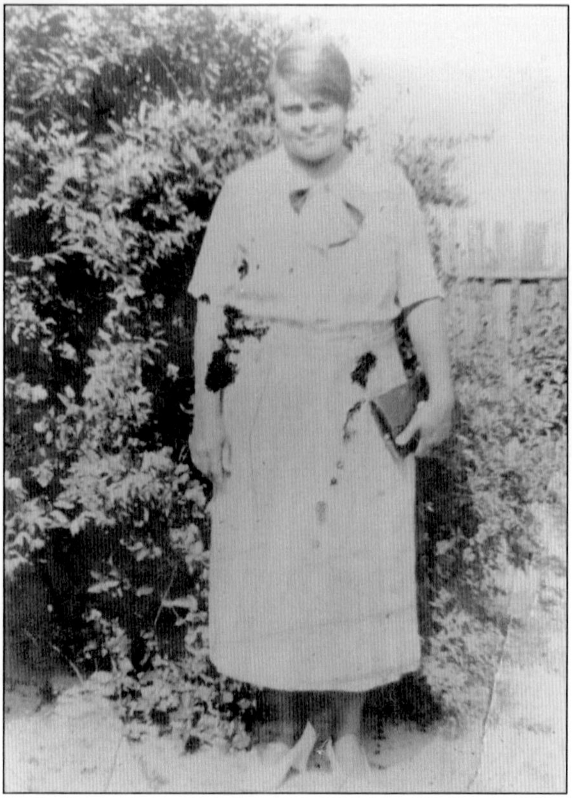

Mrs. M.C. Warley was fondly remembered by children as "the lady with the candy store" in the St. Paul area, *c.* 1920.

Hampton Anderson Sr. poses with cigar in hand in 1939.

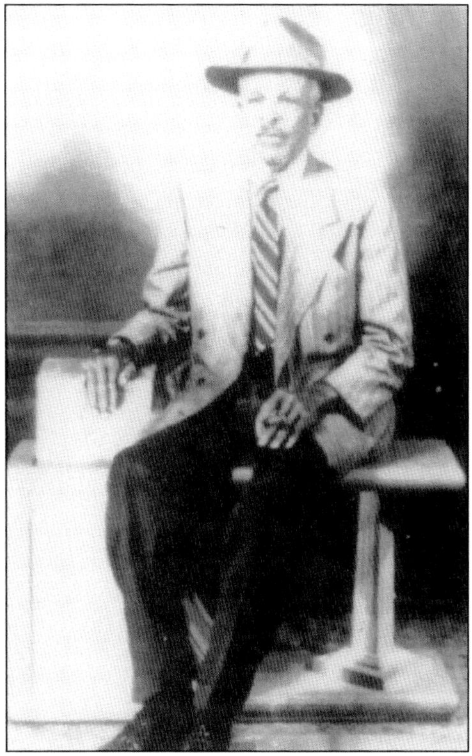

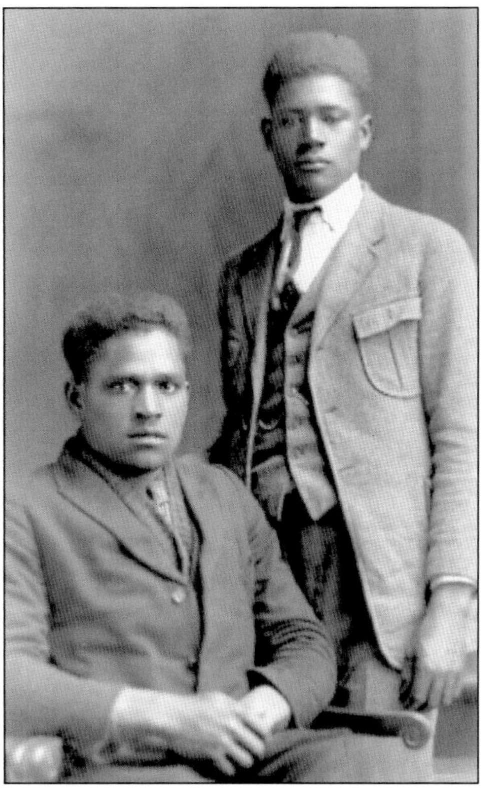

Lewis De Laine and his nephew, Henry Coe of Manning, are captured on film in 1920.

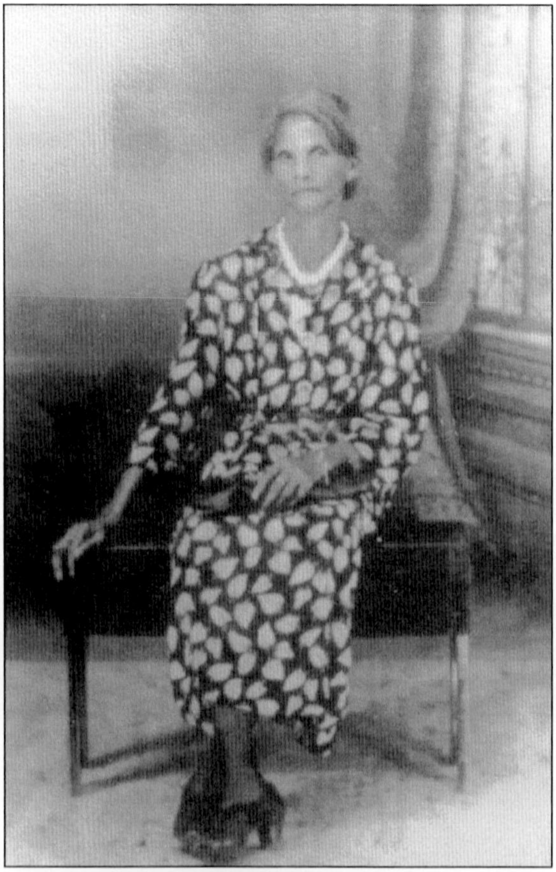

Irene Palmer Anderson of Summerton sits for the camera in 1939

The Tourist Inn is located in Manning on U.S. Route 301. Establishments such as these were prevalent in many small towns before the proliferation of motels. These inns as well as other public facilities in the south were restricted to whites only.

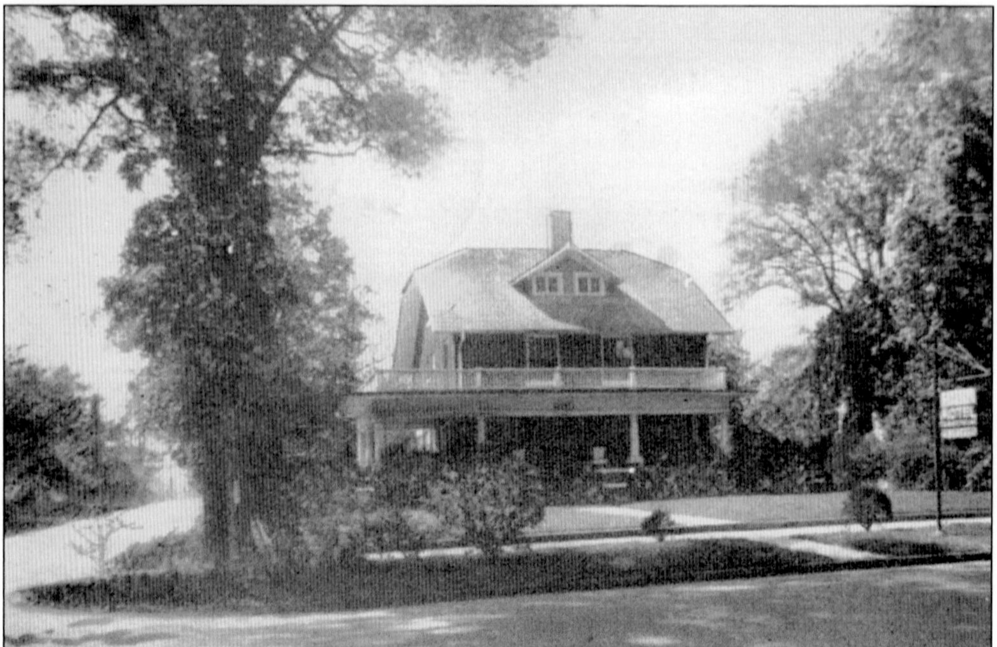

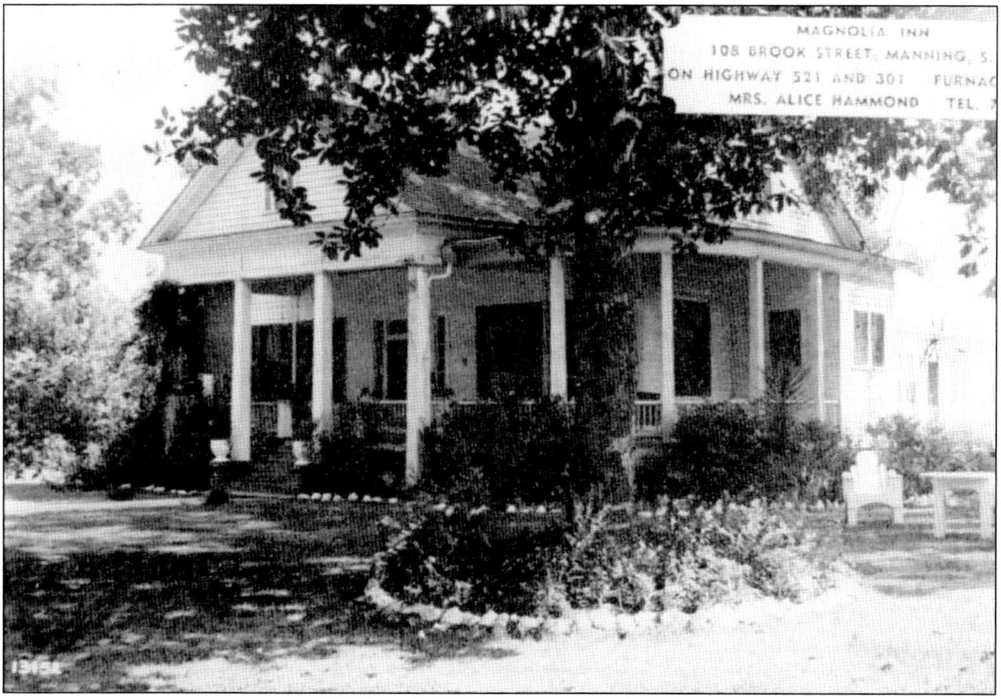

The Magnolia Inn located in Manning on Route 301 is another example of tourist inns located on major road arteries.

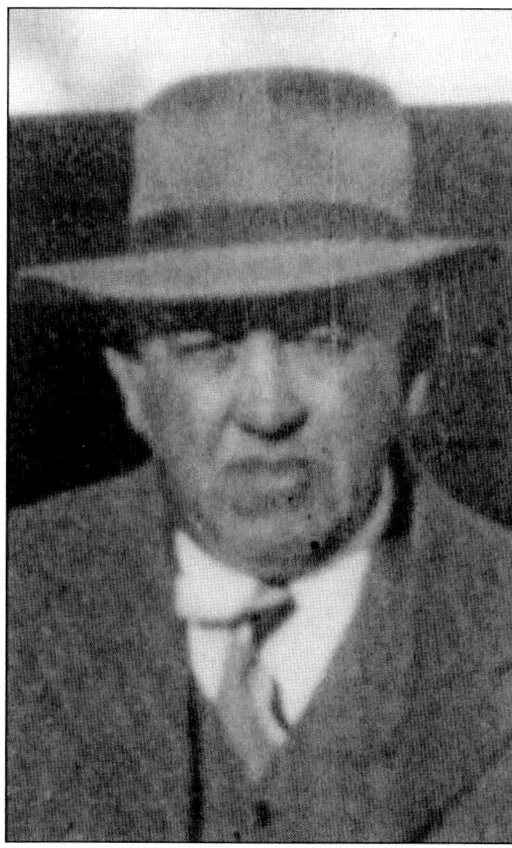

Charlie McDonald operated one of the larger farms in the county. His daughters are pictured on page 90.

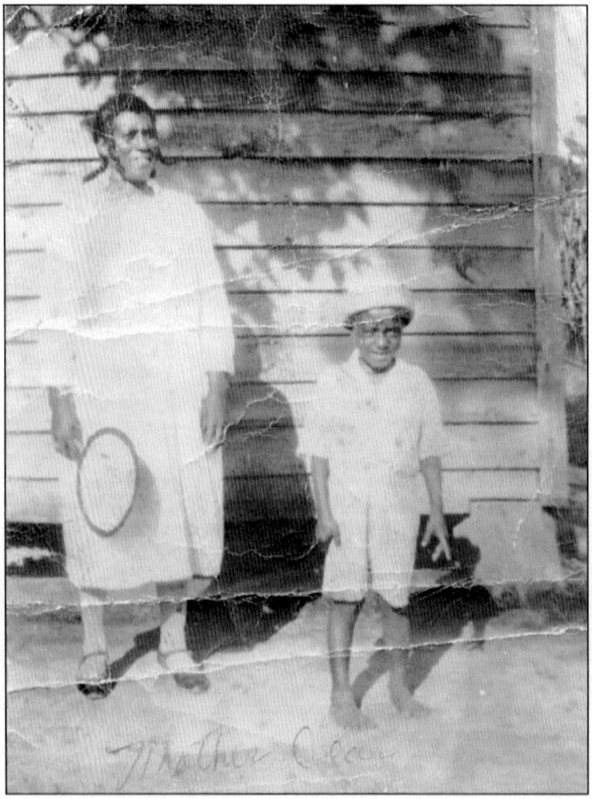

Charlotte Ragin Richardson and her daughter, Gussie, stop for a moment to be captured on film in the yard of their home in Summerton. Rural women frequently carried fans during the summer months, primarily to keep flies, gnats, and mosquitoes away.

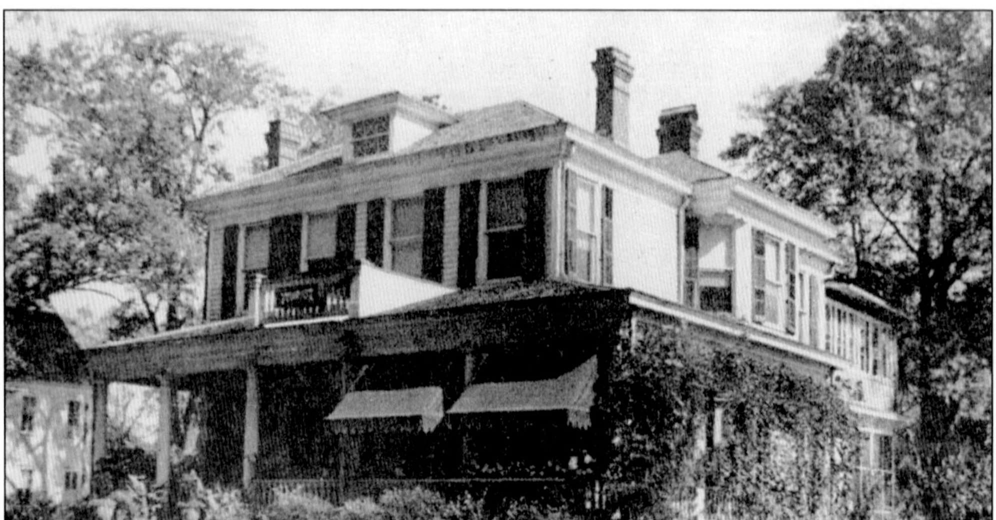

Lesesne Lodge on Highway 301 in Manning was a popular stopping place for tourists traveling north and south on this artery. Lodges like the Lesesne were the forerunners of today's motels. Popularity of the Manning lodges and inns declined with the opening of Interstate 95.

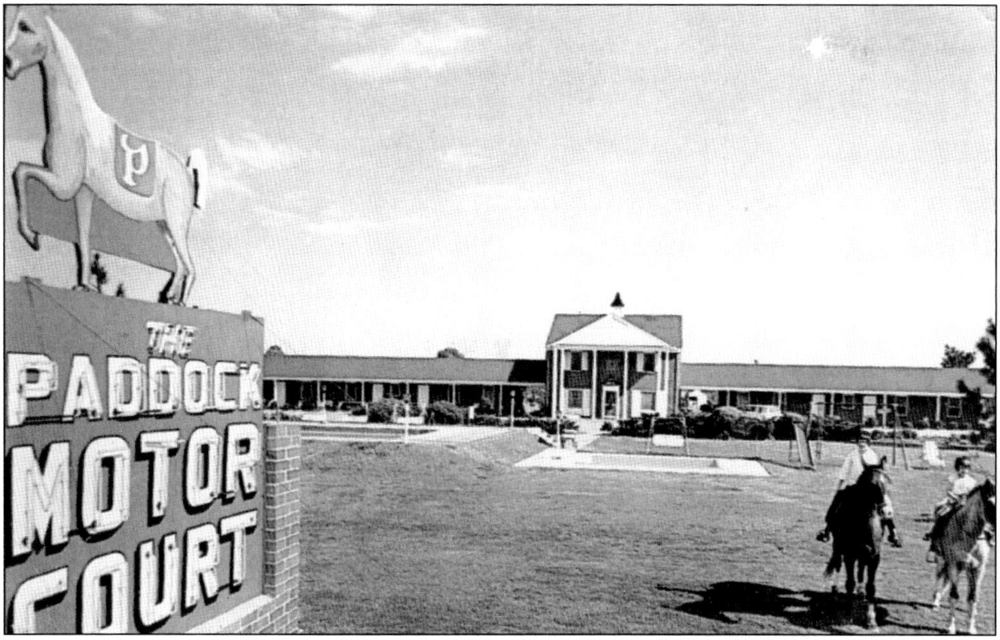

Located in the Summerton area, The Paddock Motor Court welcomed guests traveling on U.S. Route 301. Children had the opportunity to taking pony rides during their stay.

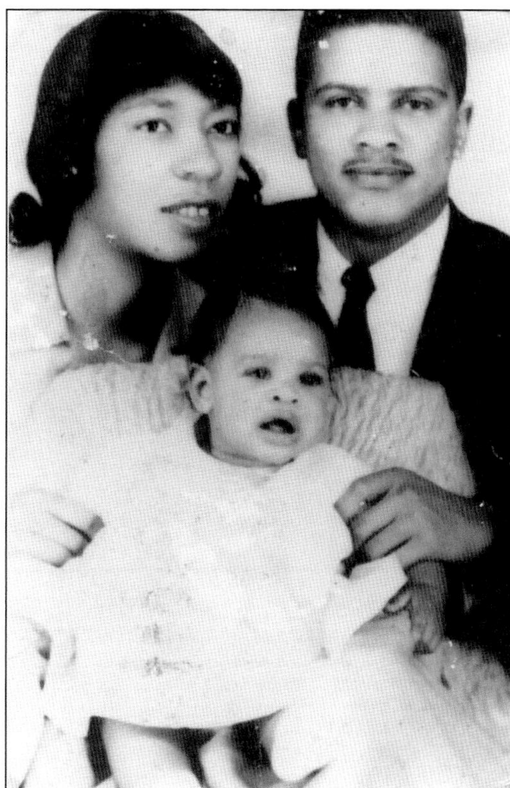
Joe L. Anderson is pictured here with his wife and infant child in 1948.

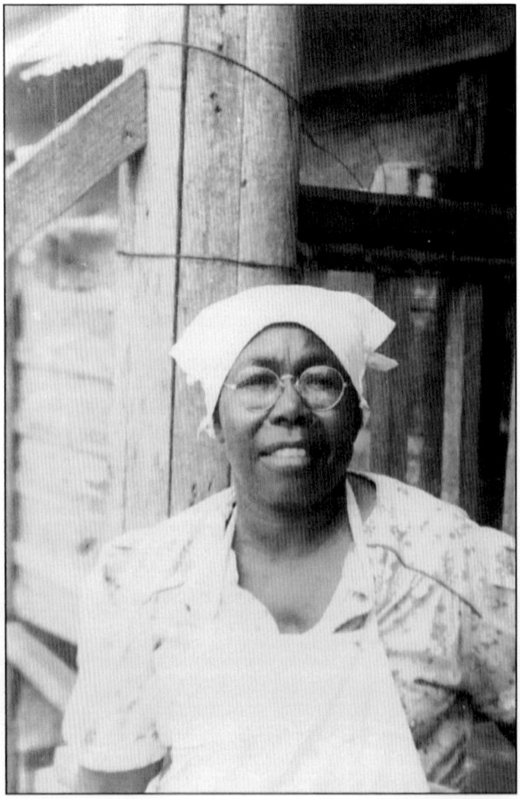

Laura Briggs, shown here *c*. 1940, is the mother of Harry Briggs Sr., who was one of the petitioners from Clarendon County in the *Briggs* school desegregation case.

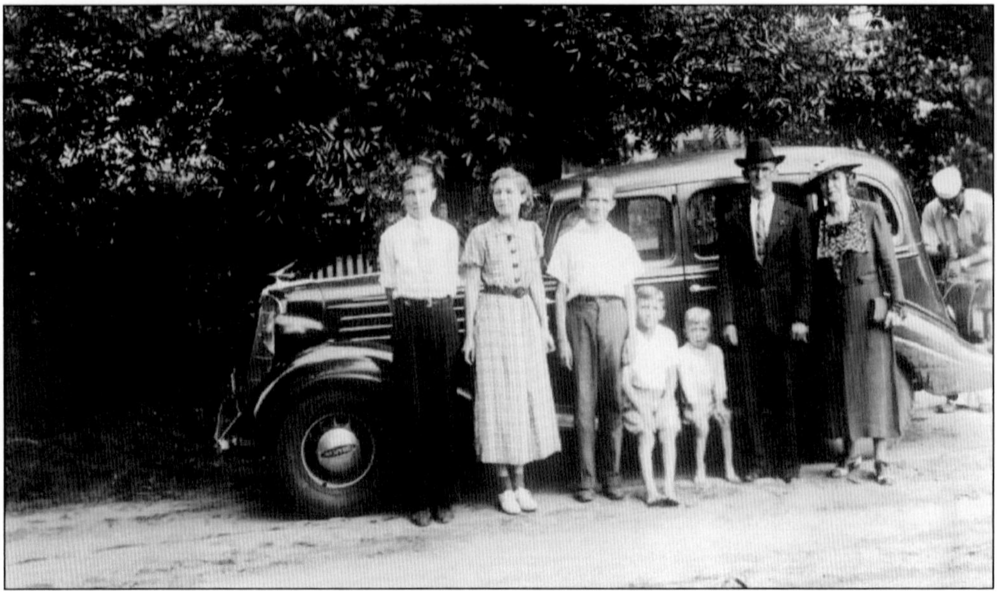

Rev. Roy Brown of Manning and his family gather for a family picture in 1937.

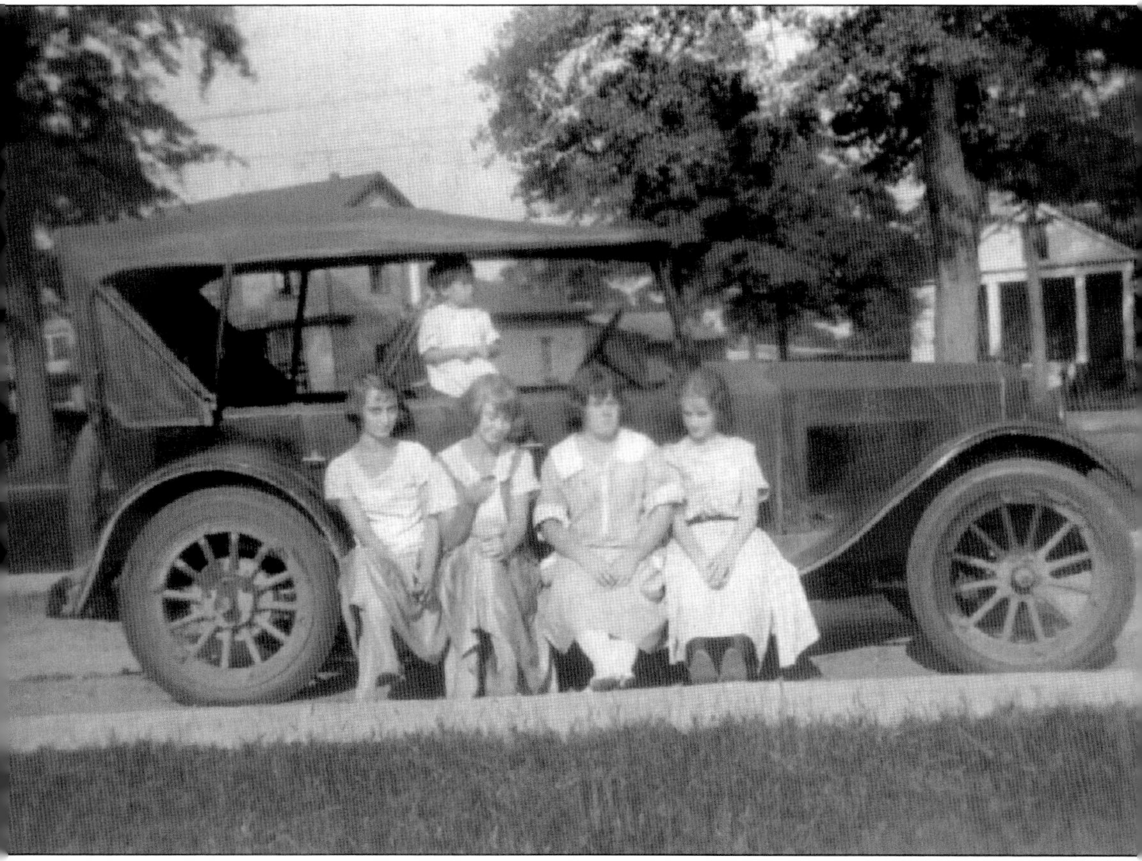

Winnie Plwden (Green) and friends pose for a photograph by the automobile in Manning.

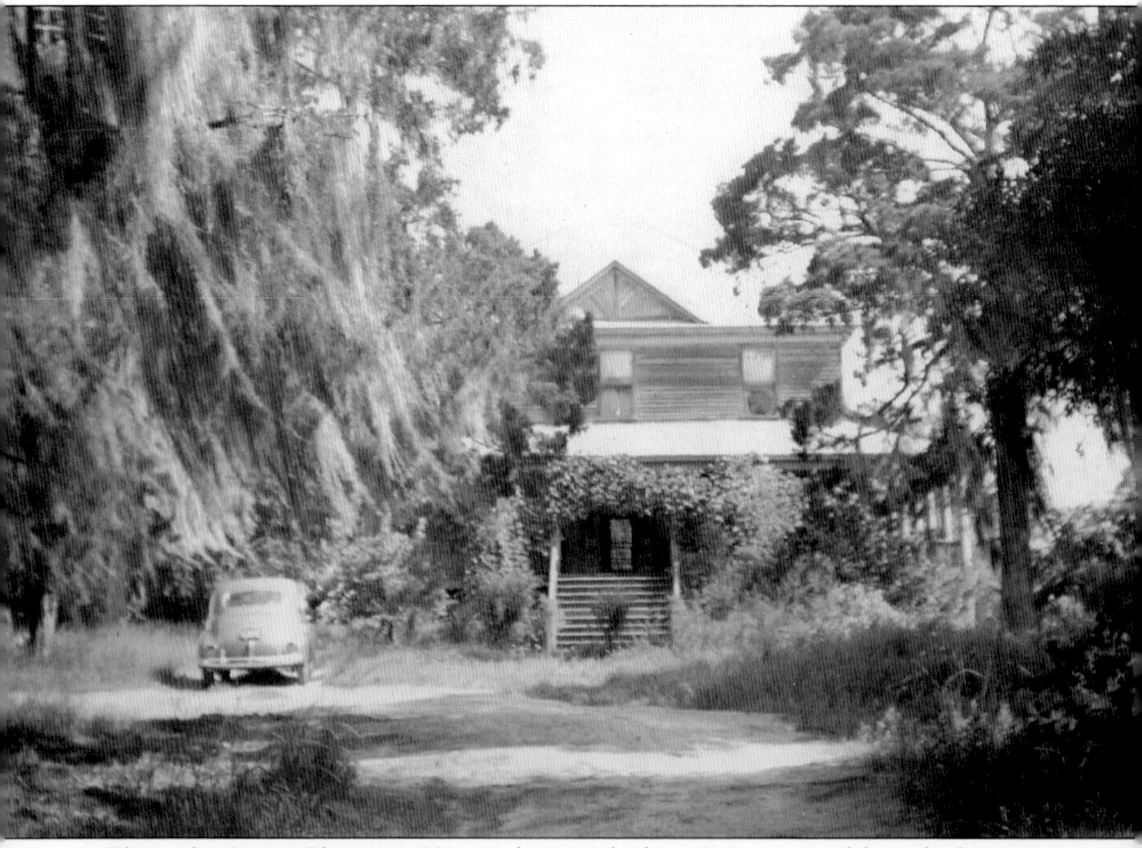

This is the Cantey Plantation House, photographed in 1945, as viewed from the lane entering the property. Note the moss-covered trees that are typical of the surrounding area. The main portion of the home (excluding the porch) was built around 1790.

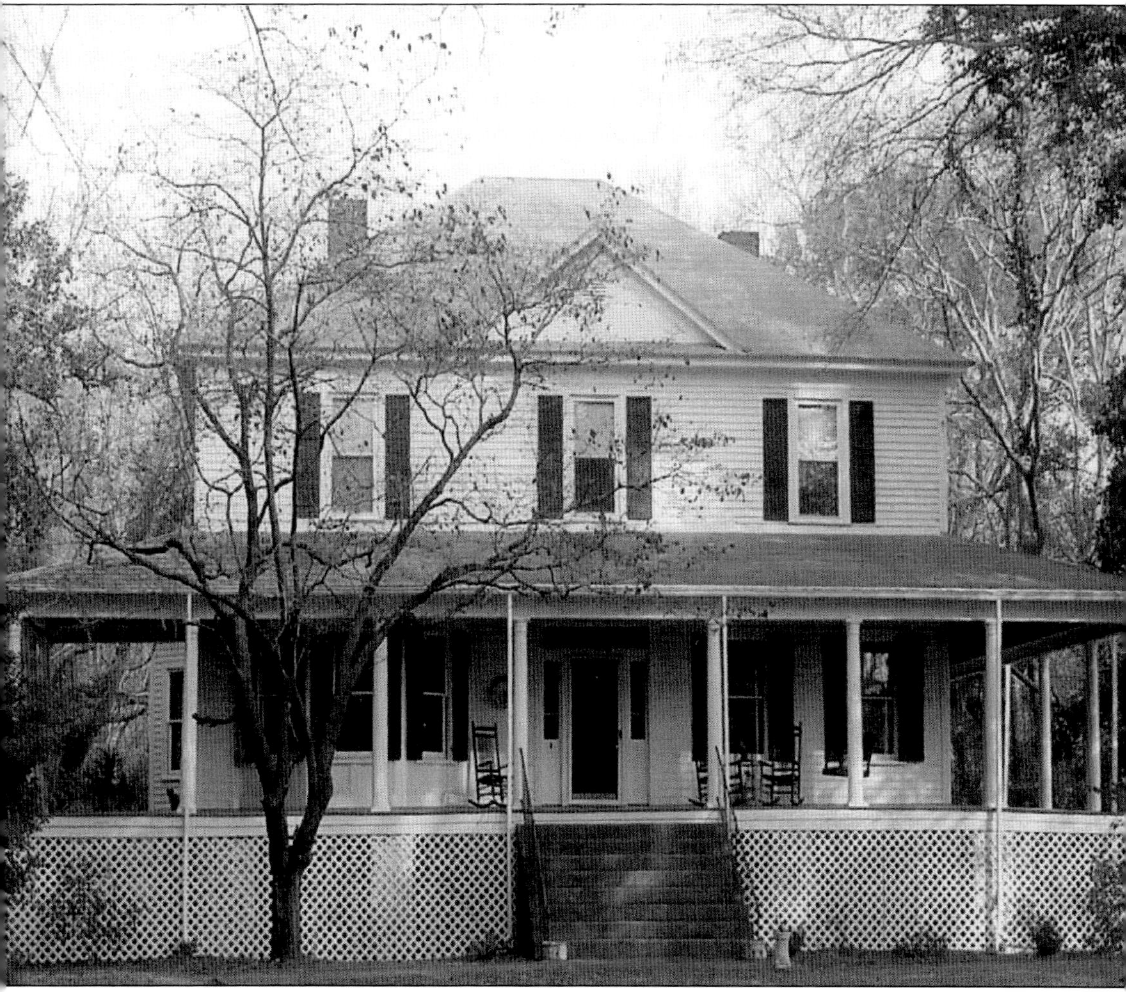

Descendants of the original owners are the present owner/occupants of the Cantey House. Mr. and Mrs. Joe Elliott recently restored the structure as a modern residence. The house is located in the town of Summerton.

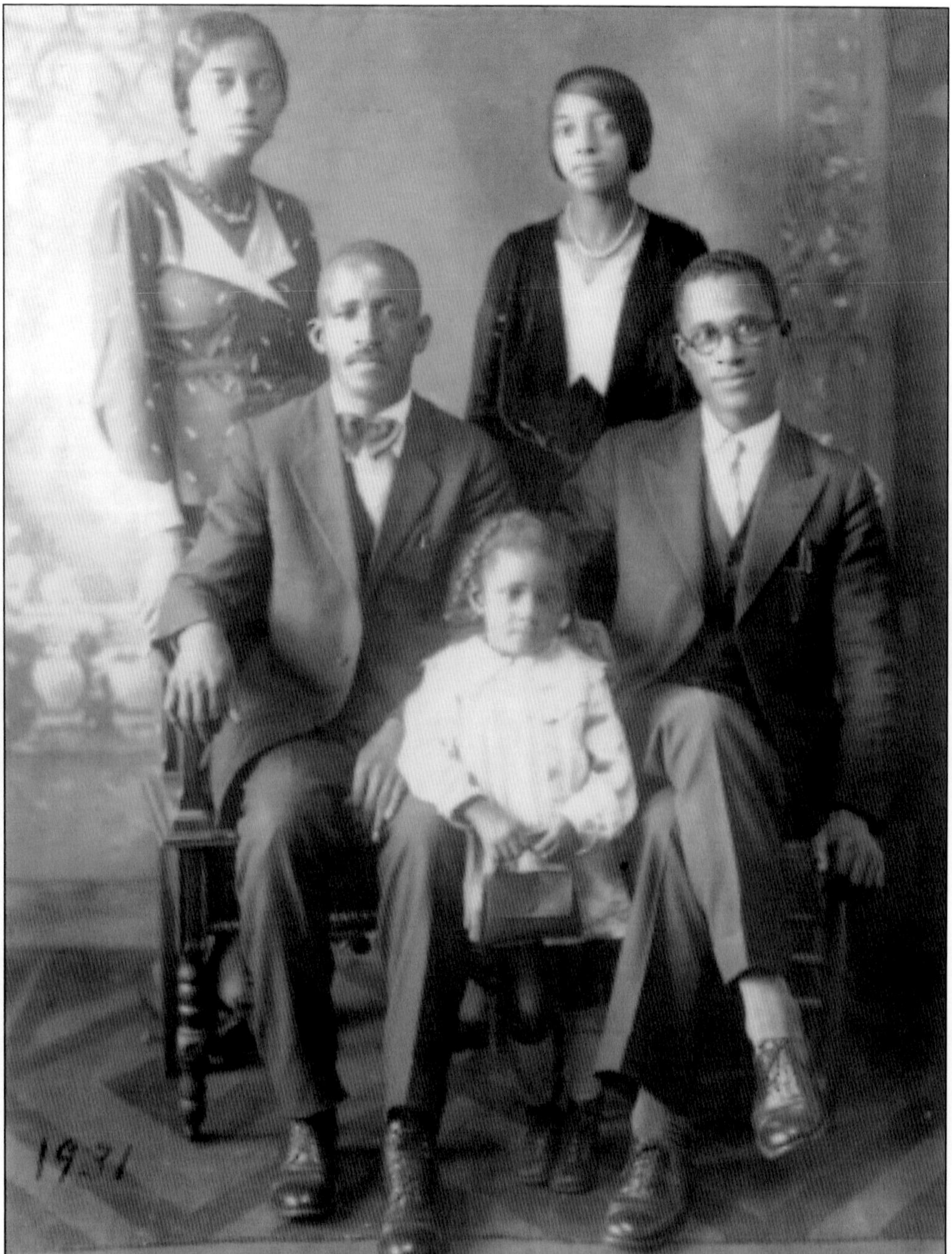

This is a photo of the Oliver and De Laine families in 1931. Pictured from left to right are (front row) William Oliver, Gwendolyn Oliver, and Rev. J.A. De Laine; (back row) Wilvera De Laine (niece of the two men) and Mattie De Laine.

Levi Pearson is shown here *c*. 1950. Pearson, a local farmer in the Davis Station area, initiated a quest for bus transportation for black children in 1947, which ultimately led to a challenge on the legality of the "Separate but Equal" doctrine enforced in the south.

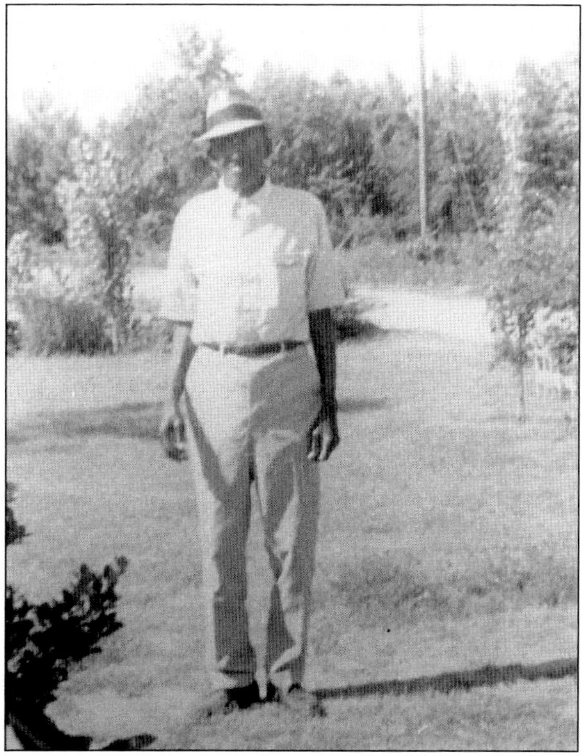

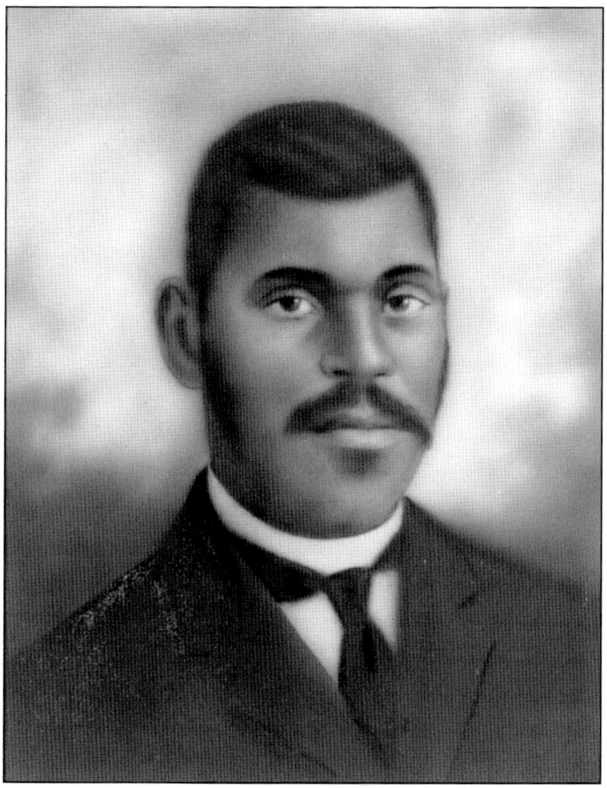

Rev. Henry Charles De Laine was pastor of Liberty Hill AME Church in Summerton for approximately 14 years between 1902 and 1916. He resided in Manning and was the father of Rev. J.A. De Laine. This photo was taken in 1880.

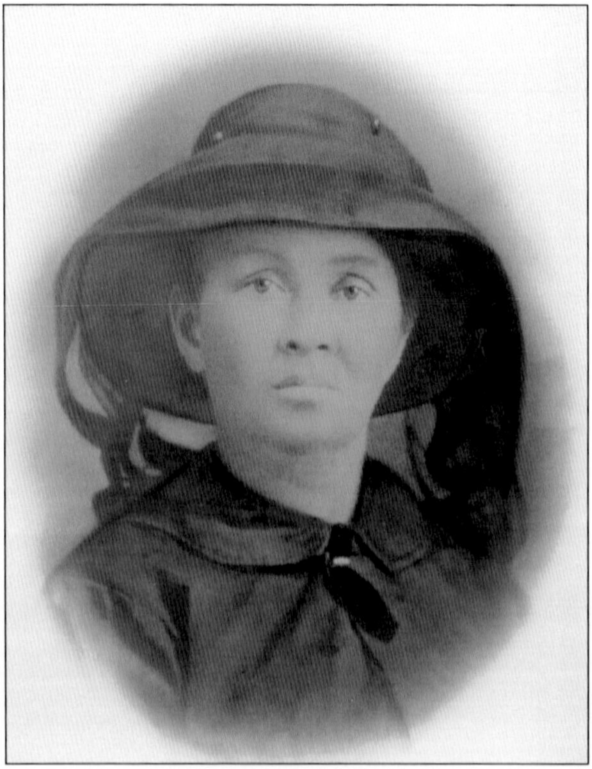

Tisbia Gamble De Laine was the wife of Rev. H.C. De Laine and the mother of Rev. J.A. De Laine. She is pictured *c.* 1920.

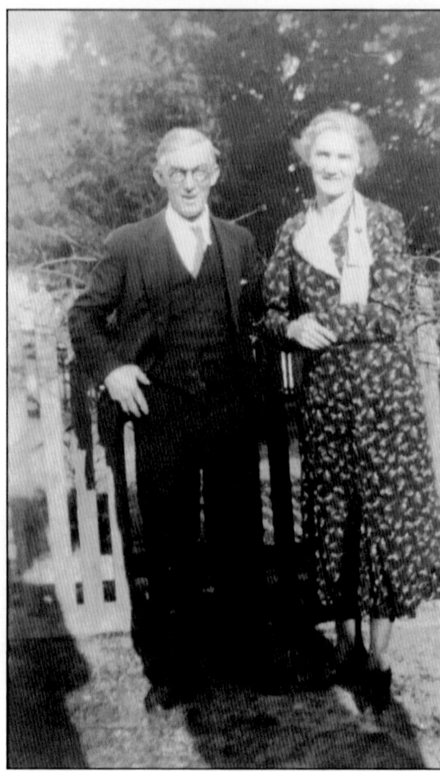

Ernest Rose and his wife, Vida Rose, are seen at their Manning home.

Rev. William Mood is a former pastor of the Manning Methodist Church.

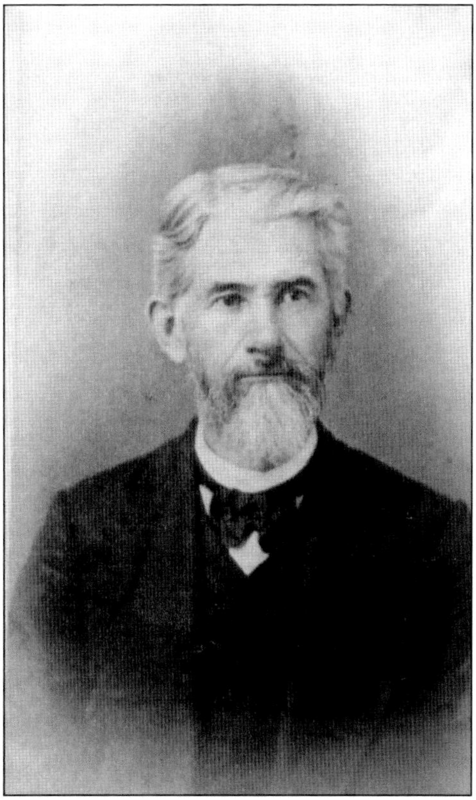

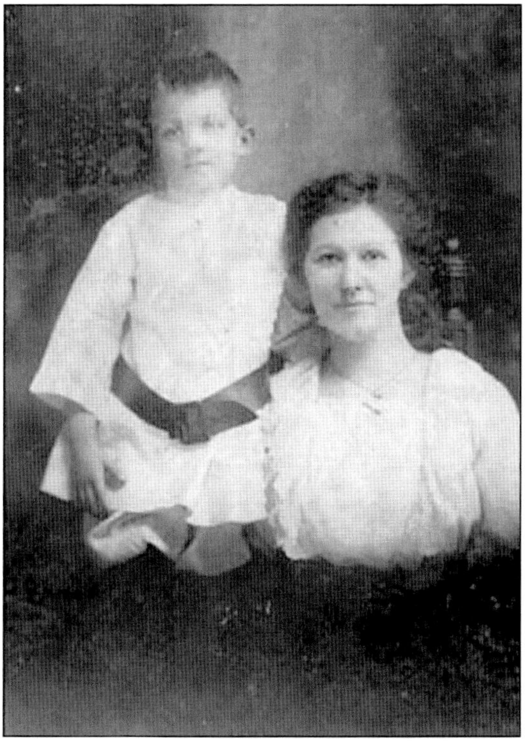

Arrie Rose Doty of Manning is pictured with her son.

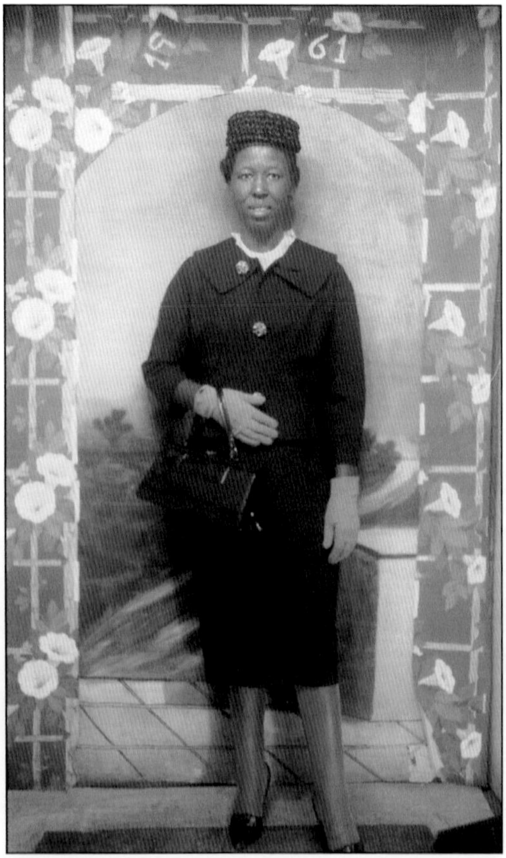

Etherlene Bethune is conservatively dressed for church in 1948.

This is a scene of Main Street (Brooks Street) in Manning. The date of the photograph is unknown, but the lack of automobiles on the street suggests that the picture may have been taken before cars became more than a novelty.

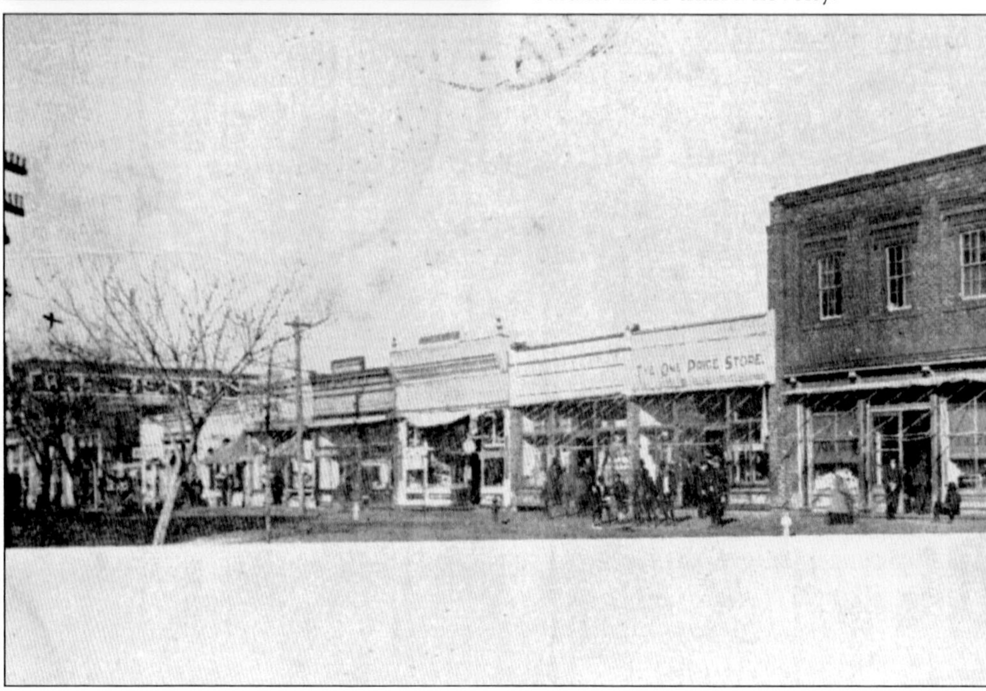

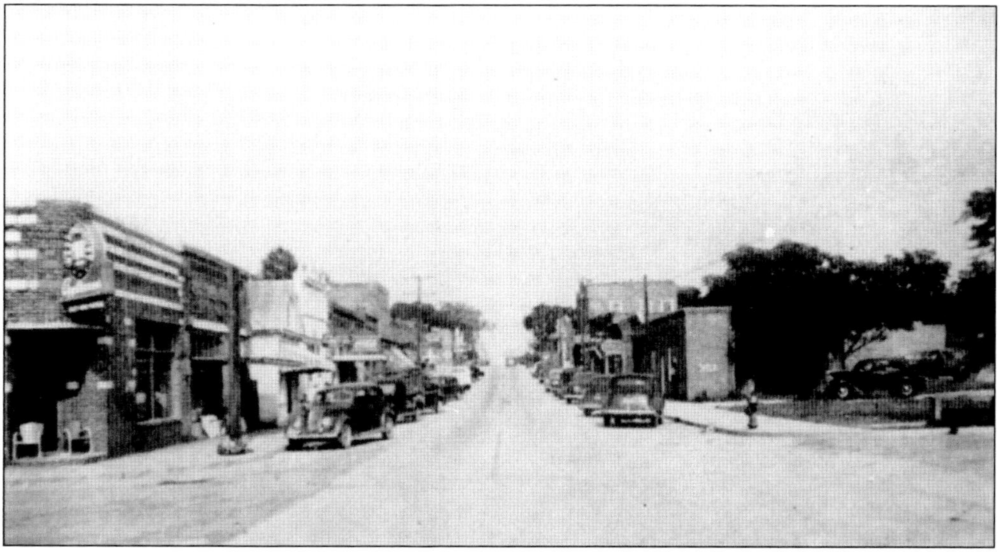

Main Street in Summerton is pictured as it appeared in 1939 or 1940. The street is U.S. Route 301 looking north toward Manning.

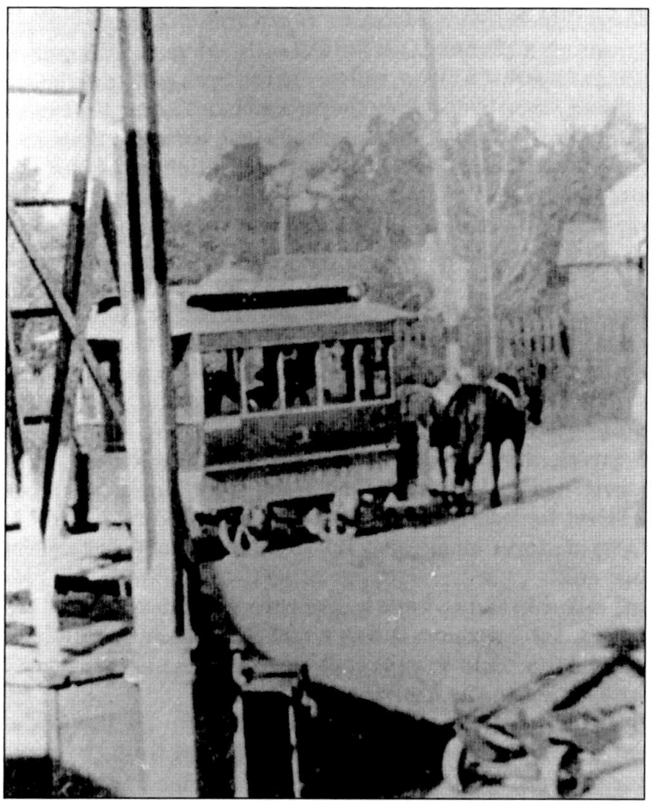

A horse-drawn trolley is captured on film as it traverses the streets of Manning.

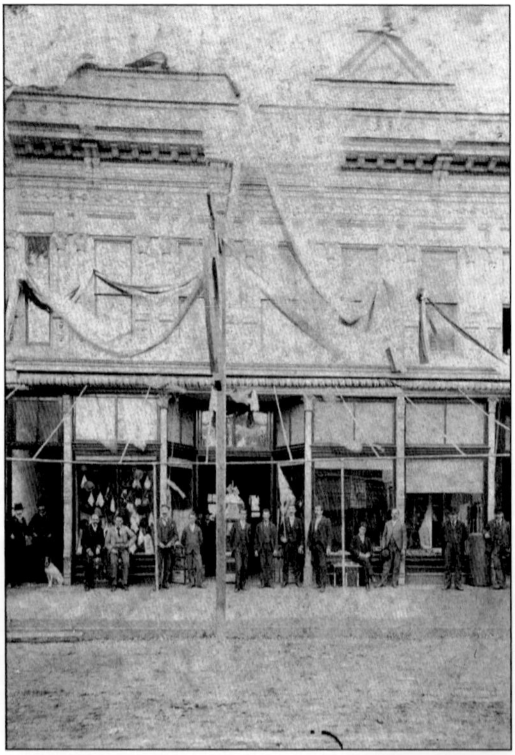

Once thought to be a photograph of "Alderman's 20 Stores in 1" on Brooks Street that opened in 1919, this building is representative of the style that proliferated in Manning prior to the turn of the 20th Century. Very few of those buildings survived the fire of 1894 and the tornado of 1915.

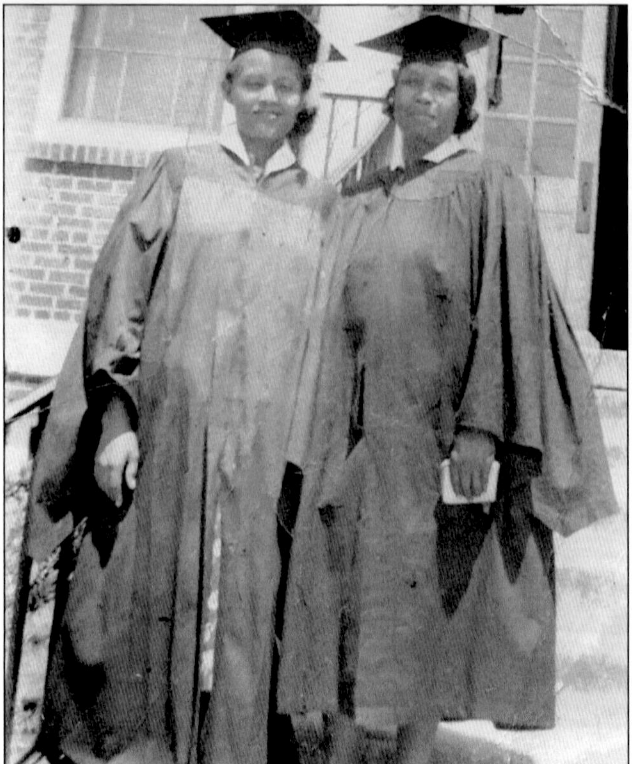

Lula M. Green De Laine and daughter Arlonial De Laine are both receiving their Bachelor's Degree from Allen University in 1949. They resided in Manning.

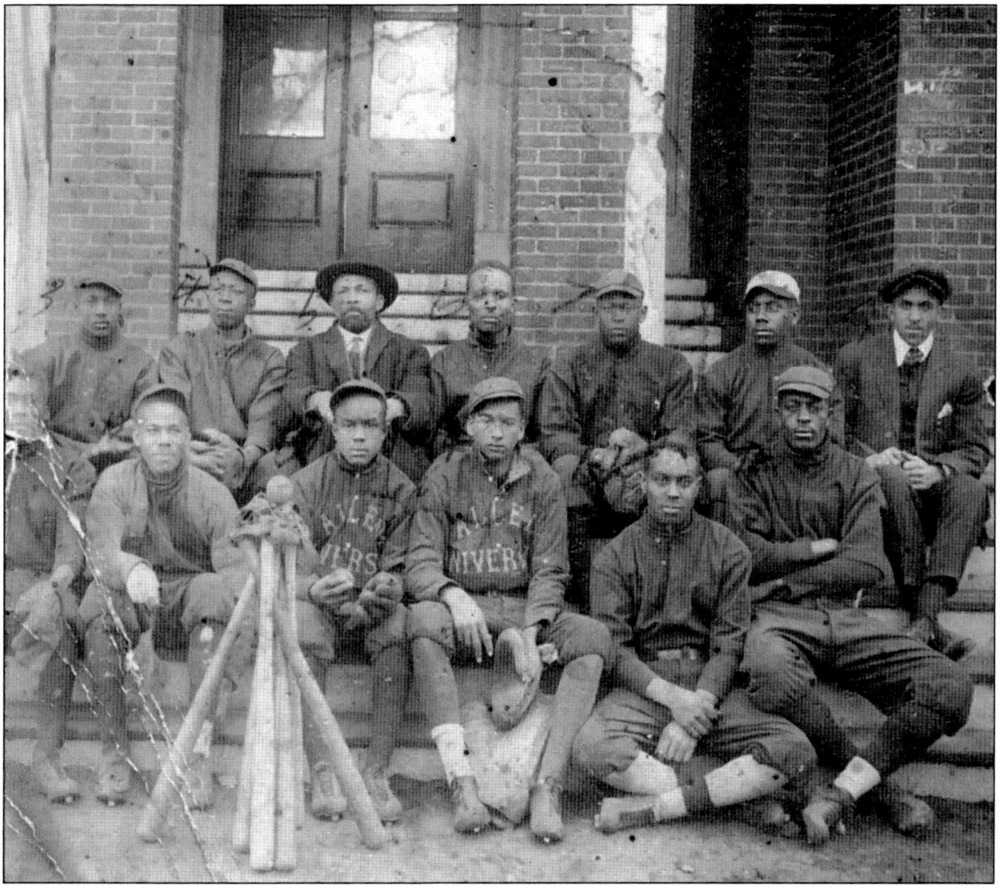

This photograph is of a baseball team believed to be from Clarendon County.

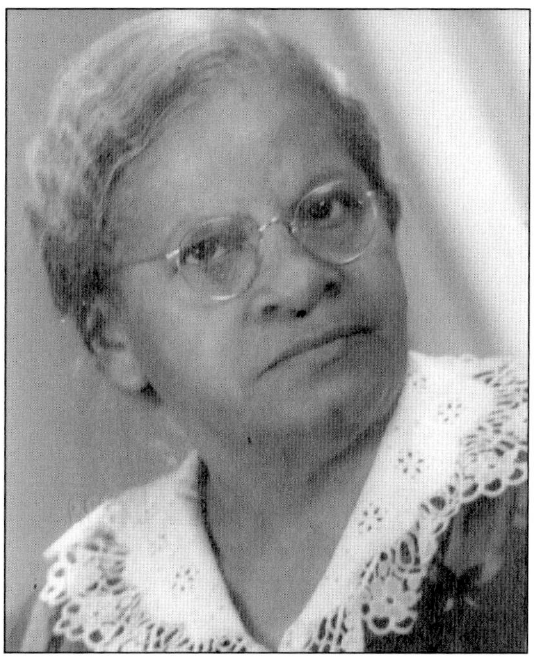

Josie Brown Ragin, shown here *c.* 1940, was a native of Summerton and taught at the Scott's Branch School for many years. Her husband was Charles Ragin.

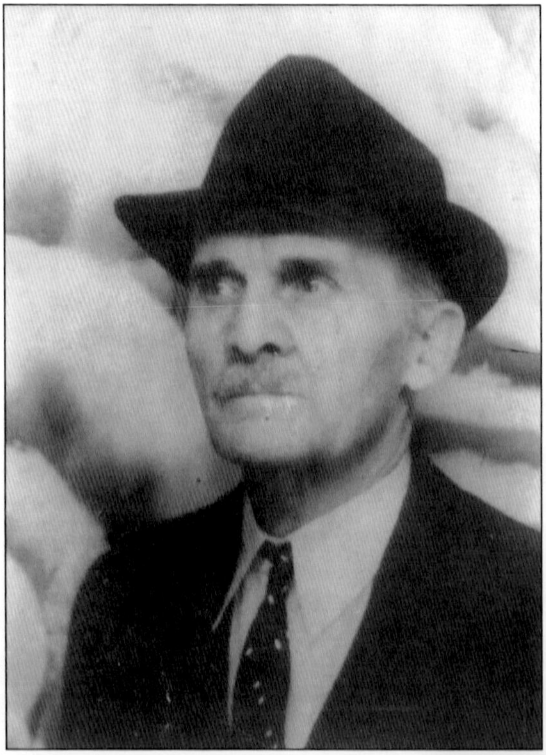

Charles Ragin was a farmer in the Summerton area. This photograph was taken around 1940.

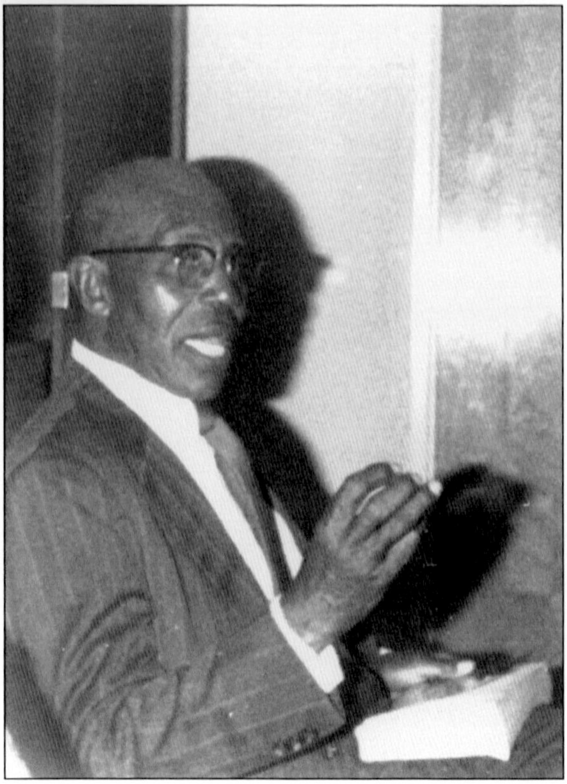

Joseph Lemmon was a farmer in the Jordan area and was active in the Civil Rights movements during the 1940s, 1950s, and 1960s.

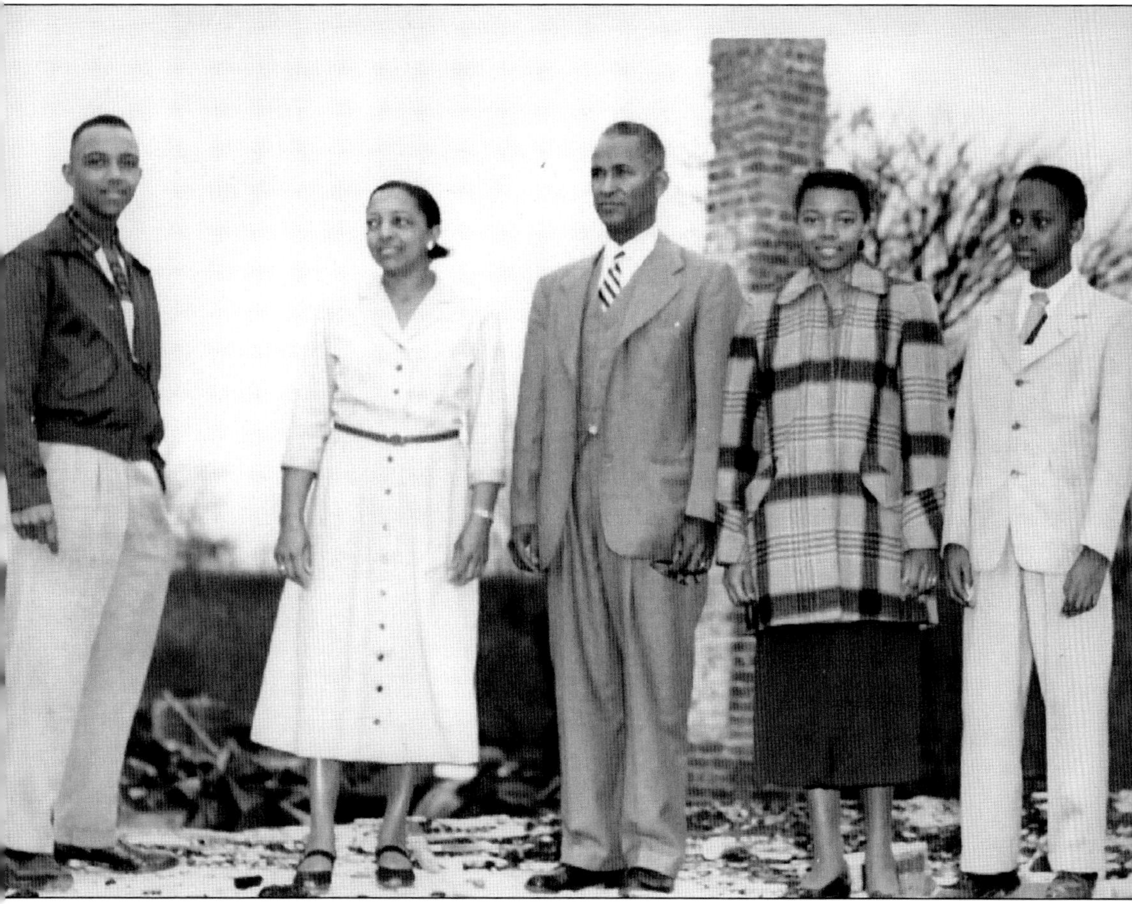

The family of Rev. J.A. De Laine stands in front of their home after it was destroyed by fire in 1951. It was widely believed that the destruction was caused by arson, resulting from Reverend De Laine's active role in the Civil Rights movements within the county. The fire department, although present, refused to extinguish the fire because the structure was a few feet outside of the town's border.

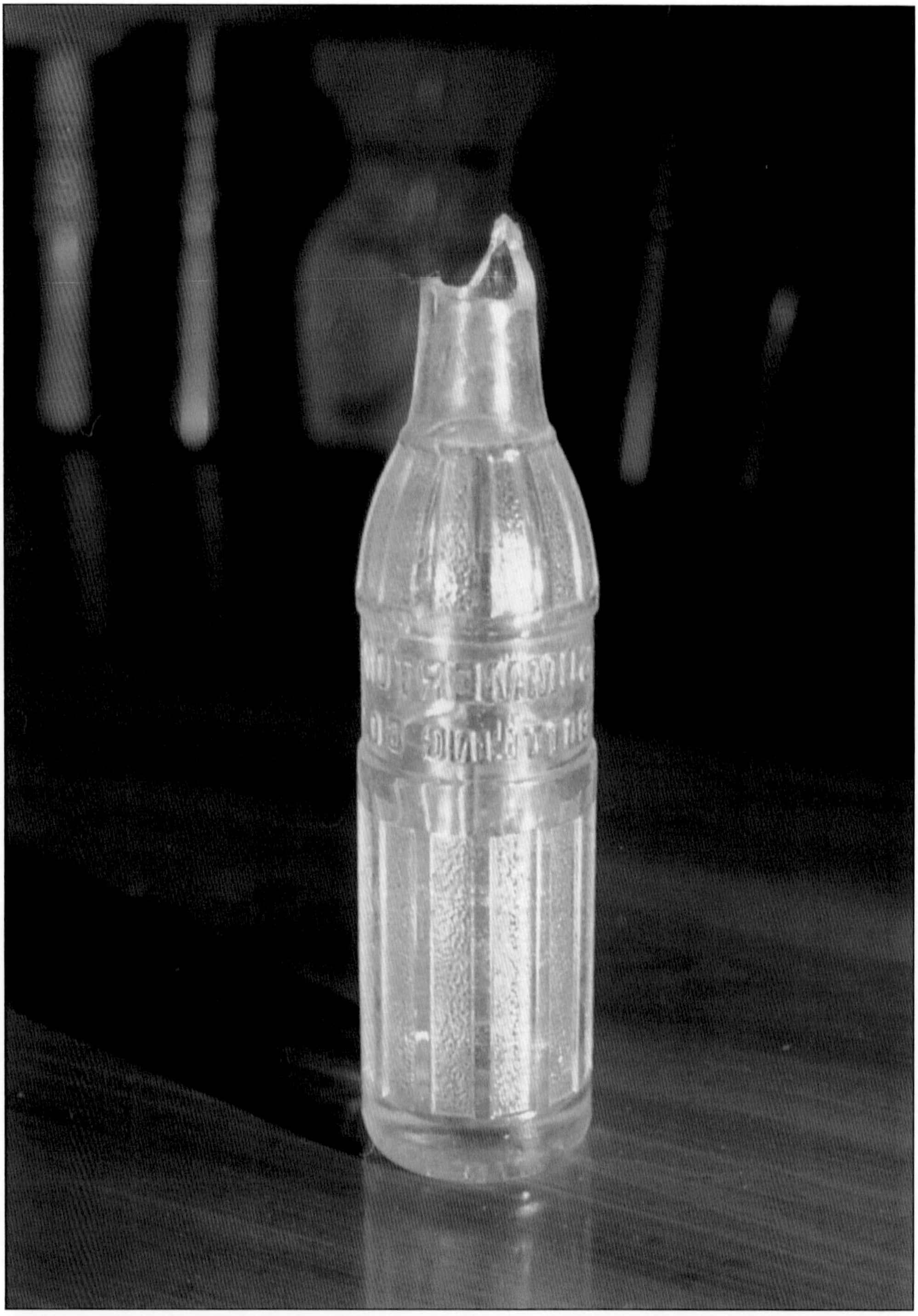

The inscription on this bottle suggests that it was manufactured in Summerton at least 100 years ago. During that era, there was a bottling plant adjacent to the Senn Grist Mill that produced soft drinks for the community. Joe Elliott recently found this bottle in the Scott's Branch Creek area.

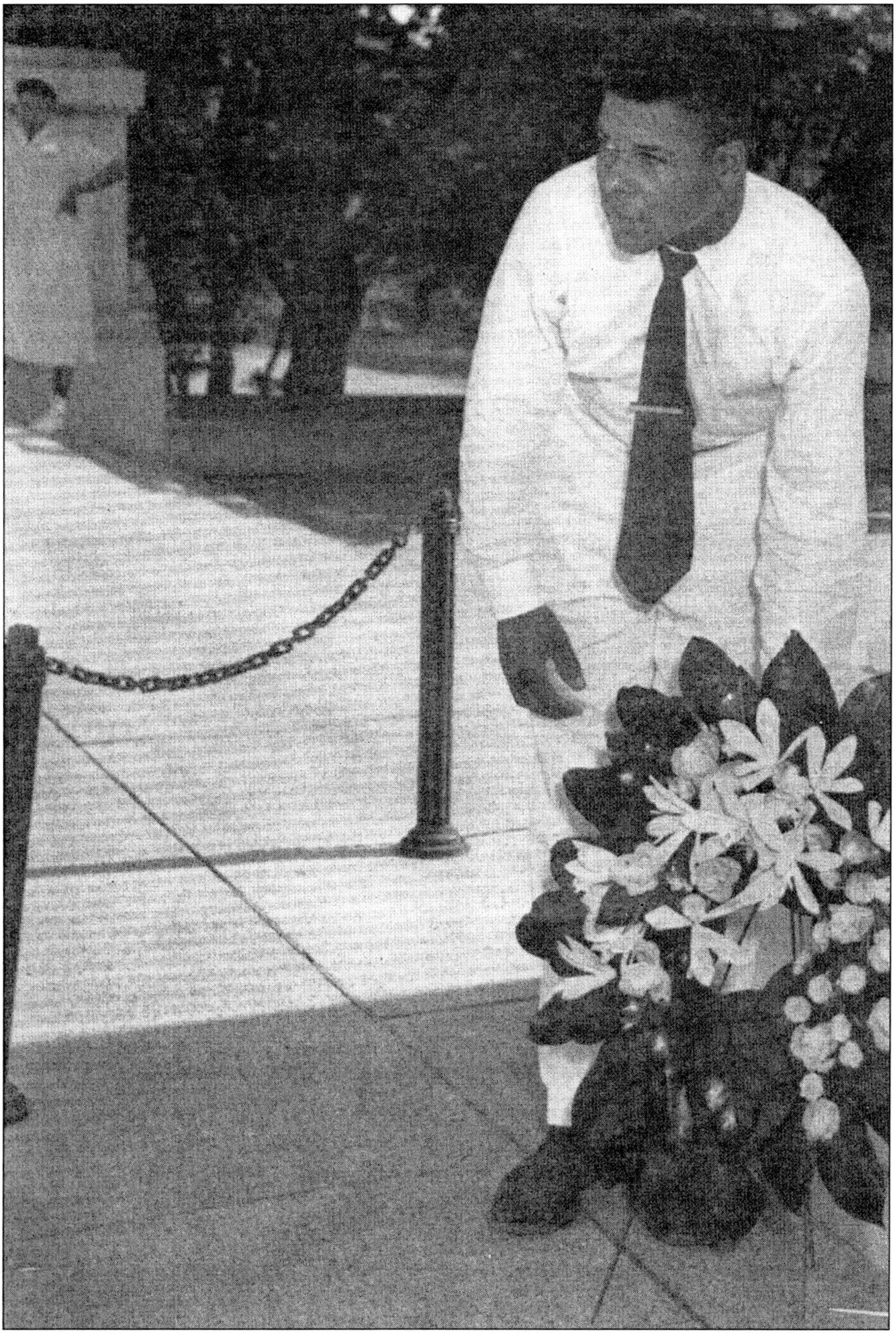

Willie Gibson, a resident of Clarendon County, places a wreath on the grave of the Unknown Soldier in Washington, D.C.

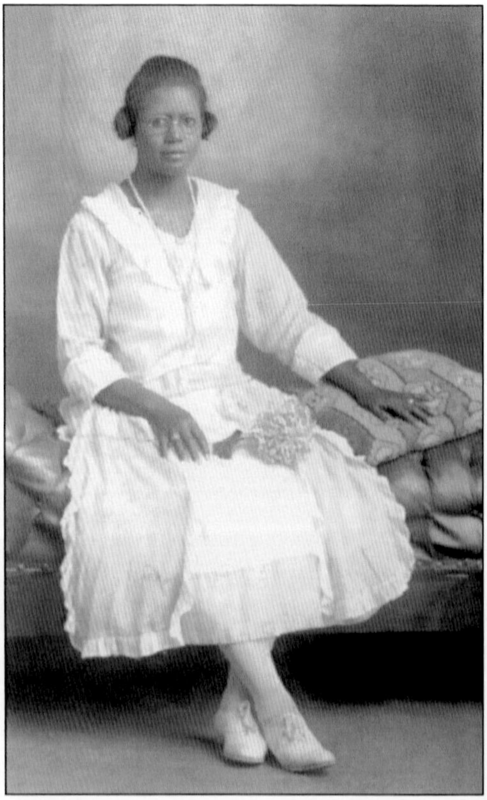

Lula Mae Green in this c. 1920 photograph is dressed in white lace with stockings and shoes. The picture was taken while she was in college. She later married Lewis De Laine and taught in public schools for 40 years.

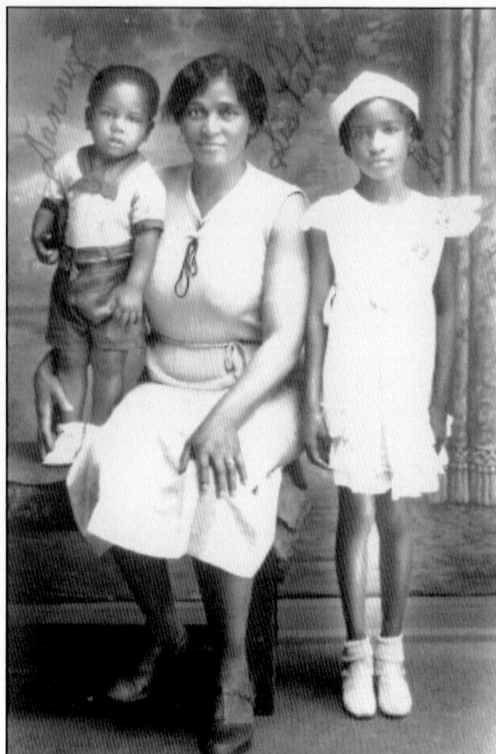

Arlonial De Laine Gibson Potter poses with her son, Danny, and niece, Gwendolyn Oliver. Potter was a beautician. She was unorthodox in many ways and had an independent spirit.

Luther and Lucille McDowell, residents of Manning, were the last members of Mt. Carmel Presbyterian Church before it closed in 1943. The Presbyterian Church was located on the corner of Church and Dinkins Streets. McDowell operated a barbershop in downtown Manning that catered to a white clientele.

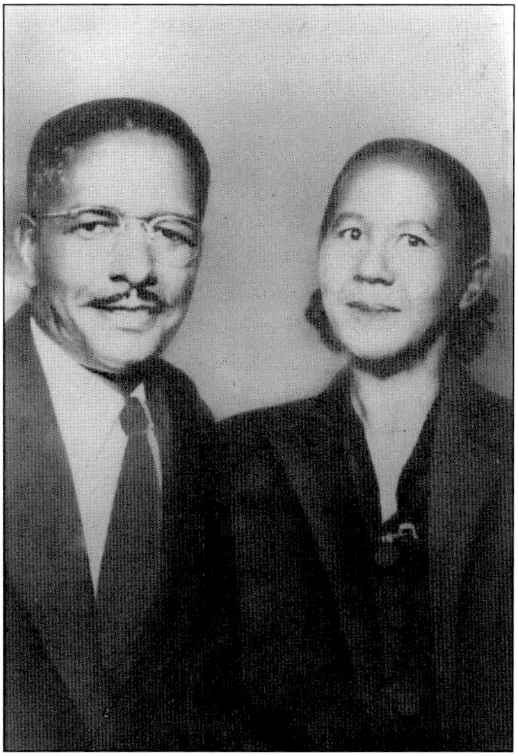

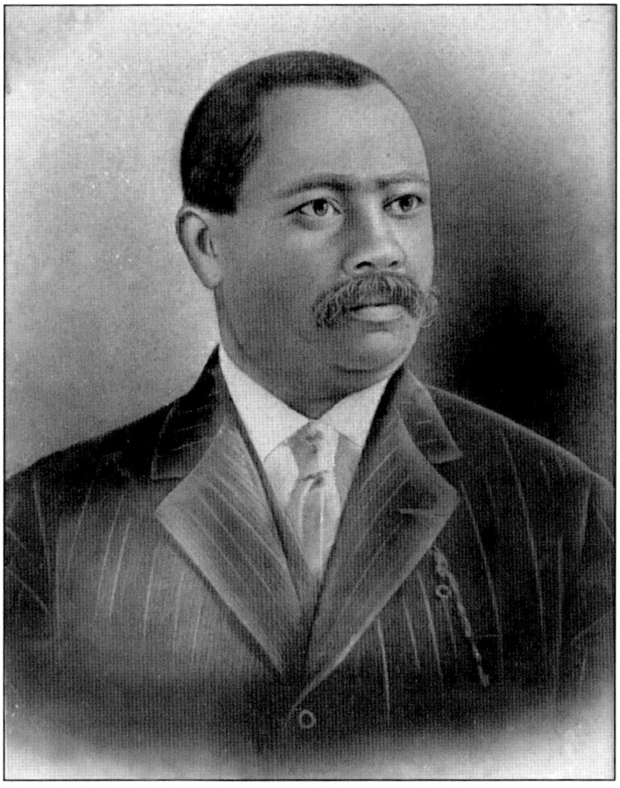

Robert Allen White (1862–1931), a businessman from Manning, was also the "District Grand Worthy of the Household of Ruth."

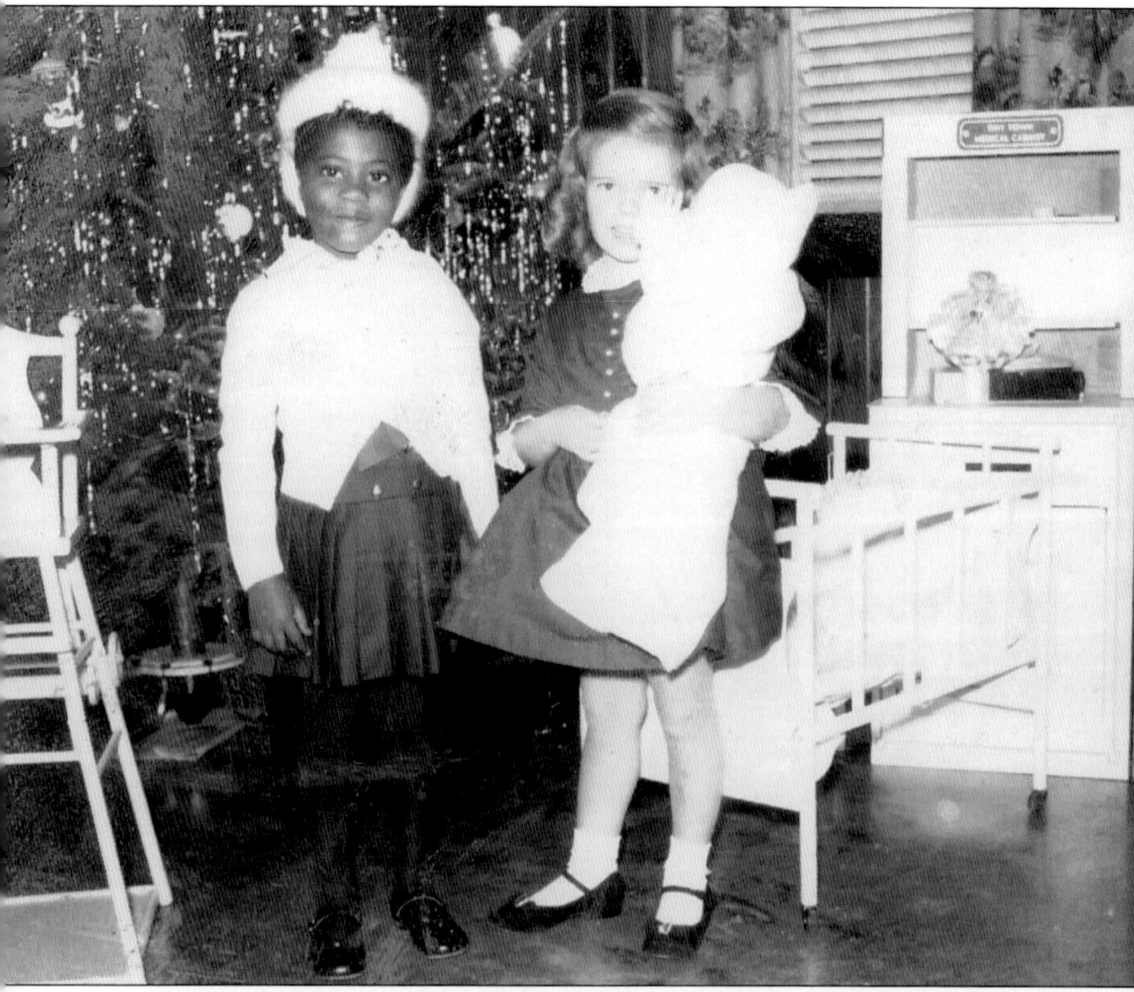

Playmates Shelia Pearson and Becki Davis pose for a snapshot in 1950. Although the practices of those days demanded strict separation of the races, it seems that this learned behavior had not yet influenced these young ladies.

Five

Civil Rights Movement of the 1950s

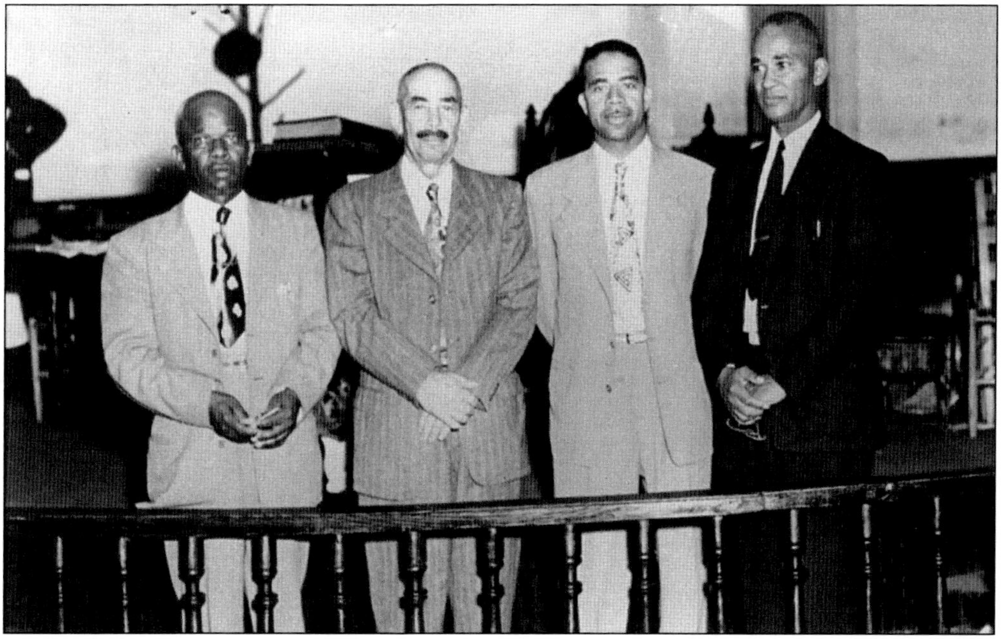

The primary leaders of the county's Civil Rights movement during the late 1940s and early 1950s were the Reverends J.W. Seals, E.E. Richburg, and J.A. De Laine and J.T. Boyd. The case *Briggs v. Elliott* became one of the five cases known as *Brown, et al. v. Board of Education, et al.* The decision in the case was rendered by the United States Supreme Court on May 17, 1954.

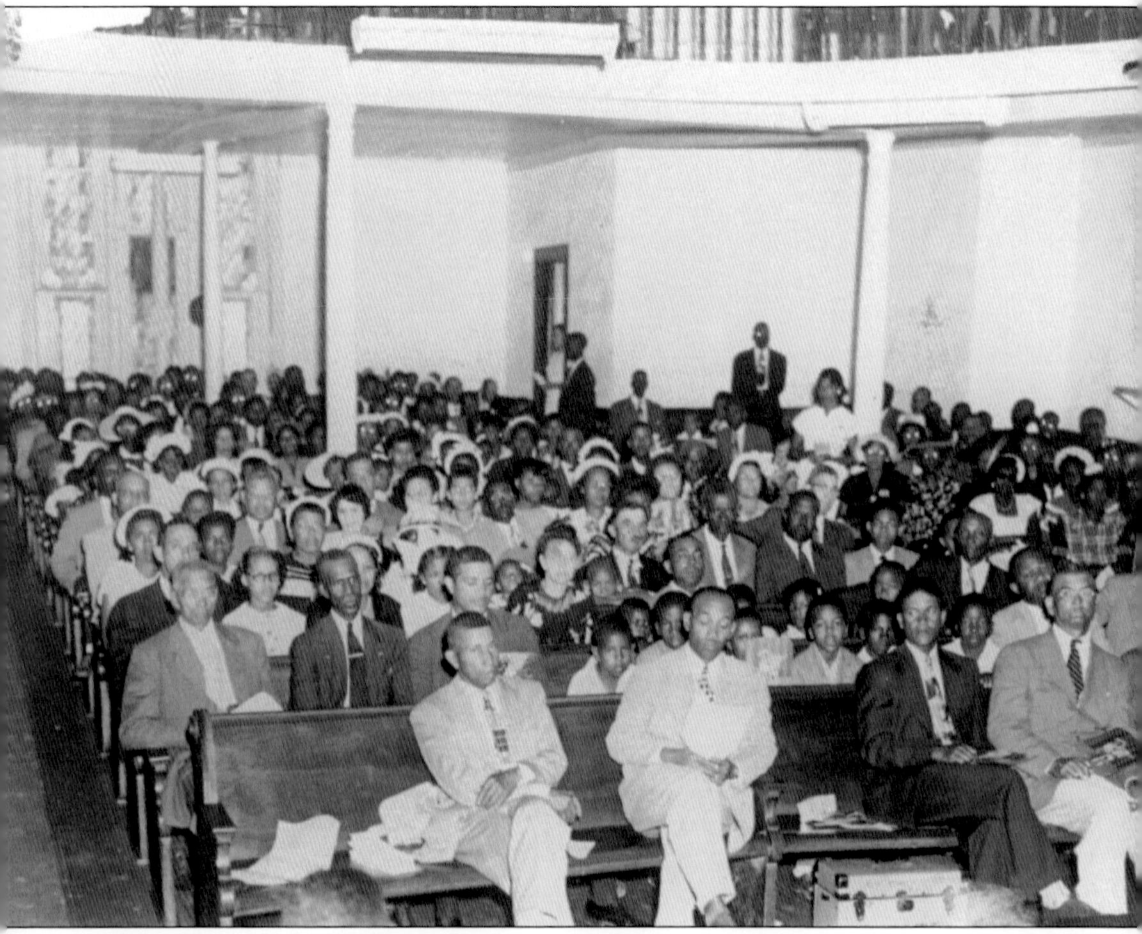

The audience was captivated during a Civil Rights meeting at the Liberty Hill Church in 1950.

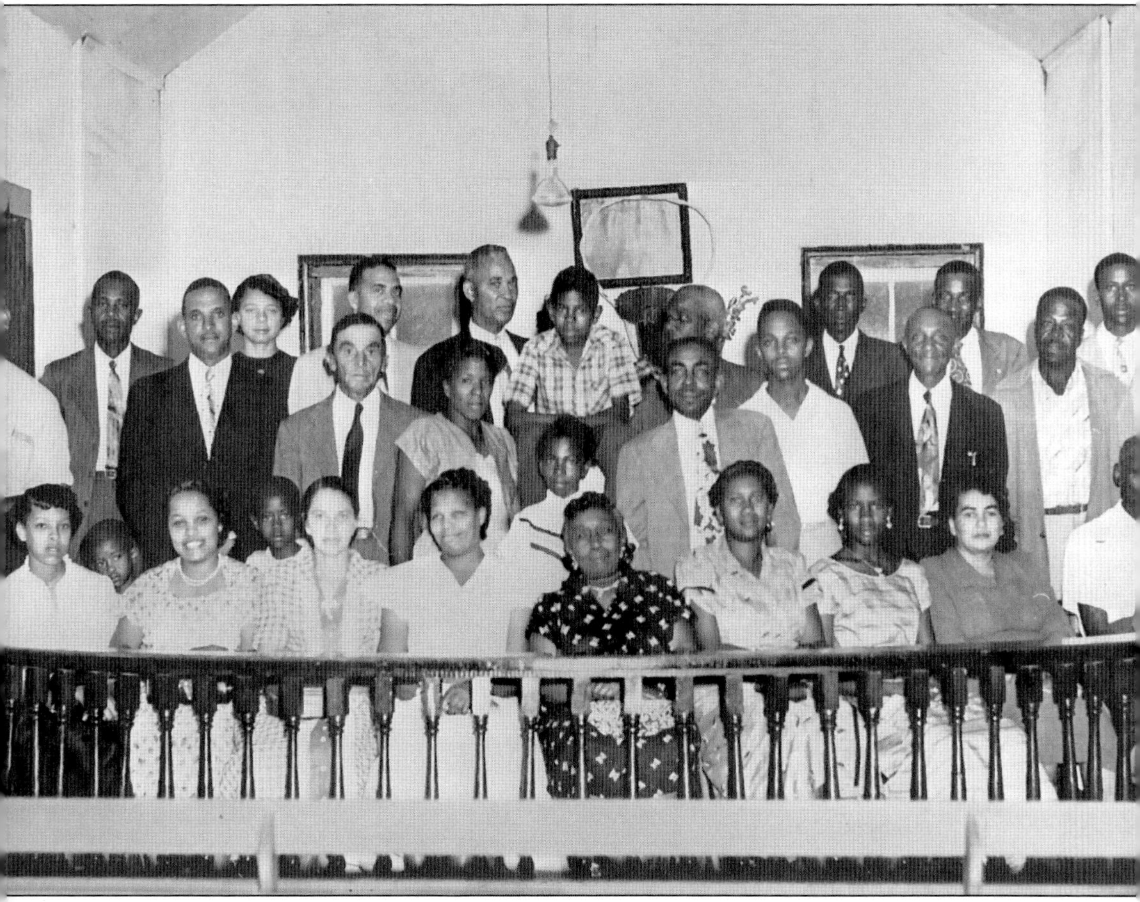

This is a group picture of the plaintiffs and supporters of the *Briggs* case taken in 1950. From left to right are (front row) Celestine Parsons, Jessie Pearson, Plummie Parsons, Sheila Pearson, Sarah Ragin, Mary Oliver, Esther Fludd, Annie Gibson, Maxine Gibson, Rebecca Richburg, and Jimmie Bennett; (back row) Gilbert Henry, Joseph Lemon, Bennie Parsons, Charlotte Pearson, Edward Ragin, E.E. Richburg, Eliza Briggs, J.A. De Laine, Harry Briggs Jr., J.W. Seals, Harry Briggs Sr., Brumit De Laine, Levi Pearson, Robert Georgia, Hammett Pearson, Lee Richardson, and Jessie Pearson.

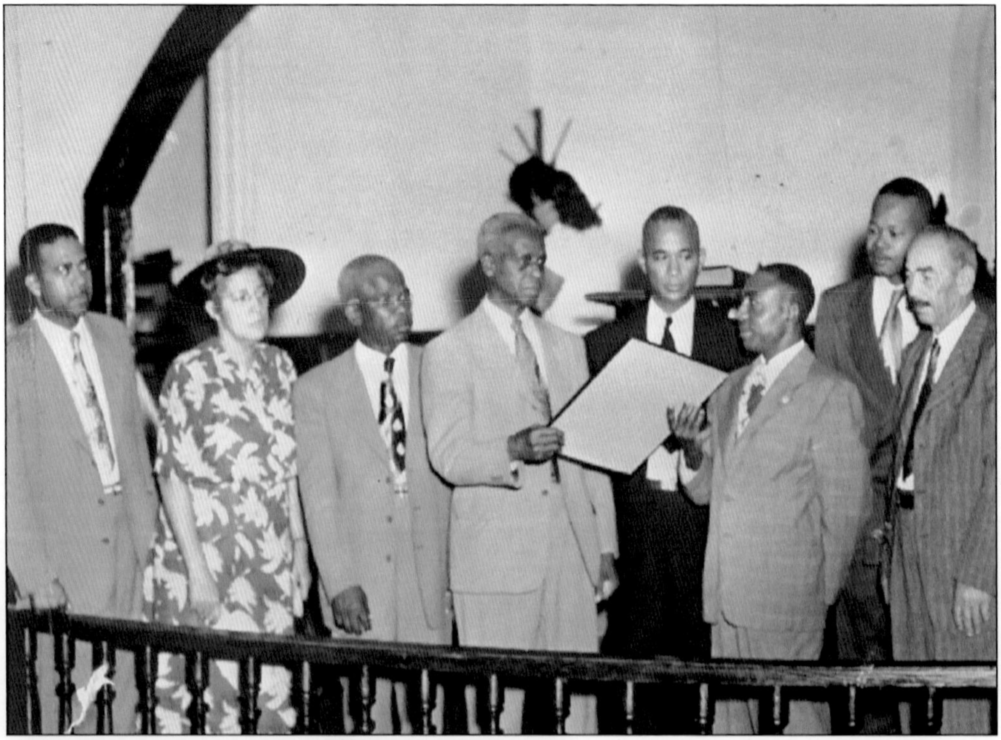

On June 17, 1951, the NAACP executive committee presented certificates of merit to plaintiffs of the *Briggs* case. Individuals in this photograph, from left to right, are Rev. E.E. Richburg, Mrs. Modjeska Simpkins, Rev. J.W. Seals, S.J. McDonald, Rev. J.A. De Laine, Harry Briggs, John McCray, J.M. Boyd, James Hinton, and Eugene A.R. Montgomery.

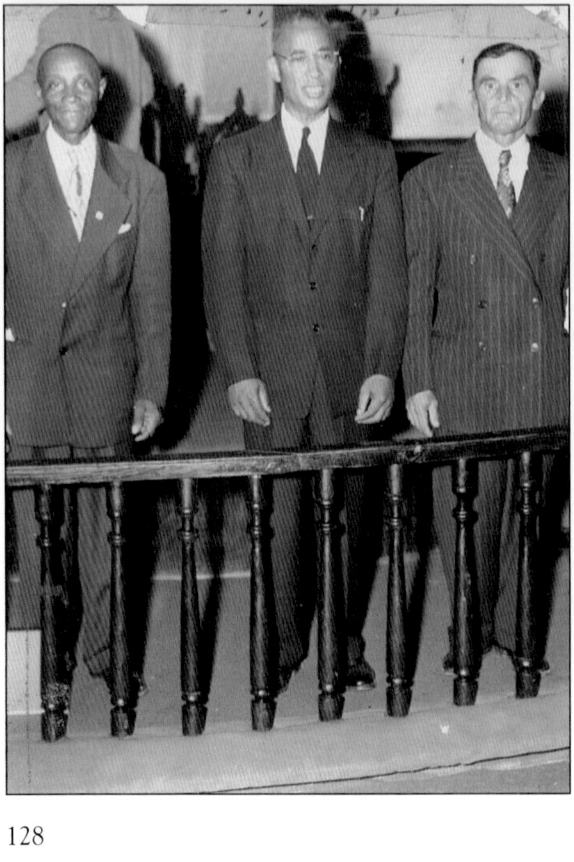

Robert Georgia, Rev. J.A. De Laine, and Edward Ragin are pictured here at St. Mark AME Church in 1949.